W9-AYV-312

MAYFLOWER FAMILIES

Through

Five Generations

DESCENDANTS OF THE PILGRIMS
WHO LANDED AT
PLYMOUTH, MASS. DECEMBER 1620

VOLUME EIGHTEEN PART III

FAMILY OF

RICHARD WARREN

**The fifth generation descendants
of his children Abigail, Nathaniel and Joseph**

Compiled by
Robert S. Wakefield, F.A.S.G

Published by
General Society of Mayflower Descendants
2001

4 Winslow Street
Plymouth, MA 02360

First Printing, 2001

Library of Congress Cataloging-in-Publication Data (Revised for Volume 18 Part III)

Mayflower Families Through Five Generations

Edited by L. M. Kellogg and others. Includes bibliographical references and indexes

Contents:

v.1. Families: Francis Eaton, Samuel Fuller, William White
v.2. Families: James Chilton, Richard More, Thomas Rogers
v.3. Family: George Soule
v.4. Family: Edward Fuller, by Bruce Campbell MacGunnigle, CG
v.5. Families: Edward Winslow, by Ruth C. McGuyre & Robert S. Wakefield
John Billington by Harriet W. Hodge
v.6. Family: Stephen Hopkins by John D. Austin
v.7. Family Peter Brown by Robert S. Wakefield, FASG
v.8. Family Degory Priest by E. Townsend, R.S. Wakefield, FASG & M.H. Stover, CG
v.9. Family Francis Eaton by L.D. Van Antwerp, MD, CG & R.S. Wakefield, FASG
v.10. Family S. Fuller by R.S. Wakefield, FASG
v.11. Family Edward Doty by Peter B. Hill (3 Volumes)
v.12. Family Francis Cook by Ralph Van Wood, Jr.
v.13. Family William White by Robert M. Sherman, FASG & Ruth W. Sherman,FASG,
Robert S. Wakefield, FASG
v.14. Family Myles Standish by Russell L. Warner & Robert S. Wakefield, FASG
v.15. Families James Chilton by Robert M. Sherman, FASG & Verlo Delano Vincent,
revised by Robert S. Wakefield, FASG
Richard More by Robert M. Sherman, FASG, Robert S. Wakefield,
FASG, & Lydia Dowfinlay
v.16 Family John Alden by Esther Littleford Woodworth-Barnes & Alicia Crane
Williams
v.17 Family Isaac Allerton by Robert S. Wakefield, FASG & Margaret Harris Stover, CG
v.18 Family Richard Warren by Robert S. Wakefield, FASG (3 Volumes)
v.19 Family Thomas Rogers by Alice Westgate, revised by Ann T. Reeves
v.20 Family Henry Samson by Robert M. Sherman, FASG, Ruth W. Sherman, FASG &
Robert S. Wakefield, FASG

1. Pilgrims (New Plymouth Colony): Genealogy
2. Massachusetts: Genealogy
I. Kellogg, Lucy Mary
II General Society of Mayflower Descendants

F63 M39 929' .2'0973 75-30145

ISBN No. 0-930270-33-9

DEDICATION

To the Memory of Morton Wells Saunders

1916 – 1998

Distinguished son, husband, father, professional, pilgrim, researcher, volunteer, the cycle of life has been completed preserving the posterity his memory and benevolence. His multidimensional service to the Mayflower Society included holding the office of Governor of the Rhode Island Society, DDG & AG of the General Society, Chairman of the Publications Committee, and chairman of numerous boards within the society. His final contribution was the publication, after his death, of the Kempton/Kimpton Families of North America, and the donation of his Canadian research books to the Mayflower Library.

HISTORY OF THE FIVE GENERATIONS PROJECT OF THE GENERAL SOCIETY OF MAYFLOWER DESCENDANTS

The concept of this genealogical project was first formally conceived by Herbert Folger in San Francisco and George E. Bowman in Boston around the turn of the century. The format was a version of the Alden Memorial published in 1867. The project officially began when it was approved at the annual meeting of the General Board of the Society on September 11, 1959.

In the first twenty-one years of the project there were three volumes of genealogies published entitled "Mayflower Families Through Five Generations". The families of seven Mayflower passengers are included in these genealogies.

Since 1990 many volumes have been added to the series. Many of the early volumes have been rewritten to bring them up to current day standard. In addition, second updated editions have been published for some families.

The Society is also publishing a series of booklets called "Mayflower Families in Progress" (MFIP), Which contain four or five generations of the families we have yet to publish in the hard cover format. These genealogies contain all the information we currently have while further research continues.

The goal of the Project is to provide documentation from primary sources for all data contained in our genealogies. Our aim is to make this material available to the general public and in doing this work we are fulfilling the objects of our Society.

Edith Bates Thomas, Director of the Five Generations Project

THE SOCIETY EXPRESSES THANKS

The Mayflower Society is grateful to many people for their assistance in preparing this volume for publication. Many names have unfortunately escaped the record, but the contribution of each is appreciated and herewith is acknowledged.

The Mayflower Society wishes to thank Claude W. Barlow, F.A.S.G., Janice a. Beebe, Ann S. Lainhart, Barbara L. Merrick, Ann T. Reeves, Mrs. Robert M. Sherman, F.A.S.G., Edith Bates Thomas and Neil D. Thompson, F.A.S.G.

INDEX: Roger D. Joslyn, FASG

PREVIEWED BY: Ann S. Lainhart

COMPUTERIZED BY: Cathryn P. Lanham

PUBLICATION: Robert Allen Greene

OFFICERS OF THE GENERAL SOCIETY

1999 - 2002

GOVERNOR GENERAL	Mr.Eugene A. Fortine
ASSISTANT GOVERNOR GENERAL	Col. William T. Lincoln
SECRETARY GENERAL	Mrs. Carol Smith Leavitt
TREASURER GENERAL	Mr. Marlin W. Brossart
HISTORIAN GENERAL	Mrs. Caroline Lewis Kardell
ELDER GENERAL	The Reverend John H. Case
CAPTAIN GENERAL	Mr. Robert E. Davis
SURGEON GENERAL	Dr. Dennis E. Ward, MD
COUNSELLOR GENERAL	Ms. Aseneth M. Kepler

EXECUTIVE COMMITTEE MEMBERS AT LARGE

Mrs. Edith Bates Thomas
Mrs. Mary Ellen Byrne
Mrs. Patricia King Davis

FIVE GENERATIONS PROJECT COMMITTEE

2000

Director, Mrs. Edith Bates Thomas
Col. Robert Allen Greene
Mrs. Caroline Lewis Kardell
Mrs. Frank W. Lanham
Mr. Robert S. Wakefield

ROBERT S. WAKEFIELD

Robert S. Wakefield is one of the most respected genealogists in the country. Born in San Mateo, California, he was employed for many years by the Southern Pacific Transportation Company. He is descended from both Stephen Hopkins and John Howland and in 1973 joined the California Society of Mayflower Descendants. He holds the prestigious title of Fellow of the American Society of Genealogist. Many of his articles have appeared in leading genealogical publications. Mr. Wakefield has been an active member of the Five Generations Project of the General Society of Mayflower Descendants since 1976, when he undertook preparation of the Richard More manuscript for publication in Mayflower Families Two. In 1977 he began work on the Peter Brown family which was published in 1992. He co-authored the Edward Winslow family in Mayflower Families Five.

Since that time he has contributed substantially to many more Project families as author, co-author, editor and advisor. He has been a member of the Five Generations Project Committee for many years.

TO THE READER

No five generation genealogy is ever complete. The authors have assembled the family as correctly and as completely as circumstances permitted. The work is based largely on carefully researched articles in genealogical journals and family histories, together with probate and land records, and town and church vital statistics. Family tradition, in the absence of confirmatory evidence, has not been accepted as proof of a line. This has, regretfully, resulted in the rejection of a few lines which the society accepted in its early years, but were based on insufficient or erroneous evidence. On the other hand, many new potential lines have been uncovered.

Paucity of records sometimes renders it virtually impossible to follow a family or individual to another town: An entire family disappears, or one or more children are labelled "n.f.r." (no further record found). The author often offers tentative identifications using the word probably, when evidence is nearly conclusive, and possibly, when evidence is merely suggestive. This is done in the hope that a reader, tracing back his ancestry through such clues, may come upon real proof and so establish the new line.

Spelling was far from consistent even after the Revolution. To a great extent names in this book have been spelled as found in each record. This often provides different spellings of an individual's name at his birth, upon marriage, and in a deed or will. For example, Hayward is found as Heywood and even Howard for the same person; Marcy and Mercy are many times interchangeable. With variant spellings so commonplace, use of "[sic]" is restricted to exceptional examples. To assist the reader, most variant spellings of a name are lumped together in the Index, rather than separately alphabetized.

A reader who finds either an error or additional information regarding any family or individual in this volume down to the birth of sixth generation children, but not beyond, is urgently requested to send such material, with documentation, to:

FIVE GENERATIONS PROJECT, P. O. BOX 3297, PLYMOUTH MA 02361

TABLE OF CONTENTS

FIFTH GENERATION - PART III

683 LYDIA SMITH[5] (Abigail Skeefe[4], Lydia Snow[3], Abigail[2] Warren, Richard[1]) b. Sandwich 4 Oct. 1685; d. 8 Nov. 1748 ae 63.

She m. JAMES SKIFF, b. Chilmark 10 March 1689; d. there 6 Jan. 1724; son of Nathan and Hepzibah (Cadman) Skiff.

No Dukes Co. PR for James Skiff.

Children (SKIFF) b. Chilmark:

i STEPHEN[6] b. 8 May 1718
ii JAMES b. 15 July 1722

References: VR CHILMARK pp. 29(b. James; b. ch.), 93(d. James). MARTHA'S VINEYARD BY BANKS 3:435.

684 DORCAS SMITH[5] (Abigail Skeefe[4], Lydia Snow[3], Abigail[2] Warren, Richard[1]) b. Sandwich 7 Jan. 1686/7.

She m. Sandwich 15 May 1712 BENJAMIN BURGES, b. Sandwich; son of Jacob and Mary (Nye) Burgess.

No Barnstable or Dukes Co. PR for Benjamin Burgess.

Children (BURGES) last 3 b. Vinyard Haven, Dukes Co.:

i BENJAMIN[6] b. Sandwich 19 Jan. 1712/3
ii THOMAS b. 15 Nov. 1715
iii SHUBAEL b. 13 July 1718
iv ABIGAIL b. 22 Aug. 1720

References: MARTHA'S VINEYARD BY BANKS 3:46(b. last 3 ch.). SANDWICH VR 1:92(m.), 95(b. Benj.).

685 REMEMBER SMITH[5] (Abigail Skeefe[4], Lydia Snow[3], Abigail[2] Warren, Richard[1]) b. Sandwich 9 Feb. 1688/9; d. there 23 Jan. 1717/18 ae 28.

She m. Sandwich 20 Jan. 1713 SAMUEL JENNINGS, b. Sandwich 18 Feb. 1684; d. there 13 May 1764 in 80th yr.; son of John and Ruhamah (Turner) Jennings. He m. (2) bef. 18 Sept. 1724 Deborah Perry by whom he had Samuel, Esther and John.

The will of Samuel Jennings of Sandwich dated 28 May 1760, names son John; dau. Ruhama; dau. Esther; granddau. Remember Ellis; son-in-law Elisha Bassett.

Children (JENNINGS) b. Sandwich:

i LYDIA[6] b. 6 Feb. 1713/4
ii RUHAMAH b. 1 May 1716

References: MD 29:23(deaths), 86(b. Samuel). Barnstable Co. PR 13:34-5(Samuel Jennings). SANDWICH VR 1:26(b. Samuel), 92(m.), 98(b. ch.); 2:1530(d. Remember, Samuel).

686 ABIGAIL SMITH[5] (Abigail Skeefe[4], Lydia Snow[3], Abigail[2] Warren, Richard[1]) b. Sandwich 5 May 1691; d. aft. 10 Feb. 1733/4 (father's will).

She m. Sandwich 27 Oct. 1709 BARNABAS GIBBS, b. Sandwich 24 June 1684; d. bef. 5 May 1724; son of John and Jane (Blackwell) Gibbs.

The inventory of the estate of Barnabas Gibs of Sandwich, dec. was dated 5 May 1724. On 7 May 1724 Abigail Gibs was appointed administratrix of the estate of Barnabas Gibs.

Children (GIBBS) b. Sandwich:

i CALEB[6] b. 13 Sept. 1710
ii SUSANNAH b. 28 Sept. 1712
iii REMEMBER b. 20 Aug. 1714
iv ABIGAIL b. 4 April 1717
v DEBORAH b. 12 Dec. 1718; d.y.
vi JANE b. 24 Oct. 1720
vii BARNABAS b. 21 Oct. 1722
viii DEBORAH b. 4 Dec. 1724

References: NEHGR 123:129-30. Barnstable Co. PR 4:184-5 (Barnabas Gibbs). MD 14:111(b. Barnabas). SANDWICH VR 1:14(b. Barnabas), 84(m.), 90(b. ch.).

687 SHUBAL SMITH[5] (Abigail Skeefe[4], Lydia Snow[3], Abigail[2] Warren, Richard[1]) b. Sandwich 19 Feb. 1702/3; living 1759.

He m. Chilmark 23 Jan. 1723/4 MARTHA MAYHEW, b. Chilmark 20 Feb. 1705/6; living 1759; dau. of Paine and Mary (Rankin) Mayhew.

In 1759 Shubael Smith gave power of attorney to wife Martha to dispose of his lands in NY and NH "or elsewhere."

No Dukes Co. PR for Shubal Smith.

Children (SMITH) b. Chilmark:

i ABIGAIL[6] b. 24 Oct. 1724
ii SARAH b. 4 Feb. 1728

References: VR CHILMARK p. 23(b. Martha), 29(b. ch.), 73(m.). Dukes Co. LR 8:627(Shubael Smith). MARTHA'S VINEYARD BY BANKS 3:450. MAYFLOWER SOURCE RECORDS p. 88(m.).

688 MARY PRESBURY[5] (Deborah Skeefe[4], Lydia Snow[3], Abigail[2] Warren, Richard[1]) b. Sandwich 28 Aug. 1694.

She m. Edgartown 29 Jan. 1712/3 THOMAS WEST, b. ca. 1687; d. bef. 7 May 1728; son of Thomas and Elizabeth (-----) West.

On 7 May 1728 Stephen Presbury was appointed administrator of the estate of Thomas West.

Children (WEST) b. Tisbury:

i WILLIAM[6] b. 4 April 1714
ii NATHAN b. 17 Aug. 1715; d. bef. 1732
iii THOMAS b. 22 Feb. 1716/7
iv LYDIA b. 6 June 1718
v JOHN b. 21 Oct. 1719; d.y.
vi MARY b. 2 June 1721
vii PAUL b. ca. 1723
viii SETH b. ca. 1726

References: MARTHA'S VINEYARD BY BANKS 3:501. VR TISBURY pp. 92-3(b. first 6 ch.). VR EDGARTOWN p. 191(m.).

689 DORCAS PRESBURY[5] (Deborah Skeefe[4], Lydia Snow[3], Abigail[2] Warren, Richard[1]) b. prob. Edgartown ca. 1698; d. bef. 16 March 1735/6.

She m. ELISHA WOLLEN, b. ca. 1687; d. bet. 16 March 1735/6 and 20 April 1736; son of Thomas Wollen.

The will of Elisha Woolen of Edgartown dated 16 March 1735/6, proved 20 April 1736, mentions his wife is dead; son Presbury Woolen and daughters Mary, Elizabeth, Drucilla and Deborah.

Children (WOLLEN) b. Edgartown; first 4 bp. 12 Oct. 1729:

i MARY[6] b. ca. 1715
ii DRUSILLA b. ca. 1717
iii PRESBURY b. ca. 1719
iv DEBORAH b. 29 July 1721
v ELIZABETH bp. 20 Aug. 1732

References: MARTHA'S VINEYARD BY BANKS 3:515. VR EDGARTOWN p. 85(bp. ch.). Dukes Co. PR 3:66(Elisha Woolen).

690 JOHN PRESBURY[5] (Deborah Skeefe[4], Lydia Snow[3], Abigail[2] Warren, Richard[1]) b. prob. Edgartown ca. 1700; d. Tisbury 20 Sept. 1728 in 28th yr.

He m. ca. 1719 ABIGAIL COTTLE, b. Tisbury 6 June 1702; d. 29 April 1780; dau. of Edward and Esther (Daggett) Cottle. She m. (2) Edgartown 20 March 1730/1 Benjamin Luce. She m. (3) Samuel Lambert.

On 16 Oct. 1728 Abigail Presbury was appointed administratrix of the estate of her husband John Presbury of Edgartown. On 21 March 1739 the estate was divided between the widow Abigail Luce and daughter Mariah Presbury.

Child (PRESBURY) b. Edgartown:

i MARIA[6] b. ca. 1720; bp. Edgartown 23 Aug. 1730

References: MARTHA'S VINEYARD BY BANKS 3:230(Lambert), 250 Luce), 411. VR EDGARTOWN pp. 66(bp. Maria). Dukes Co. PR 2:48-9; 3:111(John Presbury). VR TISBURY pp. 29(b. Abigail), 236(d. John).

691 ABIGAIL PRESBURY[5] (Deborah Skeefe[4], Lydia Snow[3], Abigail[2] Warren, Richard[1]) b. prob. Edgartown ca. 1703; d. Sandwich 25 June 1749.

She m. ca. 1728 EBENEZER PERRY, b. Sandwich 5 March 1705/6; d. bet. 19 June 1780 and 4 July 1780; son of Samuel and Esther (Taber) Perry, a descendant of Pilgrim Francis Cooke. He m. (2) Rochester 11 Jan. 1749/50 Abigail Hammond by whom he had Nathan. He m. (3) Harwich 12 Feb. 1754 Elizabeth Freeman.

The will of Ebenezer Perry of Hardwick, gentleman, dated 19 June 1780, proved 4 July 1780, names wife Elizabeth; sons Nathan, Samuel and Seth; James, Thomas, Elizabeth, Lois, Lucy and Sarah Perry, the heirs of son Stephen Perry dec.; Samuel Fessenden and Deborah Haskell [son and dau. of his dau. Deborah Fessenden dec.]; dau. Abigail Lewis, wife of David Lewis; and dau. Mary Eggry, wife of Daniel Eggry.

Children (PERRY) b. Sandwich:

i STEPHEN[6] b. 4 April 1729
ii SAMUEL b. 27 June 1731
iii DEBORAH b. 27 March 1733
iv SETH b. 27 June 1735
v THOMAS b. 6 April 1737; d. 25 Sept. 1738
vi THOMAS b. 16 Aug. 1739; d. 6 Sept. 1739
vii ABIGAIL b. 5 June 1741
viii MARY b. 21 April 1743

References: NEHGR 115:193-4(Perry). SANDWICH VR 1:59(b. Ebenezer), 134(b. Stephen), 135(b. Samuel thru Mary), 149(d. both sons Thomas), 172(d. Abigail). HARWICH VR p. 117(3rd m.). VR ROCHESTER 2:239(2nd m.). MD 30:61(b. Ebenezer). Worcester Co. PR #46092; 17:75-7(Ebenezer Perry). MF 12:335-6.

692 DRUSILLA PRESBURY[5] (Deborah Skeefe[4], Lydia Snow[3], Abigail[2] Warren, Richard[1]) b. prob. Edgartown ca. 1708; d. Rochester 14 March 1763 in 56th yr.

She m. THOMAS WEST, b. Tisbury 26 Aug. 1708; d. Rochester 14 July 1790 in 82nd yr.; son of Abner and Jane (Look) (Cottle) West. He m. (2) Rochester 30 Nov. 1763 Priscilla (Sprague) Hammond. He m. (3) Rochester 29 April 1780 Deborah Freeman.

Thomas West was pastor of the 3rd church in Rochester.

The will of Thomas West of Rochester, clerk, dated 9 May 1788, proved 5 Oct. 1790, names sons Thomas, Samuel, Benjamin and Timothy; daughters Keturah, Drucilla and Sarah; children of son John deceased; widow Sarah Freeman; "son" Enoch Hammond.

Children (WEST) b. Tisbury:

i DEBORAH[6] b. 18 Sept. 1729; d. 25 Jan. 1733/4
ii ABNER b. 13 June 1731
iii KETURAH b. 14 March 1733
iv JOHN b. 10 April 1735
v THOMAS b. 28 Feb. 1736/7
vi SAMUEL b. 18 Nov. 1738
vii DEBORAH b. 19 Oct. 1740; d. 29 Nov. 1747
viii DRUSILLA b. 22 Aug. 1742
ix BENJAMIN b. 30 June 1744; d. 13 July 1745
x BENJAMIN b. 28 March 1746
xi SARAH b. 12 May 1748
xii TIMOTHY b. ca. 1750 (named in will)

References: VR ROCHESTER 2:314(his 2nd & 3rd m.), 443(d. Drusilla, Thomas). VR TISBURY pp. 90-3(b. 1st 11 ch.), 93(b. Thomas), 241(d. Benjamin, both Deborahs). MARTHA'S VINEYARD BY BANKS 3:501-2. Plymouth Co. PR 31:274-6 (Thomas West).

693 CONTENT PRESBURY[5] (Deborah Skeefe[4], Lydia Snow[3], Abigail[2] Warren, Richard[1]) b. prob. Edgartown ca. 1711; d. Tisbury 9 Sept. 1773 in 63rd yr.

She m. Tisbury 5 Sept. 1735 STEPHEN LUCE, b. Tisbury 25 Sept. 1714; d. there 13 May 1801 ae 86y 5m 18d; son of Zephaniah and Hope (Norton) Luce.

The will of Stephen Luce of Tisbury dated 7 Feb. 1799, proved 11 April 1801, names sons Timothy, Zephaniah and Elijah Luce; daughters Jedidah Norton and Jane Doty.

Children (LUCE) b. Tisbury:

i JANE[6] b. 5 Aug. 1736
ii KETURAH b. 18 Feb. 1738 (not in will)

iii ELIJAH b. 18 May 1740
iv TIMOTHY b. 27 Aug. 1742
v JEDIDIAH b. 8 Sept. 1744
vi STEPHEN b. 8 Sept. 1747; d. 22 April 1760 ae 12y 8m 14d
vii EZEKIEL b. 5 Feb. 1750 (not in will)
viii ZEPHANIAH b. 5 April 1752
ix DEBORAH b. 27 Nov. 1754 (not in will)

References: VR TISBURY pp. 59-66(b. ch.), 65(b. Stephen), 159(m.), 222(d. Content), 226(d. Stephen, son Stephen). Dukes Co. PR 9:75(Stephen Luce).

694 SARAH PRESBURY[5] (Deborah Skeefe[4], Lydia Snow[3], Abigail[2] Warren, Richard[1]) b. prob. Edgartown ca. 1713; d. Tisbury 30 Jan. 1793 in 80th yr.

She m. Edgartown 18 Feb. 1730/1 TIMOTHY LUCE, b. 18 March 1704; d. 6 May 1782; son of Experience and Elizabeth (Manter) Luce.

On 29 March 1746 Timothy Luce of Tisbury, weaver, and wife Sarah and Drucilla Woollin of Tisbury and Deborah Woollin of Edgartown sold to Stephen Luce of Edgartown, weaver, their parts of the land of their father Stephen Presbury.

On 8 April 1762 Timothy Luce of Tisbury, husbandman, sold 7 acres in Tisbury to son Josiah Luce of Tisbury, cordwainer.

On 26 March 1779 Timothy Luce of Tisbury, yeoman, deeded all his estate to sons Benjamin, John and Moses Luce of Tisbury, laborers, in consideration of their maintaining him and his wife for life.

No Dukes Co. PR for Timothy Luce.

Children (LUCE) 1st 4 bp. Edgartown 7 May 1738:

i REUBEN[6] b. 1731
ii LYDIA b. ca. 1733
iii MARTHA b. 13 Dec. 1735
iv JOSIAH bp. 7 May 1738
v BENJAMIN b. ca. 1740
vi JOHN (named in 1779 deed)
vii MOSES (named in 1779 deed)
viii EXPERIENCE
ix GAMALIEL
x ZACHARIAH
xi LITCHFIELD b. ca. 1758
xii DORCAS
xiii DRUSILLA

References: MARTHA'S VINEYARD BY BANKS 3:254(names of ch.). VR EDGARTOWN p. 142(m.). Dukes Co. LR 7:394(to

Stephen); 11:417(to sons); 12:341(to Josiah). VR TISBURY p. 226(d. Sarah).

695 JAMES CHIPMAN[5] (Marcy Skeefe[4], Lydia Snow[3], Abigail[2] Warren, Richard[1]) b. Sandwich 18 Dec. 1694; living 23 Jan. 1728/9 (deed).

He m. (1) Stonington CT 28 Oct. 1717 MARY MINOR; b. Stonington CT 31 July 1699; living 10 Feb. 1725/6; dau. of Benjamin and Mary (Saxton) Minor. The 7 July 1721 distribution of the estate of Benjamin Minor names Mary Minor, now Mary Chipman.

He m. (2) ELIZABETH ----- (named in CHIPMAN GEN, but no evidence found.)

On 30 Jan. 1721/2 James Eldredg and wife Marcy of Kingstown RI sold 26 acres in Stonington to James Chipman of Groton [CT].

On 8 April 1725 James Chipman of Stonington and wife Mary sold 11 acres in Stonington to Lt. James Minor. On 10 Feb. 1725/6 James Chipman of New London, clothier, and wife Mary sold 10 acres in Stonington to Benjamin Minor.

On 14 May 1725 Benjamin Gorton of New London sold land in New London to James Chipman of Stonington. On 23 Jan. 1728/9 James Chipman of New London sold land in New London to Lt. James Harris of Colchester.

No further record of James Chipman has been found.

Children (CHIPMAN) rec. b. Stonington CT*:

i JAMES[6] b. 10 Aug. 1719 (also rec. in Lebanon CT)
ii MARY b. 11 June 1722
iii DEBORAH b. 17 July 1724

References: CHIPMAN GEN (1970) p. 19. Stonington CT VR 2:16(b. Mary), 63(1st m.; b. ch.). Lebanon CT VR 1:45(b. son James). New London CT PR 4:195(Benjamin Minor). DIARY OF JOSHUA HEMPSTEAD OF NEW LONDON CT, New London CT 1901, p. 161 (d. of child). Stonington CT LR 3:346(James Eldredg); 4:21, 79(James Chipman). New London CT LR 8:265(Benjamin Gorton); 9:91(James Chipman).

*Joshua Hempstead's diary under 12 Oct. 1725 mentions "a child of James Chipman died".

696 JOHN CHIPMAN[5] (Marcy Skeefe[4], Lydia Snow[3], Abigail[2] Warren, Richard[1]) b. Sandwich 18 Sept. 1697; d. there 30 Dec. 1757.

He m. Sandwich 26 Sept. 1723 HANNAH FESSENDEN, apparently dau. of Nicholas and Margaret (-----) Fessenden.

The will of John Chipman of Sandwich dated 29 Dec. 1757, proved 4 April 1758, names wife Hannah; dau. Bethia Chipman; sons Benjamin and Stephen.

Children (CHIPMAN):

i MARY^{6} b. 20 Dec. 1724; d. 24 Jan. 1730 ae 6 yrs.
ii BENJAMIN b. 7 Nov. 1726
iii BETHIAH b. 9 Dec. 1728
iv HANNAH b. ca. 1730 (not in will)
v STEPHEN b. 5 Aug. 1737

References: CHIPMAN GEN (1970) p. 20. Barnstable Co. PR 9:371 -2(John Chipman). SANDWICH VR 1:130(b. ch. except Hannah); 2:1521(d. Mary), 1618(m.).

697 MARY CHIPMAN^{5} (Marcy Skeefe^{4}, Lydia Snow^{3}, Abigail^{2} Warren, Richard^{1}) b. Sandwich 11 Dec. 1699.

She m. Sandwich 6 Sept. 1725 SHUBAL SMITH, b. Sandwich 20 Nov. 1699; d. bef. 17 Jan. 1731(adm.); son of Thomas and Abigail (-----) Smith.

On 17 Jan. 1731 Samuel Smith of Sandwich, yeoman, was appointed administrator of the estate of Shubal Smith, late of Sandwich.

On 6 Aug. 1738 the children were bp. at the Sandwich First Church.

Children (SMITH):

i MARY^{6} b. Sandwich 24 July 1726
ii ISAAC b. Newport RI 14 Nov. 1727

References: SANDWICH VR 1:34(b. Shubal), 127(m.), 131(b. dau. Mary), 132(b. Isaac); 2:1386(bp. ch.), 1618(m.). Sandwich First Church recs. p. 19(bp. ch.). Barnstable Co. PR 3:642(Shubal Smith).

698 BETHIA CHIPMAN^{5} (Marcy Skeefe^{4}, Lydia Snow^{3}, Abigail^{2} Warren, Richard^{1}) b. Sandwich 11 Dec. 1699.

She m. Sandwich 6 Oct. 1717 SAMUEL SMITH, b. Sandwich 18 Jan. 1688/9; son of Thomas and Abigail (-----) Smith.

On 6 Aug. 1738 Abigail, Bethia, Mary, John, Rebecca and Deborah, the children of Samuel and Bethiah Smith were baptized at the Sandwich First Church.

No Barnstable Co. PR for Samuel Smith.

Children (SMITH) b. Sandwich:

i THOMAS^{6} b. 7 Sept. 1718
ii SAMUEL b. 19 Feb. 1720

iii ABIGAIL b. 16 Dec. 1722
iv BETHIAH b. 10 Dec. 1724
v MARY b. 18 May 1727
vi JOHN b. 12 Sept. 1729
vii REBECCA b. 19 July 1731
viii SHUBAEL b. 10 June 1733
ix STEPHEN b. 30 May 173[5]; d. 16 Feb. 1735/6 ae 9m 14d
x DEBORAH b. 6 May 1737
xi STEPHEN b. 30 May 1739
xii LUCY (twin) b. 3 Nov. 1741; d.y.
xiii LYDIA (twin) b. 3 Nov. 1741

References: Sandwich First Parish Church Baptisms p. 19. CAPE COD HIST 2:84(b. ch.). SANDWICH VR 1:34(b. Samuel); 2:1386(bp. Abigail thru Deborah), 1538(d. Stephen). CHIPMAN GEN (1970) p. 12(m.).

NOTE: The births of the children were recorded in Sandwich VR but that page has been lost. Dates are taken from CAPE COD HIST.

699 PEREZ CHIPMAN[5] (Marcy Skeefe[4], Lydia Snow[3], Abigail[2] Warren, Richard[1]) b. Sandwich 28 Sept. 1702; d. Delaware bet. 5 Aug. 1780 and 14 Sept. 1781.

He m. (1) 1722 ELIZABETH PERRY, d. 1724.

He m. (2) ca. 1725 MARGARET WHEELER, dau. of Keziah Wheeler.

He m. (3) MARGARET HINCKLEY.

He m. (4) JUDITH (or JUDAH) DRAPER, living 5 Aug. 1780 (will).

Perez (or Paris) Chipman was in Sussex Co., Delaware as early as 4 May 1732 when his earmark was recorded.

The will of Paris Chipman of Sussex Co. and State of Delaware, blacksmith, dated 5 Aug. 1780, proved 14 Sept. 1781, names wife Judah; son Draper Chipman; dau. Sarah Chipman; dau. Betsy Chipman; dau. Memory Chipman; son Paris Chipman; daus. Lovey Chipman, Milley Chipman and Mary Chipman.

No Perez Chipman deeds to children.

Children (CHIPMAN) first 7 by 2nd wife, last 5 by fourth wife; most born Sussex Co., Delaware:

i JAMES[6] b. ca. 1725; served in the French & Indian war and was killed in 1757
ii JOHN b. ca. 1727 (not in will)
iii STEPHEN b. ca. 1728 (not in will)
iv PEREZ b. ca. 1729
v BETSY
vi MEMORY (called KEZIAH in CHIPMAN GEN.)

vii BENJAMIN b. ca. 1738 (not in will)
viii DRAPER b. ca. 1742
ix LOVEY
x MILLEY (or MELLICENT)
xi MARY
xii SARAH b. 30 Oct. 1757 (Bible rec.)

References: CHIPMAN GEN (1970) p. 20. Sussex Co. DE LR F-6:166(earmark). Sussex Co. DE Wills C:269(Paris Chipman). SOME RECORDS OF SUSSEX COUNTY, DELAWARE, Rev. C. H. B. Turner, Philadelphia PA, 1909 p. 333(b. of Sarah in Bible).

NOTE: Sons John, Stephen and Benjamin are from CHIPMAN GEN. If they existed, they died before their father.

700 DEBORAH CHIPMAN[5] (Marcy Skeefe[4], Lydia Snow[3], Abigail[2] Warren, Richard[1]) b. Sandwich 6 Dec. 1704; d. bef. 4 Jan. 1756 (Seth's 2nd m.).

She m. (1) int. Harwich 17 March 1721/2 NICHOLAS NICKERSON, b. Eastham 19 March 1693/4; reported to be captured by pirates bef. 1722; d. bef. 1724; son of William and Mary (Snow) Nickerson, a descendant of Pilgrim Stephen Hopkins.

She m. (2) Harwich 23 Dec. 1726 SETH BANGS, b. Harwich 29 July 1705; son of Samuel and Mary (Hinckley) Bangs. He m. (2) Harwich 4 Jan. 1756 Thankful Stone.

In 1724 Deborah Nickerson and Ebenezer Nickerson brought suit to recover a debt due the estate of Nicholas Nickerson.

No Barnstable Co. PR for Seth Bangs.

Children (BANGS) b. Harwich:

i CHIPMAN[6] b. 20 June 1727; d. 4 April 1750
ii SOLOMON b. 23 May 1729
iii ELIJAH b. 3 June 1731
iv SAMUEL b. 9 April 1733
v PERIS b. 20 Feb. 1735/6
vi SETH b. 14 July 1738
vii JOHN b. 17 Feb. 1744 [sic]
viii DEBORAH b. 5 Feb. 1744 [sic]
ix CHIPMAN b. 8 Aug. 1750

References: HARWICH VR pp. 5(b. Seth), 29(int. 1st m.), 38 (2nd m.), 46(b. ch.), 118(2nd m. Seth). MD 4:33(b. Nicholas). MF 6:39-40.

701 STEPHEN CHIPMAN[5] (Marcy Skeefe[4], Lydia Snow[3], Abigail[2] Warren, Richard[1]) b. Sandwich 9 June 1708; d. Nevis West Indies 27 April 1735.

He m. Aug. 1733 MARY GRIFFIN, b. 18 May 1718; dau. of James Griffin.

No known issue according to CHIPMAN GEN.

No Barnstable Co. PR for Stephen Chipman.

References: CHIPMAN GEN (1970) p. 21.

702 LYDIA CHIPMAN[5] (Marcy Skeefe[4], Lydia Snow[3], Abigail[2] Warren, Richard[1]) b. Sandwich 9 June 1708; d. Wilmington VT 23 June 1790 in 78th yr. (g.s.).

She m. Sandwich 30 Sept. 1725 ZEPHANIAH SWIFT, b. Sandwich 6 March 1702/3; d. Wilmington VT 9 May 1781 in 78th yr.; son of Jirah and Abigail (Gibbs) Swift, a descendant of Pilgrim Richard Warren.

See #865 for an account of this family.

References: MD 30:99(b. Zephaniah). SANDWICH VR 1:69(b. Zephaniah), 127(m.).

703 EBENEZER CHIPMAN[5] (Marcy Skeefe[4], Lydia Snow[3], Abigail[2] Warren, Richard[1]) b. Sandwich 13 Nov. 1709; d. 1745.

He m. Dartmouth 3 Dec. 1730 MARY ADAMS. She m. (2) Harwich 29 April 1755 John Gage.

No Barnstable Co. PR for Ebenezer Chipman.

Children (CHIPMAN):

i WILLIAM[6] b. Sandwich 6 May 1731
ii JOHN b. Falmouth 10 April 1733
iii MARY bp. Falmouth 30 March 1735
iv STEPHEN bp. Falmouth 13 March 1737
v EBENEZER b. Barnstable 18 Nov. 1738

References: VR DARTMOUTH 2:115(m.). MD 30:100(b. Wm.); 33:121(b. Eben.); 34:28(her 2nd m.). FALMOUTH VR p. 22(b. John; bp. Mary, Stephen). CHIPMAN GEN (1970) p. 21. HARWICH VR p. 118(her 2nd m.). SANDWICH VR p. 70(b. William).

NOTE: No evidence found for sons Samuel and Perez listed in CHIPMAN GEN.

704 LYDIA WINSLOW[5] (Lydia Snow[4], Josiah[3], Abigail[2] Warren, Richard[1]) b. Marshfield 24 June 1693; d. there 3 Jan. 1780 ae 86.

She m. Marshfield 10 Dec. 1718 JOSEPH THOMAS, b. Marshfield ca. 1690; d. there 25 Jan. 1759 ae 68; son of Samuel and Mercy (Ford) Thomas.

The will of Joseph Thomas of Marshfield, yeoman, dated 13 Feb. 1758, proved 6 March 1759, names wife Lidiah; grandson Joseph and unborn grandchild of son Joseph dec.; son Samuel Thomas; dau. Zilpha Thomas.

Children (THOMAS) b. Marshfield:

i JOSEPH[6] b. 2 Nov. 1719
ii SAMUEL b. 5 Sept. 1721
iii ZILPHA b. 5 Aug. 1725

References: THOMAS GEN p. 166. Plymouth Co. PR #20389(Joseph Thomas). MARSHFIELD VR pp. 35(m.), 78(b. Zilpha), 84(b. Joseph, Sam.), 110(d. Joseph), 111(d. Lydia).

705 THANKFUL WINSLOW[5] (Lydia Snow[4], Josiah[3], Abigail[2] Warren, Richard[1]) b. Marshfield 3 Feb. 1695.

She m. Marshfield 27 Oct. 1725 NATHANIEL KEEN, b. Duxbury 11 Nov. 1692; living 20 March 1765; son of Josiah and Lydia (Baker) Keen, a descendant of Pilgrim Richard Warren (see #394).

On 20 March 1765 Nathaniel Keen of Pembroke, yeoman, gave his sons Asa Keen and Snow Keen, both of Pembroke, yeomen, land in Marshfield.

No Plymouth Co. PR for Nathaniel Keen.

Children (KEEN) b. Pembroke:

i NATHANIEL[6] b. 2 Sept. 1726
ii JOSHUA b. 13 Dec. 1730
iii ASA b. 28 Nov. 1732
iv SNOW b. 7 March 1734
v THANKFUL b. 11 Dec. 1737

References: VR DUXBURY p. 101(b. Nathaniel). VR PEMBROKE pp. 127-32(b. ch.). MARSHFIELD VR p. 145(m.). MD 28:6(Keen). Plymouth Co. LR 49:236-7(Nathaniel Keen).

706 SNOW WINSLOW[5] (Lydia Snow[4], Josiah[3], Abigail[2] Warren, Richard[1]) b. Marshfield 13 May 1698; d. there 31 Jan. 1770 ae 72.

He m. (1) Marshfield 6 Nov. 1728 DEBORAH BRYANT, b. Scituate 17 June 1709; d. bef. 24 Nov. 1742 (2nd m.); dau. of John and Deborah (Barstow) Bryant.

He m. (2) Marshfield 24 Nov. 1742 LYDIA CROCKER.

The will of Snow Winslow of Marshfield, yeoman, dated 3 Nov. 1769, proved 5 Feb. 1770, names son Snow Winslow who was to pay dower to his grandmother Deborah Winslow*; son Josiah Winslow; daus. Lidia and Deborah Winslow.

Children (WINSLOW) by first wife, b. Marshfield:

i SNOW[6] b. 30 Aug. 1729; d. Marshfield 25 July 1810 ae 80; unm. No PR.
ii LYDIA b. 23 Sept. 1731; d. Marshfield 12 Jan. 1816 ae 84; unm. No PR.
iii JOSIAH b. 25 Sept. 1733
iv DEBORAH b. 5 April 1736

References: MARSHFIELD VR pp. 49(b. Snow, Josiah), 89(b. Lydia), 92(b. Deborah), 146*(1st m.), 159(2nd m.), 414(d. dau. Lydia). Plymouth Co. PR 20:323, 346(Snow Winslow). VR SCITUATE 1:58(b. Deborah). WINSLOW MEMORIAL 1:172(d. Snow, Lydia). TAG 17:235(d. Snow).

*Deborah Winslow is Deborah (Barstow) (Bryant) Winslow.

707 OLIVER WINSLOW[5] (Lydia Snow[4], Josiah[3], Abigail[2] Warren, Richard[1]) b. Marshfield 24 Nov. 1702; d. bef. 7 May 1759.

He m. (1) Marshfield 10 Dec. 1733 AGATHA BRYANT, b. Scituate 16 July 1712; dau. of John and Deborah (Barstow) Bryant.

He m. (2) Hanover 5 Dec. 1749 BETHIA PRIOR of Hanover; living 28 Oct. 1765.

The inventory of the estate of Oliver Winslow was dated 7 May 1759.

On 7 May 1759 Nathaniel, Ruth and John Winslow chose Benjamin Barstow as guardian. Bethia Winslow, widow, was appointed guardian to Bethia, Oliver and Joseph.

In the final account dated 28 Oct. 1765 Nathaniel Winslow, eldest son, was to make payments to John, Agatha, Ruth, Bethiah, Joseph and Oliver and after the widow Bethia Winslow's death to make further payments.

Children (WINSLOW) five by first wife:

i AGATHA[6] b. Marshfield 6 Dec. 1734; d. unm. after 28 Oct. 1765
ii OLIVER b. Marshfield 26 Dec. 1736; d. in battle 3 July 1756 in 20th yr.
iii RUTH b. Scituate 11 July 1739
iv NATHANIEL b. Hanover 6 Oct. 1741
v JOHN b. Hanover 23 Jan. 1743
vi BETHIAH b. 23 Sept. 1751; d. 19 May 1808; unm.
vii JOSEPH bp. Scituate 28 Oct. 1753
viii OLIVER bp. Scituate Sept. 1757

References: VR SCITUATE 1:42(b. Agatha), 413(b. Ruth, bp. Joseph, Oliver). MARSHFIELD VR pp. 90(b. Agatha), 92 (b. Oliver). WINSLOW MEMORIAL 1:173(b. Nath., John, Bethiah; d. Agatha, Oliver). Plymouth Co. PR 15:133, 181; 19:337, 339(Oliver Winslow); 15:151, 174, 176, 177, 181 (gdns.). HANOVER FIRST CH pp. 91(2nd m.), 124(bp. Nathaniel), 126(bp. John).

708 DEBORAH WINSLOW[5] (Lydia Snow[4], Josiah[3], Abigail[2] Warren, Richard[1]) b. Marshfield 21 March 1708; living 16 Dec. 1783 (acknowledged deed).

She m. Pembroke 15 Dec. 1742 JOB CROOKER; b. Marshfield 27 Dec. 1708; living 6 Jan. 1785; son of Daniel and Margery (-----) Crooker.

On 9 April 1783, acknowledged 16 Dec. 1783, Job Crooker and wife Deborah sold "the farm on which I live" in Duxbury to John Neal.

On 6 Jan. 1785 Job Crooker made an agreement with neighbors concerning the boundaries of a lot.

No Plymouth Co. PR for Job Crooker.

Child (CROOKER) b. Marshfield:

i ELIZABETH[6] b. 30 Oct. 1748

References: MARSHFIELD VR pp. 49(b. Job), 95(b. Elizabeth), 351(m.). VR PEMBROKE p. 260(m.). Plymouth Co. LR 62:168; 65:6(Job Crooker).

NOTE: VR PEMBROKE & MARSHFIELD VR p. 351 both say he m. ABIGAIL WINSLOW. However, dau. Elizabeth was born to DEBORAH.

709 NATHANIEL WINSLOW[5] (Lydia Snow[4], Josiah[3], Abigail[2] Warren, Richard[1]) b. Marshfield 9 Sept. 1712; d. there 19 Jan. 1786 ae 73y 4m "wanting a day."

He m. LYDIA FORD, b. Marshfield 2 July 1716; d. there 31 Aug. 1793; dau. of Thomas and Ruth (Bradish) Ford.

The will of Nathaniel Winslow of Marshfield, yeoman, dated 24 Dec. 1785, proved April 1786, names wife Lydia; only child Ruth Wadsworth; grandchildren Winslow, Ichabod and Nathaniel Wadsworth; son-in-law Luke Wadsworth.

Children (WINSLOW) b. Marshfield:

i SARAH[6] b. 24 Jan. 1746; d. 14 Jan. 1754 "almost 8 years"
ii NATHANIEL b. 25 March 1748; d. 13 Feb. 1754 ae 5y 10m
iii RUTH b. 19 Aug. 1751
iv SARAH d. 19 Jan. 1754 ae 14d
v HANNAH b. 14 Sept. 1755; d. 27 Jan. 1756 ae 4m 13d

References: MARSHFIELD VR pp. 38(b. Lydia), 94(d. Nath., Lydia), 95(b. 1st 2 ch.), 96(b. 1st 3 ch.), 108(d. ch.), 414(deaths). Plymouth Co. PR 30:65(Nathaniel Winslow). WINSLOW MEMORIAL 1:173-4.

710 ISSACHAR WINSLOW[5] (Mercy Snow[4], Josiah[3], Abigail[2] Warren, Richard[1]) b. Marshfield 19 Feb. 1699; d. No. Yarmouth ME 7 July 1741.

He m. int. Kingston 24 Sept. 1726 MARY MITCHELL.

On 6 April 1737 Issacher Winslow of Marshfield, husbandman, sold land in Marshfield to Anthony Winslow of Marshfield; signed by Issacher and Mary Winslow.

On 13 Dec. 1741 Elsie, Gilbert, Elisabeth and Issachar, children of widow Mary Winslow were bapt.

On 19 June 1760 Gilbert Winslow Jr., tanner; Issacher Winslow, husbandman; Elsie Winslow, spinster; William Low, husbandman & Betty his wife all of N. Yarmouth, sold to Job Winslow of Marshfield land in Marshfield given by their grandfather Gilbert Winslow to their father Issacher Winslow and his heirs in his will.

Children (WINSLOW) first 3 b. Marshfield:

i ELSIE[6] b. 8 Nov. 1730
ii GILBERT b. 8 June 1732
iii ELIZABETH b. 29 Oct. 1734
iv ISSACHAR b. No. Yarmouth ME 27 July 1738

References: MARSHFIELD VR p. 50(b. Gilbert, Eliz.). NO. YARMOUTH ME VR pp. 111(b. 4 ch.), 343(d. Issachar). VR KINGSTON p. 305(int.). OLD TIMES pp. 613(bp. ch.), 1103. Plymouth Co. LR 32:128(Issacher Winslow); 47:236-7(Gilbert Winslow). NO YARMOUTH ME VR Supplement p. 59(corrects d. Issachar).

711 BARNABAS WINSLOW[5] (Mercy Snow[4], Josiah[3], Abigail[2] Warren, Richard[1]) b. Marshfield 24 Feb. 1701; d. No. Yarmouth ME 8 April 1765.

He m. MERCY GLASS, b. No. Yarmouth ME 15 Nov. 1705; dau. of John and Esther (Chandler) Glass.

Barnabas Winslow was town clerk of No.Yarmouth ME from 1733 to 1762, except one year.

Children (WINSLOW) b. No. Yarmouth ME:

i REBECCA[6] b. 9 March 1735
ii ESTHER b. 8 Dec. 1736; d. 16 Dec. 1736
iii STEPHEN b. 2 May 1738; d. 8 June 1738
iv SARAH b. 29 July 1739
v ASENATH b. 1 April 1743; d. 29 Oct. 1753

vi BARNABAS b. 1 March 1745

References: NO. YARMOUTH ME VR pp. 110(b. 1st 4 ch.), 111(b. last 2 ch.), 343(deaths). OLD TIMES p. 1103.

712 GILBERT WINSLOW[5] (Mercy Snow[4], Josiah[3], Abigail[2] Warren, Richard[1]) b. Marshfield 26 July 1704; d. No. Yarmouth ME 9 Jan. 1777.

He m. ca. 1733 PATIENCE SEABURY, b. Duxbury 10 Aug. 1710; dau. of Samuel and Abigail (Allen) Seabury.

On 30 July 1724 Gilbert Winslow of North Yarmouth purchased Lot No. 33 in No. Yarmouth from Edward King.

Children (WINSLOW) b. No. Yarmouth ME:

i SEABURY[6] b. 1 Oct. 1734; d. 3 Oct. 173-
ii BENJAMIN b. 16 Aug. 1737; d. 17 June 1738
iii BENJAMIN b. 26 April 1739
iv LYDIA b. 23 Sept. 1740
v ABIGAIL b. 1 March 1741
vi SEABURY b. 2 March 1742/3
vii SAMUEL b. 12 June 1747
viii PATIENCE b. 29 Aug. 1749
ix HANNAH b. 5 June 1751; d.y.
x GILBERT b. 5 June 1753

References: NO. YARMOUTH ME VR pp. 111(b. of ch.), 343(d. of 2 ch.). ADDENDUM TO NO. YARMOUTH ME VR pp. 19, 59 (corrections). VR DUXBURY p. 150(b. Patience). WINSLOW MEMORIAL 1:186 (d. Gilbert, Hannah). OLD TIMES pp. 435, 794(1724 deed), 1103-4.

713 ANTHONY WINSLOW[5] (Mercy Snow[4], Josiah[3], Abigail[2] Warren, Richard[1]) b. Marshfield 24 April 1707; d. Bridgewater 17 May 1789 ae 83.

He m. Pembroke 7 Jan. 1729 DEBORAH BARKER, b. Scituate 25 Dec. 1710; d. Bridgewater 26 May 1773 ae 63; dau. of Ebenezer and Deborah (Randall) Barker.

No Plymouth Co. PR for Anthony Winslow.

Children (WINSLOW) b. Marshfield:

i LUSANNAH[6] b. 2 April 1730
ii PRISCILLA b. 19 Jan. 1737
iii DEBORAH b. 7 Dec. 1743

References: VR E. BRIDGEWATER p. 403(deaths). VR PEMBROKE p. 376(m.). VR SCITUATE 1:121(b. Deborah). MARSHFIELD VR pp. 89(b. Lusannah), 94(b. last 2 ch.), 351 (m.).

714 MERCY WINSLOW[5] (Mercy Snow[4], Josiah[3], Abigail[2] Warren, Richard[1]) b. Marshfield 1 Aug. 1710; living 3 March 1784.

She m. ca. 1736 WILLIAM HOWLAND, b. Marshfield 12 Feb. 1707/8; d. bet. 3 March 1772 and 17 March 1784; son of Thomas and Mary (-----) Howland.

The will of William Howland of Pembroke, housewright, dated 3 March 1772, proved 17 March 1784, names wife Mercy; son William and daughter Rebecca Keen.

Children (HOWLAND):

i REBECCA[6] b. Marshfield 14 June 1737
ii WILLIAM b. Pembroke 2 Nov. 1741

References: MARSHFIELD VR pp. 27(b. William), 78(b. Rebecca). VR PEMBROKE p. 114(b. son William). Plymouth Co. PR 29:115(William Howland).

715 REBECCA WINSLOW[5] (Mercy Snow[4], Josiah[3], Abigail[2] Warren, Richard[1]) b. Marshfield 3 Jan. 1712; d. bef. 22 March 1761.

She m. ca. 1736 ADAM RICHARDSON, b. Woburn 10 April 1709; d. Brunswick ME 1758; son of Stephen and Bridget (Richardson) Richardson.

Adam Richardson graduated from Harvard in 1730.

On 22 March 1761 Winslow Richardson, Rebekah Richardson and Stephen Richardson, as heirs of Rebekah Richardson, quitclaimed to Job Winslow of Marshfield land in Marshfield.

No ME PR for Adam Richardson.

Children (RICHARDSON) b. Groton:

i WINSLOW[6] b. 14 Dec. 1737
ii REBECKAH b. 13 July 1740
iii STEPHEN b. 6 Aug. 1743

References: VR GROTON 1:199(b. ch.). HARVARD GRADS 8:776-7. VR WOBURN p. 212(b. Adam). Plymouth Co. LR 52:72-3(Winslow Richardson, etc.).

716 JOB WINSLOW[5] (Mercy Snow[4], Josiah[3], Abigail[2] Warren, Richard[1]) b. Marshfield 2 June 1715; d. there 19 May 1787 in 72nd yr.

He m. Marshfield 20 March 1740 ELIZABETH MACOMBER, b. Marshfield 20 Feb. 1715; d. there 16 March 1800 in her 85th yr.; dau. of Thomas and Joanna (Tinkham) Macomber, a descendant of Pilgrim Peter Brown.

On 20 Dec. 1787 Daniel Lewis, housewright of Marshfield, and wife Marcy and Charles Hatch of Scituate and wife Joanna, divided equally the estate of their father Job Winslow dec., reserving to their mother widow Elizabeth Winslow her thirds.

No Plymouth Co. PR for Job or Elizabeth Winslow.

Children (WINSLOW) b. Marshfield:

i MERCY[6] b. 11 March 1741
ii BENJAMIN b. ca. 1745; d. 4 Dec. 1761 in 17th yr.
iii JOANNA b. 18 March 1755

References: MARSHFIELD VR pp. 38(b. Eliz.), 77(b. Mercy, Joanna), 171(m.), 414(d. Job, Eliz., Benj.). Plymouth Co. LR 68:103(Daniel Lewis, etc.). MF 7:83-4.

717 SAMUEL BAKER[5] (Sarah Snow[4], Josiah[3], Abigail[2] Warren, Richard[1]) b. Marshfield 12 June 1701; d. there 4 Nov. 1792 in 91st yr.

He m. Marshfield 9 Nov. 1726 HANNAH FORD, b. ca. 1705; d. Marshfield 28 April 1800 in 95th yr.; dau. of James and Hannah (Dingley) Ford.

On 16 May 1731 Samuel Baker joined the Marshfield First Church; wife Hannah joined 13 June 1731.

The will of Samuel Baker of Marshfield dated 3 Aug. 1790, proved 2 Dec. 1793, names wife Hannah; sons James, Thomas, Charles and Elijah; daus. Eleanor, Hannah, Bethia and Abigail (no surnames).

Children (BAKER) b. Duxbury:

i ELEANOR[6] b. 21 Sept. 1727
ii HANNAH b. 25 Feb. 1729
iii BETHIA b. 11 May 1733
iv JAMES b. 4 Jan. 1737
v THOMAS b. 27 Jan. 1739
vi CHARLES b. 26 April 1741
vii ELIJAH b. 1 July 1744
viii ABIGAIL b. 24 Sept. 1746

References: MARSHFIELD VR p. 145(m.). Plymouth Co. PR 33:498, 559(Samuel Baker). MD 31:170(Samuel, Hannah join); 32:15(bp. James), 16(bp. Thomas), 17(bp. Charles), 20(bp. Elijah). VR DUXBURY pp. 21-2(b. ch.).

718 JOSHUA BAKER[5] (Sarah Snow[4], Josiah[3], Abigail[2] Warren, Richard[1]) b. Marshfield 16 Sept. 1711; d. bef. 6 Aug. 1753(adm.).

He apparently m. Pembroke 3 Sept. 1730 SARAH CUSHING.

On 6 Aug. 1753 Sarah Baker, widow, and Edward Thomas, yeoman, were appointed to administer the estate of Joshua Baker of Pembroke, blacksmith.

Children (BAKER) b. Pembroke:

i DANIEL[6] bp. 25 Aug. 1737
ii SNOW b. 7 July 1739; bp. 19 Aug. 1739

References: Plymouth Co. PR 13:57(Joshua Baker). VR PEMBROKE pp. 22(bp. Daniel), 23(b. Snow), 230(m.).

NOTE: He would be just under 19 at time of mar. which is young, but they had a child SNOW b. Pembroke 7 July 1739 (VR) which makes the identification quite likely.

719 SARAH BAKER[5] (Sarah Snow[4], Josiah[3], Abigail[2] Warren, Richard[1]) b. Marshfield 25 Feb. 1713.

She m. Newbury 30 Nov. 1733 FOBES LITTLE, b. Marshfield 9 March 1712/3; d. Little Compton RI May 1801; son of John and Constant (Fobes) Little, a descendant of Pilgrims John Alden and Richard Warren.

See #509 for an account of this family.

References: MARSHFIELD VR p. 33(b. Fobes). VR NEWBURY 2:291 (m.).

720 ELISHA BAKER[5] (Sarah Snow[4], Josiah[3], Abigail[2] Warren, Richard[1]) b. Marshfield 10 July 1715; d. bef. 11 April 1788.

He m. (1) prob. Falmouth ME 2 Nov. 1737 SARAH WILSON of Falmouth ME; bp. Kittery ME 10 Oct. 1730 (prob. as an adult); dau. of Gowan and Ann (Shepherd) Wilson.

He m. (2) bef. 13 Oct. 1765 (deed) HANNAH -----; living 30 Aug. 1787.

On 19 Nov. 1736 Elisha Baker of Pembroke sold seven acres in Marshfield to Nathan Thomas of Marshfield. On the same date he sold land to Samuel Thomas.

On 18 Oct. 1737 Elisha Baker of North Yarmouth, Mass. Bay Colony sold 43 acres in Duxbury and Pembroke to Henry Ford Jr.

On 19 June 1740 Elisha Baker of Falmouth, blacksmith, bought 6 acres in Falmouth [ME] from Thomas Westbrook.

On 8 April 1763 Elisha Baker, husbandman, mortgaged 77 acres in Brunswick [ME] to Jabez Jones of Falmouth. The mortgage says Elisha bought this land 18 Aug. 1760 from Benjamin Thompson of Georgetown [ME].

On 13 Oct. 1765 Elisha Baker of Brunswick, blacksmith, and wife Hannah sold 4 acres in Brunswick to John Pattin.

On 29 March 1784, ack. same day, Elisha Baker of Brunswick, yeoman, sold land in Brunswick to Hosea Baker.

On 30 Aug. 1787 Josiah Baker of Falmouth, Elisha Baker of Brunswick, Ichabod Baker of Wales, John and Elizabeth Welsh of Wales and John and Olive Andrus of Brunswick sold 70 acres in Brunswick to Alexander Thompson of Wales, subject to the widow's thirds which would also pass to him at her death.

The 11 April 1788 settlement of the estate of Elisha Baker went to children Josiah, Elisha, Ann Shepard, Ichabod, Sarah, Elizabeth, Joseph, Benjamin, Hannah and Olive.

Children (BAKER) all b. prob. Falmouth ME, all or most by Sarah:

- i ELISHA[6] b. ca. 1737 (based on age at death)
- ii ANN SHEPARD bp. Falmouth ME 1739
- iii JOSIAH b. ca. 1740 (based on age at death)
- iv ICHABOD bp. Falmouth ME 1744
- v SARAH
- vi ELIZABETH
- vii JOSEPH
- viii BENJAMIN
- ix HANNAH
- x OLIVE

References: Plymouth Co. LR 31:39(to Nathan Thomas), 124(to Henry Ford); 32:33(to Samuel Thomas). NEHGR 14:223(int. 1st m.). BOSTON EVENING TRANSCRIPT 10 Oct. 1719 #5183(1st m.; settlement). First Church Kittery ME(bp. Sarah). ME NH GEN DICT p. 761(Wilson). First Church Falmouth ME p. 53(bp. Ann, Ichabod). York Co. ME LR 22:220(from Thomas Westbrook). Cumberland Co. ME LR 5:432(mort.); 13:14(to Hosea Baker); 19:363(sale by ch.), 445(to John Patten). Poplar Ridge Cemetery, Falmouth ME(g.s. son Elisha). Eastern Cemetery of Portland ME(g.s. of Josiah). OLD TIMES p. 395(int. 1st m.).

721 NATHANIEL BAKER[5] (Sarah Snow[4], Josiah[3], Abigail[2] Warren, Richard[1]) b. Marshfield 28 May 1719; d. bef. 2 June 1760 (adm.).

He m. (1) Pembroke 29 Dec. 1740 SUSANNAH LINCOLN, b. Pembroke; d. bef. 4 June 1750; dau. of John and Susannah (Nichols) Lincoln. The 4 June 1750 division of the estate of John Lincoln mentions children of Susannah Baker, dec.

He m. (2) ca. 1750 SARAH NICHOLS, b. Hingham 22 Feb. 1715; d. bef. 6 Dec. 1762; dau. of Ephraim and Susanna (Waterman) Nichols. The will of Susannah Nichols dated 19 Nov. 1750 names dau. Sarah executrix. She was Sarah Baker 2 June 1760 when she filed an account of her mother's estate.

On 11 March 1740/1 Nathaniel Baker of Pembroke, cordwainer, sold 82 acres in Duxbury to Samuel Thomas of Marshfield.

On 30 Dec. 1743 Nathaniel Baker of Pembroke, cordwainer, sold meadow in Marshfield to Nathaniel Keen of Pembroke.

On 2 June 1760 Seth Jacobs of Pembroke was appointed administrator of the estate of Nathaniel Baker. On 4 Aug. 1760 he reported the estate insolvent. No mention of a widow.

Children (BAKER) b. Pembroke, first 3 by Susanna:

i BENJAMIN[6] b. 10 June 1741
ii JOHN b. 22 May 1743
iii SUSANNA b. 28 July 1747
iv NICHOLS b. 20 Sept. 1751
v ABIGAIL b. 25 Sept. 1753
vi BETTY b. 6 Nov. 1756

References: VR PEMBROKE pp. 22-3(b. ch.), 230(1st m.). HINGHAM HIST 2:85(b. Sarah). Plymouth Co. LR 33:235; 36:164(Nathaniel Baker). Plymouth Co. PR 11:357(John Lincoln); 12:292; 15:521, 532(Susanna Nichols), 572(Nathaniel Baker).

722 BETHIAH SPRAGUE[5] (Bethiah Snow[4], Josiah[3], Abigail[2] Warren, Richard[1]) b. prob. Marshfield ca. 1707; living 21 July 1755 (deed).

She m. Duxbury 14 Dec. 1732 DAVID CURTIS, b. Scituate 26 June 1708; living 21 July 1755 (deed); son of Benjamin and Mary (Silvester) Curtis.

On 6 Jan. 1748 David Curtis of Hanover, yeoman, sold land in Scituate to David Jenkins. On 12 Oct. 1750 David Curtis of Hanover, husbandman, sold land in Scituate to William Whitten and Thomas Whitten.

On 21 July 1755 David Curtis of N. Yarmouth, county of York [ME], yeoman, sold his farm in Hanover to Joseph Soper. Bethiah Curtis, wife of David, surrendered her right to dower; acknowledged same day.

Children (CURTIS) b. Hanover:

i NEHEMIAH[6] b. 3 Jan. 1733
ii EZEKIEL b. 30 April 1735
iii PAUL b. 29 May 1737
iv MICHAEL b. 30 April 1739
v DAVID b. 23 Aug. 1741
vi RUTH b. 31 July 1743

References: NEHGR 124:120(Sprague). HANOVER VR p. 20(b. ch.). VR DUXBURY p. 238(m.). VR SCITUATE 1:107(b. David). Plymouth Co. LR 44:201; 47:172; 52:27(David Curtis).

723 JOHN SPRAGUE[5] (Bethiah Snow[4], Josiah[3], Abigail[2] Warren, Richard[1]) b. prob. Duxbury ca. 1709; d. Duxbury Sept. 1784.

He m. Duxbury 5 Dec. 1744 DEBORAH (BISHOP) SIMMONS b. Pembroke 6 Aug. 1712; living 14 March 1770 (deed); dau. of

Ebenezer and Amy (Stetson) Bishop. She m. (1) Pembroke 27 May 1731 Zachariah Simmons by whom she had Lorah.

On 14 March 1770 John Sprague of Duxborough, yeoman, and Deborah his wife sold land in Duxborough to John Peterson.

No Plymouth Co. PR for John Sprague.

Children (SPRAGUE) b. Duxbury:

i BETHIAH[6] b. 23 April 1745
ii SNOW b. 28 May 1749; d. 28 Feb. 1749/50

References: VR DUXBURY pp. 168(b. Bethiah), 169(b. Snow), 315(m.), 426(d. John), 427(d. Snow). VR PEMBROKE pp. 36(b. Deborah), 347(her 1st m.). NEHGR 124:120(Sprague). Plymouth Co. LR 55:103(John Sprague).

724 REBECCA SPRAGUE[5] (Bethiah Snow[4], Josiah[3], Abigail[2] Warren, Richard[1]) b. prob. Duxbury ca. 1711; d. Duxbury 20 or 25 Oct. 1805 ae 94y 8m 8d.

She m. Duxbury 27 July 1732 EZRA ARNOLD, b. Duxbury 30 July 1707; d. there 18 Feb. 1780; son of Edward and Mercy (Brewster) Arnold, a descendant of Pilgrims William Brewster and James Chilton.

The will of Ezra Arnold of Duxbury, yeoman, dated 1 Nov. 1779, proved 6 March 1780, names wife Rebecca; sons Seth and Gamaliel; dau. Lucy Freeman, wife of Edmund Freeman; sons William and Edward.

Children (ARNOLD) b. Duxbury:

i SETH[6] b. 12 June 1733
ii GAMALIEL b. 8 Aug. 1735
iii LUCY
iv WILLIAM
v EDWARD

References: NEHGR 124:120(Sprague). MF 15:110. VR DUXBURY pp. 19(b. Ezra, b. ch.), 214(m.), 348(d. Rebecca, Ezra). Plymouth Co. PR 25:416-8(Ezra Arnold).

725 JOANNA SPRAGUE[5] (Bethiah Snow[4], Josiah[3], Abigail[2] Warren, Richard[1]) b. prob. Duxbury ca. 1715; d. Duxbury 19 March 1766 ae 50y 11m.

She m. Duxbury 19 Feb. 1734/5 JAMES ARNOLD, bp. Marshfield 20 Oct. 1700; d. Duxbury 24 Sept. 1755 ae 55; son of Seth and Elizabeth (Gray) Arnold, a descendant of Pilgrim James Chilton.

On 6 Oct. 1755 Joanna Arnold of Duxboro was appointed administratrix of the estate of James Arnold late of Duxboro. On 7 May 1759 all the real estate was alloted to eldest son

Bildad Arnold, after reserving his mother's dower; he was to pay his brothers Luther, James and Benjamin Arnold.
No Plymouth Co. PR for Joanna Arnold.

Children (ARNOLD) b. Duxbury:

i BILDAD[6] b. 20 Nov. 1735
ii LUTHER b. Sept. 1737
iii JAMES b. 23 Sept. 1740; d. 9 Sept. 1742 ae 1y 11m 16d
iv JAMES b. 1745
v BENJAMIN bp. 12 April 1752

References: VR DUXBURY pp. 19(b. & bp. ch.), 214(m.), 348 (deaths). MD 11:122(bp. James). NEHGR 124:120 (Sprague). Plymouth Co. PR 13:551(James Arnold). MF 15:36.

726 PELEG SPRAGUE[5] (Bethiah Snow[4], Josiah[3], Abigail[2] Warren, Richard[1]) b. prob. Duxbury ca. 1716; d. Duxbury 28 Dec. 1754 in 38th yr.
He m. Duxbury 18 Feb. 1745/6 MERCY CHANDLER, b. ca. 1726; d. Duxbury 28 Oct. 1815 in 89th yr.; dau. of Nathaniel and Zerviah (Sprague) Chandler. She m. (2) ca. 1755 Phinehas Sprague by whom she had Peleg, Seth, Mercy and Ruth. She m. (3) Duxbury Aug. 1781 Ichabod Simmons.
On 3 Feb. 1755 Marcy Sprague was named administratrix of the estate of Peleg Sprague of Duxbury.

Children (SPRAGUE) b. Duxbury:

i NATHANIEL[6] b. 15 Nov. 1747
ii PELEG b. 25 May 1751; d. 6 May 1756 ae abt. 5
iii JOHN bp. Duxbury 14 Sept. 1755, son of Mercy, widow

References: VR DUXBURY pp. 168(bp. John), 169(b. 1st 2 ch.), 307(her 3rd m.), 315(m.), 417(d. Mercy), 426(d. Peleg, son Peleg). Plymouth Co. PR 13:377, 452(Peleg Sprague). NEHGR 124:120(Sprague).

727 ASENATH SPRAGUE[5] (Bethiah Snow[4], Josiah[3], Abigail[2] Warren, Richard[1]) b. prob. Duxbury ca. 1723; d. Hanover 14 Sept. 1757.
She m. Duxbury 20 April 1742 SIMEON CURTIS, b. Scituate 1 June 1720; d. Hanover 7 March 1800 ae 79; son of Samuel and Anna (Barstow) Curtis. He m. (2) Hanover 9 Jan. 1759 Lucy (Barker) Macomber by whom he had Lucy, Mary and Barker.
The will of Simeon Curtis of Hanover, gentleman, dated 4 March 1794, proved 31 March 1800, names wife Lucy; sons

Melzar, James, Simeon and Barker Curtis; dau. Mary Young; granddau. Asenath Stetson; grandson Charles Stetson.

Children (CURTIS) b. Hanover:

i SIMEON[6] b. 4 July 1743; d.y.
ii MELZAR b. 17 April 1745
iii JAMES b. 17 July 1747
iv ASENATH b. 21 Nov. 1749
v SUSANNA b. 25 Nov. 1753
vi SIMEON b. 11 Oct. 1756

References: VR DUXBURY p. 238(m.). VR SCITUATE 1:114(b. Simeon). HANOVER VR pp. 18(b. ch.), 120(2nd m.), 187(d. Asenath), 194(d. Simeon). NEHGR 124:120(Sprague). Plymouth Co. PR 37:214, 245, 365(Simeon Curtis).

728 ASAPH TRACY[5] (Lusannah Snow[4], Josiah[3], Abigail[2] Warren, Richard[1]) b. Marshfield 12 Oct. 1723; d. Pembroke 6 July 1799 in 76th yr.

He m. Pembroke 21 Dec. 1749 MARY JACOB, b. 21 Dec. 1725; d. Pembroke 5 Dec. 1786 ae 61 yrs. wanting 16 days; dau. of Samuel and Susanna (-----) Jacob.

On 9 Nov. 1796 Asaph Tracy of Pembroke, yeoman, gave his son Jacob Tracy of Pembroke, cordwainer, all his real estate in Pembroke.

No Plymouth Co. PR for Asaph Tracy.

Children (TRACY) b. Pembroke:

i LUSANNAH[6] b. 21 Aug. 1750
ii THOMAS b. 26 Nov. 1752; d. there 21 Jan. 1776; unm. No PR.
iii ASAPH b. 22 Nov. 1755; d. 4 Dec. 1755
iv ASAPH b. 25 Dec. 1756
v JACOB b. 6 Aug. 1760

References: VR PEMBROKE pp. 208(b. ch.), 364(m.), 456(deaths). TRACY GEN p. 37. Plymouth Co. LR 81:58(Asaph Tracy).

729 ABIGAIL BRANCH[5] (Lydia Ford[4], Abigail Snow[3], Abigail[2] Warren, Richard[1]) b. Marshfield 1 Feb. 1692/3; living 27 March 1764.

She m. Marshfield 28 Feb. 1711/2 WILLIAM CARVER, b. Marshfield 29 Oct. 1685; d. there 1763; son of William and Elizabeth (Foster) Carver.

On 2 Jan. 1764 William Carver of Marshfield was appointed administrator on the estate of William Carver of Marshfield, yeoman. On 27 March 1764 the estate was ordered to be divided with the widow Abigail to be given her dower and the rest divided between eldest son Reuben and Lydia, Elizabeth, Deborah, Abigail, William, Huldah and Keziah.

Children (CARVER) b. Marshfield:

i dau. (worn) (LYDIA)[6] b. 24 (worn) 1712
ii ELIZABETH b. 4 Sept. 1715.
iii REUBEN b. 6 Dec. 1718
iv AMOS b. 20 March 1720; d. "Jemeco" 17 July 1748. No PR.
v DEBORAH b. 14 Jan. 1722
vi ABIGAIL b. 12 Feb. 1724
vii WILLIAM b. 29 Dec. 1727
viii HULDAH b. 22 Nov. 1730
ix KEZIAH b. 8 Jan. 1737/8

References: MARSHFIELD VR pp. 19(b. Wm.), 37(m.), 42(b. Elizabeth), 46(b. dau.), 80(b. Wm., Huldah, Keziah), 86(b. Reuben, Amos, Deborah), 98(d. Amos). Plymouth Co. PR 17:122; 19:43, 87; 20:105(William Carver).

730 THOMAS BRANCH[5] (Lydia Ford[4], Abigail Snow[3], Abigail[2] Warren, Richard[1]) b. Marshfield 20 Oct. 1695; d. bef. 14 Feb. 1731 (adm.).

He m. Plymouth 11 Oct. 1720 LYDIA BARROW, b. Plymouth 19 March 1699; d. bef. 17 Nov. 1752(adm.); dau. of Robert and Lydia (Dunham) Barrow.

On 14 Feb. 1731 Lydia Branch of Plymouth was appointed administratrix of the estate of Mr. Thomas Branch of Plymouth, dec. The estate was divided 10 Sept. 1745, with the widow receiving her dower and children John Branch; Lydia, wife of Nathaniel Shurtleff; Mary Branch; Thankful Branch and youngest dau. Experience Branch receiving their shares.

On 17 Nov. 1752 Nathaniel Shurtleff was appointed administrator of the estate of Lydia Branch dec. The estate was divided 12 Nov. 1753 between Lydia, wife of Nathaniel Shurtleff; Mary, wife of Ebenezer Churchill; Experience wife of Samuel Sherman; and Thomas Howard only child of Thomas Howard dec. [son of dau. Thankful].

Children (BRANCH) b. Plymouth:

i LYDIA[6] b. 26 Aug. 1721
ii MARCY (or MARY) b. 15 July 1723
iii JOHN b. 24 May 1725
iv THANKFUL b. 5 June 1727
v THOMAS b. 24 Nov 1729 (not in division)
vi EXPERIENCE b. 3 April 1732

References: Plymouth Co. PR 6:129, 227, 282; 10:1(Thomas Branch); 13:23, 100, 155, 169(Lydia Branch). MD 1:209(b. Lydia); 11:113(b. ch.); 14:37(m.). PLYMOUTH VR pp. 10(b. Lydia), 65(b. ch.), 92(m.).

731 WILLIAM FORD[5] (William[4], Abigail Snow[3], Abigail[2] Warren, Richard[1]) b. Marshfield Sept. 1696; d. bef. 26 Feb. 1787 (adm.).

He m. Marshfield 7 Dec. 1721 HANNAH TRUANT.

On 21 June 1766, acknowledged 7 July 1766, William Ford of Marshfield, yeoman, and wife Hannah sold land in Marshfield to Levi Ford.

On 26 Feb. 1787 Elijah Ford was appointed to administer the estate of William Ford of Marshfield.

Children (FORD) b. Marshfield:

i SILENCE[6] b. 22 Nov. 1722
ii ABNER b. 8 Nov. 1724
iii ABIGAIL b. 24 Sept. 17--
iv LEVI (date of b. worn off)
v NATHAN b. 14 Jan. 1727
vi ELIJAH b. 2 May 1731

References: MARSHFIELD VR pp. 48(b. Abigail, Levi), 88(b. Silence, Abner, Nathan), 90(b. Elijah), 143(m.). Plymouth Co. PR 27:235; 30:104, 312(William Ford). Plymouth Co. LR 64:88(Wm. Ford).

732 SAMUEL FORD[5] (William[4], Abigail Snow[3], Abigail[2] Warren, Richard[1]) b. Marshfield 11 May 1701; d. there 5 Feb. 1781 in 80th yr.

He m. Marshfield 16 Feb. 1728 SARAH ROGERS, b. Marshfield 26 Dec. 1705; d. there 13 June 1796 in 91st yr.; dau. of John and Hannah (Sprague) Rogers.

The will of Samuel Ford of Marshfield dated 18 Oct. 1765, proved June 1781, names wife Sarah; son Samuel; daus. Kezia Hall, Sarah Ford, Betty Ford; grandson Stephen Cushing; granddau. Jemima Ford Cushing.

No Plymouth Co. PR for Sarah Ford.

Children (FORD) b. Marshfield:

i JEMIMA[6] b. 18 Oct. 1729
ii KEZIA b. 14 April 1732
iii SAMUEL b. 6 June 1735
iv SARAH b. 3 July 1738
v LUKE b. 21 July 1741 (not in will)
vi BETTY b. 31 May 1747

References: MARSHFIELD VR pp. 49(b. Jemima, Kezia), 80(b. Luke), 81(b. wife Sarah, Samuel, Sarah), 102(b. Betty), 146(m.). Plymouth Co. PR 28:141(Samuel Ford).

733 ELIZABETH FORD[5] (William[4], Abigail Snow[3], Abigail[2] Warren, Richard[1]) b. Marshfield 27 Feb. 1703; living 28 Feb. 1783.

She m. Marshfield 6 April 1731 TIMOTHY TAYLOR, bp. Marshfield 3 Dec. 1704; d. bef. 2 April 1783; son of Joseph and Experience (Williamson) Taylor.

On 2 Sept. 1766 Timothy Taylor of Stoneham, Middlesex Co., housewright, sold land to Samuel Taylor of Pembroke which had been owned by his father Joseph Taylor.

The will of Timothy Taylor of Stoneham, yeoman, dated 23 Nov. 1782, proved 2 April 1783, names wife Elizabeth; son Peleg; daughter Ruth and minor grandchildren Mary and Elizabeth Taylor [daughters of dec. son Micah]. Son Peleg declined administration and on 28 Feb. 1783 the widow Elizabeth and dau. Ruth Taylor consented to Deacon Edward Bucknam as administrator.

Children (TAYLOR) b. Marshfield:

i BERIAH[6] b. 26 March 1732
ii PELEG b. 21 Oct. 1733
iii TIMOTHY b. 6 June 1735; d. 26 June 1735
iv SIMEON b. 20 Sept. 1736 (not in will)
v BENJAMIN b. 22 Sept. 1738 (not in will)
vi MICAH b. 24 April 1740
vii RUTH b. 15 June 1743; living unm. 28 Feb. 1783

References: MARSHFIELD VR pp. 95(b. ch.; d. Timothy), 140(m.). Plymouth Co. LR 60:12(Timothy Taylor). MD 11:123(bp. Timothy). Middlesex Co. PR #22255(Timothy Taylor).

734 JAMES FORD[5] (James[4], Abigail Snow[3], Abigail[2] Warren, Richard[1]) b. Marshfield ca. 1699; d. Norwich CT 5 May 1757 ae 58.

He m. ca. 1726 ELIZABETH BARTLETT, b. Marshfield Sept. 1708; d. Norwich CT 4 May 1755; dau. of Ichabod and Elizabeth (Waterman) Bartlett, a descendant of Pilgrim Richard Warren (see #255).

The will of James Ford dated 21 April 1757, proved 12 May 1757, names sons James, Joseph, Ichabod and John; daus. Ann, Elizabeth, Hannah and Sarah.

Children (FORD) last 6 b. rec. Norwich CT:

i ANN[6] bp. Marshfield 9 July 1727
ii ELIZABETH bp. Marshfield 5 Oct. 1729

iii JAMES b. 5 Sept. 1734
iv JOSEPH b. 16 Aug. 1737
v ICHABOD b. 22 Feb. 1740
vi HANNAH b. 22 Feb. 1743
vii JOHN b. 22 June 1745; d. 1763 unm.
viii SARAH b. 22 Dec. 1749

References: WATERMAN GEN 1:658-9. NORWICH CT VR 1:169(d. James, Eliz.; b. last 6 ch.). Norwich CT PR #3930(James Ford). MARSHFIELD VR p. 25(b. Eliz.). MD 31:166(bp. Ann), 168(bp. Elizabeth).

735 ABIGAIL FORD[5] (James[4], Abigail Snow[3], Abigail[2] Warren, Richard[1]) b. Marshfield 1701; living 17 July 1762 (will).

She m. Marshfield 13 March 1728/9 JOHN JOYCE, b. Marshfield 2 Oct. 1702; d. there 29 Nov. 1762 in 60th yr.; son of Thomas and Elizabeth (-----) Joyce.

The will of John Joyce of Marshfield, yeoman, dated 17 July 1762, proved 6 Dec. 1762, names wife Abigail; sons Ebenezer, John, Nathaniel and Thomas; daughters Abigail Joyce and Abiah Lapham.

No Plymouth Co. PR for Abigail Joyce.

Children (JOYCE) b. Marshfield:

i (worn) (EBENEZER)[6] b. 6 Dec. 1729
ii ABIAH b. 27 June 1731
iii JOHN b. 22 Nov. 1733
iv THOMAS bp. 3 Sept. 1738
v NATHANIEL b. 31 Aug. 1742
vi ABIGAIL b. 26 April 1744

References: MARSHFIELD VR pp. 28(b. John), 48(b. Ebenezer), 49(b. Abiah, John), 70(b. Abigail), 77(b. Nath.), 146(m.), 404(d. John). Plymouth Co. PR 16:377(John Joyce).

736 HANNAH FORD[5] (James[4], Abigail Snow[3], Abigail[2] Warren, Richard[1]) b. Marshfield 18 Oct. 1705; d. there 28 April 1800 ae 95 yrs.

She m. Marshfield 9 Nov. 1726 SAMUEL BAKER, b. Marshfield 5 Feb. 1702/3; d. there 4 Nov. 1793 in 91st yr.; son of Kenelm and Sarah (Bradford) Baker, a descendant of Pilgrim William Bradford.

The will of Samuel Baker of Duxbury, yeoman, dated 3 Aug. 1790, proved 2 Dec. 1793, names wife Hannah; sons James, Thomas, Charles and Elijah; daus. Eleanor, Hannah, Bethiah and Abigail (no surnames).

No Plymouth Co. PR for Hannah Baker.

Children (BAKER) b. Duxbury:

i ELEANOR[6] b. 21 Sept. 1727
ii HANNAH b. 25 Feb. 1729
iii BETHIAH b. 11 May 1733
iv SAMUEL b. 26 Feb. 1735; d. May 1759 "drowned at Sea Eastward," prob. unm. No PR.
v JAMES b. 4 Jan. 1737
vi THOMAS b. 24 Jan. 1739
vii CHARLES b. 26 April 1741
viii ELIJAH b. 1 July 1744
ix ABIGAIL b. 24 Sept. 1746

References: MARSHFIELD VR pp. 145(m.), 398(d. Hannah), 399(d. Samuel). VR DUXBURY pp. 21-2(b. ch.), 349(d. son Samuel). MD 11:238-9(b. ch.); 12:55(d. Samuel, Hannah). Plymouth Co. PR 33:498(Samuel Baker).

737 MICHAEL FORD[5] (James[4], Abigail Snow[3], Abigail[2] Warren, Richard[1]) b. Marshfield 23 April 1710; d. there May 1764.

He m. ca. 1738 ORPHAN WATERMAN, b. Marshfield 21 Aug. 1715; d. there 15 Feb. 1791 in 76th yr.; dau. of Anthony and Elizabeth (Arnold) Waterman, a descendant of Pilgrim Richard Warren (see #757). She m. (2) Pembroke 18 Dec. 1775 Aaron Soule.

The will of Michael Ford of Marshfield dated 3 May 1764, proved 2 June 1764, names wife Orphan; daus. Sarah Ford, Lucy Ford, Lydia Ford, Elizabeth Ford, Hannah Ford and Ann Ford; sons Seth, Waterman and Michael Ford.

The 4 Sept. 1794 division of the estate of Orphan Soul names Seth, Waterman, Lucy and Michael Ford; Elizabeth dec. wife of George Keith; Hannah, wife of Hezekiah Keene; Anna, wife of Marlborough Ford.

Children (FORD) b. Marshfield:

i SETH[6] b. 4 March 1738/9
ii SARAH b. 14 Sept. 1740; d. Marshfield 2 Sept. 1776 ae 36y wanting 12d; unm.
iii JAMES b. 28 July 1742; d.y.
iv LUCE b. 18 Sept. 1744
v WATERMAN b. 27 Jan. 1745
vi MICHEL b. 20 Feb. 1747
vii LYDIA b. 13 April 1750; d. 11 May 1784 in 34th yr.; unm.
viii ELIZABETH b. 31 Aug. 1752
ix HANNAH b. 4 Jan. 1754
x ANN b. 23 Dec. 1757

References: MARSHFIELD VR pp. 83(b. Seth, Sarah), 98(b. 8 ch.), 99(d. Orphan), 401(d. Lydia). MF 3:49. Plymouth Co. PR 9:64(Michael Ford); 35:307(division). VR PEMBROKE p. 348(her 2nd m.). MD 12:150(d. Sarah, Lydia). WATERMAN GEN 1:141-3, 658.

738 BARNABAS FORD[5] (James[4], Abigail Snow[3], Abigail[2] Warren, Richard[1]) b. Marshfield 1714; d. there 3 Sept. 1773 in 59th yr.

He m. HANNAH SPRAGUE, b. Marshfield 18 March 1722; d. Pembroke bef. 7 Nov. 1785 (inv.); dau. of James and Hannah (Black) Sprague.

The will of Barnabas Ford of Pembroke, yeoman, dated 17 Aug. 1773, proved 27 Sept. 1773, names wife Hannah; son James; dau. Olive Barker; son-in-law Thomas Barker.

The inventory of the estate of Hannah Ford, late of Pembroke, was taken 7 Nov. 1785. On 17 Nov. 1785 James Ford, administrator of the estate, swore to the inventory.

Children (FORD) named in will:

i JAMES[6]
ii OLIVE

References: MARSHFIELD VR pp. 86(b. Hannah), 401(d. Barnabas, Hannah). Plymouth Co. PR 21:566-7(Barnabas Ford); #7907(Hannah Ford). MD 12:149(d. Barnabas).

739 JONATHAN GRINNELL[5] (Abigail Ford[4], Abigail Snow[3], Abigail[2] Warren, Richard[1]) b. Little Compton 7 Feb. 1710/1; d. aft. 1777.

He m. Little Compton 30 April 1735 ALICE MIAS, b. Little Compton 13 Feb. 1710; d. aft. 20 Jan. 1772 (deed); dau. of Nicholas and Elizabeth (Nichols) Mias.

On 13 Sept. 1758 Thomas Howland of Tiverton sold 3 tracts of land in Tiverton to Jonathan Grinnell of Elizabeth Islands, Dukes Co., Mass., cordwainer.

On 6 Oct. 1768 Jonathan Grinnell of Tiverton, yeoman, sold 10 acres in Tiverton to Daniel Grinell of Tiverton, mariner; wife Alice also signed. On 20 Jan. 1772 Jonathan Grinnell of Tiverton, cordwainer, sold 80 acres in Tiverton to sons Daniel Grinnell of Tiverton, blacksmith, and Gideon Grinnell of Tiverton, cooper; wife Alice renounced her dower.

Jonathan Grinnell as over 60 in the 1777 Military Census of RI.

No probate found for Jonathan Grinell.

Children (GRINNELL) 3 b. Little Compton, rest b. Dartmouth:

i NATHANIEL[6] b. 9 Nov. 1735
ii REMINGTON b. 4 June 1738
iii ABIGAIL b. Dartmouth 17 April 1740
iv DANIEL b. 4 June 1742
v GIDEON b. Dartmouth 26 Aug. 1745

References: RIVR Little Compton 4:6:30(m.), 122(b. Nathaniel, Remington, Daniel), 138(b. Alice). LITTLE COMPTON FAMS p. 309. Tiverton RI LE 1:263(Thomas Howland); 2:112(Jonathan Grinnell). VR DARTMOUTH 1:104(b. Abigail, Gideon). RHODE ISLAND 1777 MILITARY CENSUS p. 106.

740 JOHN HEWETT[5] (Sarah Waterman[4], Sarah Snow[3], Abigail[2] Warren, Richard[1]) b. Marshfield 16 Sept. 1700; d. Norwich CT 5 April 1760.

He m. Norwich CT 5 Sept. 1727 RUTH GIFFORD, b. Norwich CT 1 Sept. 1706; living 2 April 1760; dau. of Samuel and Mary (Calkins) Gifford.

The will of John Hewett dated 2 April 1760, proved 1 May 1760, names wife Ruth; sons Solomon, John, Amos "incapable", Elisha, Benjamin and Jedediah; daus. Ruth, wife of John Griswold, and Lydia.

Children (HEWETT) b. Norwich CT:

i SOLOMON[6] b. 12 March 1729
ii JOHN b. 30 Jan. 1730/1
iii AMOS b. 5 May 1733
iv ELISHA b. 8 June 1734
v RUTH b. 25 Oct. 1737
vi LYDIA b. 27 March 1740
vii BENJAMIN b. 9 Feb. 1742/3; d. 22 Sept. 1762
viii JEDEDIAH b. 19 Nov. 1748

References: NORWICH CT VR 1:117(m.; d. John; b. ch.). Norwich CT PR 2:420; #5207(John Hewett). WATERMAN GEN 1:57, 662.

741 JOSEPH HEWETT[5] (Sarah Waterman[4], Sarah Snow[3], Abigail[2] Warren, Richard[1]) b. Marshfield 14 July 1702; d. there 3 March 1749 in 47th yr.

He m. Marshfield 19 Dec. 1728 SARAH DINGLEY, b. Marshfield 22 Feb. 1707/8; d. there 28 Aug. 1776 in her 68th yr.; dau. of John and Sarah (Porter) Dingley.

On 22 March 1748 Jacob Dingley of Duxbury was appointed to administer the estate of Joseph Hewett of Marshfield, dec. On 2 July 1750 Sarah Hewett received her dower and the rest of the estate was divided between eldest son Solomon Hewett; daus. Tabitha Hewett and Hannah Hewett; second son Joseph Hewett; third son John Hewett and youngest dau. Sarah Hewett. The estate could not be divided, so on 15 July 1759 the estate was settled on Solomon Hewett, save for his mother's dower and Solomon was to pay brothers Joseph and John and sisters Tabitha Baker, Hannah Hewett and Sarah Hewett.

Children (HEWETT) b. Marshfield:

i ABIGAIL[6] b. 26 Sept. 1729; d. 29 July 1745 in 16th yr.
ii SOLOMON bp. 20 Feb. 1730/1
iii TABITHA b. 11 March 1733/4
iv HANNAH b. 24 Dec. 1736
v JOSEPH b. 7 June 1739
vi JOHN bp. 29 Nov. 1741
vii SARAH (named in division)

References: MARSHFIELD VR pp. 29(b. Sarah), 48(b. Abigail), 80(b. Tabitha, Hannah, Joseph), 146(m.), 403(d. Joseph, Sarah, Abigail). Plymouth Co. PR 11:202, 269, 453; 12:508; 15:159, 228(Joseph Hewett). MD 31:171(bp. Solomon); 32:18(bp. John).

742 JAMES HEWETT[5] (Sarah Waterman[4], Sarah Snow[3], Abigail[2] Warren, Richard[1]) b. Marshfield 21 Nov. 1706; d. bef. 4 May 1750 (inv.).

He m. ca. 1729 ABIGAIL TISDALE, b. ca. 1711; d. Taunton May 1790 in 80th yr.; daughter of John and Abigail (Burt) Tisdale, a descendant of Pilgrim Thomas Rogers.

On 9 July 1728 James Hewett of Dighton sold to Ichabod Cushman land in Middleborough which had belonged to his father Solomon Hewett, dec.

On 3 Dec. 1729 James Hewett of Dighton sold to John Bennett land in Middleborough that he had received from his father Solomon Hewett, dec.

The inventory of the estate of James Hewett of Bridgewater, bloomer, was dated 4 May 1750.

On 4 Sept. 1759 Timothy Jones Jr. and wife Abigail; Simeon Baker and wife Sarah; Susanna Hewett, singlewoman; and Bathsheba Hewett, singlewoman, all of Raynham; Abigail, Sarah, Susanna and Bathsheba being the four daughters of James Hewett of Bridgewater, dec., sold four-sevenths of the real estate of their father to Nehemiah Lincoln.

The will of Israel Tisdale of Taunton dated 30 Aug. 1769 names Abraham Hewit son of his sister Hewit and others.

Children (HEWETT) rec. Bridgewater:

i ABIGAIL[6] b. 24 May 1730
ii SARAH b. 15 April 1732
iii SUSANNAH b. 23 Oct. 1733
iv BATHSHEBA b. 2 June 1735
v son b. 2 March 1737; d. 13 June 1737
vi ABIAH b. 25 Aug. 1739
vii ABRAHAM b. 18 June 1742

References: VR BRIDGEWATER 1:156(b. ch.). VR TAUNTON 3:103(d. Abigail). Plymouth Co. PR 11:442; 12:67(James Hewett). MF 19:174. Bristol Co. PR 21:75-7(Israel Tisdale). Plymouth Co. LR 26:4, 38(James Hewett); 47:135-6(Timothy Jones, etc.). MD 15:91(b. ch.; d. child).

743 SARAH HEWETT[5] (Sarah Waterman[4], Sarah Snow[3], Abigail[2] Warren, Richard[1]) b. Marshfield 17 Nov. 1708; d. Norwich CT 1 Jan. 1777.

She m. (1) Norwich CT 8 Feb. 1732/3 ELEAZER HYDE, b. Norwich CT 13 Dec. 1704; d. there 11 May 1772; son of John and Experience (Abell) Hyde.

She m. (2) Norwich CT 22 Sept. 1773 JOHN BIRCHARD, b. Norwich CT 12 April 1704; son of James and Elizabeth (Beckwith) Birchard. He m. (1) Norwich CT 26 March 1755 Mary Barrett.

On 16 Jan. 1734/5 Eleazer Hyde and wife Sarah Hyde of Norwich CT and Mercy Hewett of Marshfield sold land in Marshfield which had belonged to their father Solomon Hewett.

The will of Eleazer Hide of Norwich dated 26 April 1760, proved 6 June 1772, names wife Sarah; only son Issacher, daus. Zilpha and Sarah. In a 12 Feb. 1773 distribution the heirs of Issacher being both deceased, their portion of the estate was given to Zilpha, eldest dau. and her sister Sarah (Case?).

Children (HYDE) b. Norwich CT:

i ZILPHAH[6] b. 8 Nov. 1735
ii ELIAB b. 22 March 1738; d. 21 April 1760
iii SARAH b. 29 April 1740
iv ISAACHER b. 7 June 1745; d.y.
v ISAACHER b. 16 Aug. 1747

References: NORWICH CT VR 1:146(1st m.; d. Eleazer; b. ch.); 2:97(2nd m.; d. Sarah). Norwich CT PR #5712 (Eleazer Hide). Plymouth Co. LR 29:164; 35:37(Eleazer Hyde). WATERMAN GEN 1:57-8.

744 MERCY HEWETT[5] (Sarah Waterman[4], Sarah Snow[3], Abigail[2] Warren, Richard[1]) bp. Marshfield 7 Nov. 1712.

She prob. m. ca. 1733 GERSHOM THOMAS, b. Marshfield 11 April 1700; d. there 1 May 1750; son of Israel and Bethia (Sherman) Thomas.

The will of Gershom Thomas of Marshfield, yeoman, dated 28 April 1750, proved 1 July 1750, names wife Mercy; sons Noah, Zenas and Gershom; daughters Bethia and Mercy; an unborn child.

On 25 Sept. 1761 Noah Thomas, Zenas Thomas, Gershom Thomas, Bethia Thomas, Mercy Thomas and Abiah Thomas all of Marshfield, yeomen and spinsters, heirs of Gershom Thomas, late of Marshfield and others sold land in Marshfield to Thomas Waterman, Nehemiah Thomas and Thomas Ford Jr.

No Plymouth Co. PR for Mercy Thomas.

Children (THOMAS) b. Marshfield:

i ABIGAIL[6] bp. 22 April 1734; d. 1 July 1750
ii NOAH bp. 11 Jan. 1738/9
iii BETHIA b. 11 April 1740
iv ZENAS b. 25 April 1742
v MARCY b. 29 Feb. 1743
vi ISAAC b. 28 Oct. 1745; d. 4 April 1750
vii GERSHOM b. 26 April 1748
viii ABIAH b. 3 May 1750

References: MD 32:19(bp. Noah), 19(bp. Abigail). Plymouth Co. LR 57:221(Noah Thomas etc.). MARSHFIELD VR pp. 47(b. Bethiah, Isaac, Gershom), 77(b. Zenas), 98(d. Gershom, Isaac), 168(b. Marcy), 169(b. Abiah). Plymouth Co. PR 12:185-6(Gershom Thomas). THOMAS GEN p. 169.

745 LYDIA HEWETT[5] (Sarah Waterman[4], Sarah Snow[3], Abigail[2] Warren, Richard[1]) bp. Marshfield 19 June 1715; d. Norwich CT 11 April 1760 in 45th yr.

She m. Marshfield 21 March 1743 ROBERT ROATH, b. Norwich CT 19 May 1717; living 1790 (census); son of Peter and Anna (Halford) Roath. He m. (2) Amy Forsyth by whom he had Joshua, William, Amy, Robert Mason, Lydia, Joseph and Joshua.

Robert Roath was admitted to the First Church, Norwich CT 14 Aug. 1743.

The division of the land of James Forsyth of New London dated 10 March 1767 names Robert Roath of Norwich, husband of eldest dau. Amy.

On 8 June 1774 Robert Roath and wife Amy of Norwich mortgaged land to Elijah Bankes.

Robert Roath was 1-0-0 in the 1790 census of New London Co. CT.

No CT PR for Robert Roath.

Children (ROATH) b. Norwich CT:

i LYDIA[6] b. 5 March 1744
ii AZUBAH b. 18 Sept. 1745
iii RHODA b. 6 Dec. 1747
iv ELIZABETH b. 26 Oct. 1749
v EUNICE b. 27 Oct. 1751
vi LUCY b. 13 July 1754
vii ANNA b. 29 April 1756
viii SARAH b. 20 Dec. 1758

References: NORWICH CT VR 1:27(b. Robert); 2:23(m.; b. ch.). Norwich CT LR 21:470(Robert Roath). MARSHFIELD VR p. 159(m.). New London CT PR H:676(James Forsyth). First Church, Norwich CT rec. 2:213(adm.).

NOTE: Robert Roath had a dau. Mary bp. Norwich CT 30 May 1762 who could be by either wife, but is prob. by Amy. (Norwich First Church 2:150).

746 ABIGAIL WATERMAN[5] (Joseph[4], Sarah Snow[3], Abigail[2] Warren, Richard[1]) b. Marshfield 10 April 1710; d. Pembroke 4 Feb. 1791 in 81st yr.

She m. Marshfield 28 Nov. 1728 JOHN MAGOUN, b. Scituate 10 July 1705; d. Pembroke 19 Aug. 1743 ae 41; son of John and Hannah (Turner) Magoun.

The will of John Magoon of Pembroke, gentleman, dated 15 Aug. 1743, proved 5 Sept. 1743, names mother Hannah Magoon; wife Abigail; sons John and Joseph Magoon; daus. Lusanna Magoon and Abigail Magoon.

On 9 April 1794 John Magoun of Pembroke, yeoman, was appointed administrator of the estate of Abigail Magoun of Pembroke, dec.

Children (MAGOUN) b. Pembroke:

i LUSANNA[6] b. 16 Jan. 1729
ii ABIGAIL b. 28 Feb. 1732
iii JOHN b. 6 Aug. 1735
iv HANNAH b. 17 May 1737; d. 15 May 1738
v BETTY b. 19 March 1738; d. 10 April 1739
vi JOSEPH b. 28 May 1740; d. 30 Aug. 1740
vii JOSEPH b. 8 Sept. 1741

References: VR PEMBROKE pp. 145-7(b. ch.), 429-30(deaths). VR SCITUATE 1:241(b. John). WATERMAN GEN 1:132-3. Plymouth Co. PR 9:153-5(John Magoun); 27:474 (Abigail Magoun). MARSHFIELD VR p. 146(m.).

747 ABIAH WATERMAN[5] (Joseph[4], Sarah Snow[3], Abigail[2] Warren, Richard[1]) b. Marshfield 11 Dec. 1714; living 22 Sept. 1765 (2nd m.).

She m. (1) Scituate 4 June 1730 JOHN EELLS, b. Scituate 15 Feb. 1708/9; drowned in North Carolina 24 Aug. 1750; son of Nathaniel and Hannah (North) Eells. The will of Hannah Eells of Scituate dated 1 Sept. 1752, mentions children of son John dec. with specific legacies to granddaus. Hannah Eells and Abiah Eels, daus. of John.

She m. (2) Middletown CT 22 Sept. 1765 ELIJAH MILLER d. bef. 29 Sept. 1785 (inv.). He m. (1) Bathsheba ----- by whom he had Nathaniel, Jabez, Huldah, Elijah, Bathsheba, Hosea and Sarah.

On 14 Nov. 1760 Waterman Eells of Middletown CT, shipwright, was appointed administrator of the estate of John Eells late of Scituate. [Probably refers to son John.]

Children (EELS) b. Scituate:

- i WATERMAN[6] bp. 13 Aug. 1732
- ii HANNAH bp. 5 May 1734
- iii ABIAH b. ca. 1736
- iv JOHN bp. 5 March 1737/8; d. in the French War ae 22; unm.
- v LUSANNA bp. 19 Dec. 1742
- vi SARAH bp. 8 May 1743; d.y.
- vii LENTHAL bp. 19 May 1745
- viii JOSEPH bp. 21 June 1747
- ix ABIGAIL bp. 4 Nov. 1750

References: VR SCITUATE 1:142(b. John), 142-3(b. ch.); 2:112 (m.). WATERMAN GEN 1:133-4. Plymouth Co. PR 16:40 (John Eells); 17:3(Hannah Eels). CT MARR 2:91(2nd m.). Middletown CT PR #2353(Elijah Miller).

748 SARAH WINSLOW[5] (Abigail Waterman[4], Sarah Snow[3], Abigail[2] Warren, Richard[1]) b. Marshfield 3 Dec. 1704; d. Wellfleet 8 Feb. 1770 in 66th yr.

She m. (1) Marshfield 14 Oct. 1728 TOBIAS PAINE, bp. Boston 27 June 1697; d. Virgin Islands 1730; son of William and Mary (Taylor) Paine, a descendant of Pilgrim James Chilton.

She m. (2) Eastham 29 Dec. 1737 SAMUEL SMITH, b. Eastham 13 Feb. 1690/1; d. Wellfleet 18 July 1768 in 78th yr.; son of Samuel and Bershuah (Lothrop) Smith, a descendant of Pilgrim Stephen Hopkins. He m. (1) Eastham 9 Oct. 1712 Abigail Freeman by whom he had Mary, Zoath, Abigail, Martha, Bathshuah, Grace, Susanna and Samuel.

In a deed dated 23 Sept. 1747 Mary Payne "only child of Tobias Payne, late of Boston, dec." was under the guardianship of Kenelm Winslow Jr.

The will of Samuel Smith of Wellfleet, dated 18 April 1768, proved 11 Oct. 1768, names wife Sarah; heirs of son Zoeth, viz. Zoheth, Richard, Elizabeth, Samuel and Ruth Smith; heirs of dau. Bathsheba Atwood, viz. Abigail, Martha, John, William, Bathsheba, Thankful, Anna and Zoheth; heirs of dau. Martha Rich, viz. Martha Rich and Abigail Young; dau. Abigail Eldridge, wife of Jesse, dau. Susanna Atwood and son Joseph Smith.

Child (PAYNE) bp. Marshfield:

i MARY[6] b. ca. 1729; bp. 3 Jan. 1730/1

Children (SMITH) b. Eastham:

ii SARAH d. 3 June 1740 ae 1y 6m
iii JOSEPH b. 9 Sept. 1741

References: MD 6:13(b. Sam.), 206(Samuel's 1st m.; b. ch. by 1st wife; b. Joseph); 12:96(d. Sarah, Samuel, dau. Sarah); 19:100(2nd m.); 31:170(bp. Mary). MARSHFIELD VR p. 146(m.). MF 6:357; 15:133-4. Barnstable Co. PR 13:367-9(Samuel Smith). Suffolk Co. LR 74:221(John Payne et al.).

749 ABIGAIL WINSLOW[5] (Abigail Waterman[4], Sarah Snow[3], Abigail[2] Warren, Richard[1]) b. Marshfield 25 June 1707; d. Wellfleet 13 April 1776 in 69th yr.

She m. Marshfield 25 June 1730 ISAIAH LEWIS, b. Hingham 10 June 1703; d. Wellfleet 30 Oct. 1786 in 84th yr.; son of John and Hannah (Lincoln) Lewis.

Isaiah Lewis graduated from Harvard in 1723.

On 28 Dec. 1786 Winslow Lewis was appointed administrator of the estate of Rev. Isiah Lewis dec.

Children (LEWIS) b. Eastham:

i HANNAH[6] b. 25 Sept. 1731
ii WINSLOW b. 3 July 1741

References: MARSHFIELD VR p. 146(m.). Barnstable Co. PR 19:141; 26:244-5(Issiah Lewis). WINSLOW MEMORIAL 1:196. MD 12:34(deaths); 17:81(b. ch.). HINGHAM HIST 2:441(b. Isaiah).

750 NATHANIEL WINSLOW[5] (Abigail Waterman[4], Sarah Snow[3], Abigail[2] Warren, Richard[1]) b. Marshfield 21 April 1709; d. there 24 May 1734.

He m. Marshfield 3 Feb. 1731/2 SUSANNA BRYANT, b. Scituate 11 May 1714; d. 2 May 1800; dau. of John and Deborah (Barstow) Bryant. She m. (2) Marshfield 22 Dec. 1740 Ezekiel Kent by whom she had Penelope, Susanna, Ezekiel, Deborah, Benjamin, Mary, Abigail and Ann.

No Plymouth Co. PR or LR for Nathaniel Winslow.

Child (WINSLOW) b. Marshfield:

i NATHANIEL[6] b. 7 April 1733

References: VR SCITUATE 1:43(b. Susanna). MARSHFIELD VR pp. 50(b. Nath.), 76(b. Penelope), 92(b. dau. Susanna), 109(b. last 6 Kent ch.), 140(m.), 159(her 2nd m.). MD 10:51(d. Nath.).

751 FAITH WINSLOW[5] (Abigail Waterman[4], Sarah Snow[3], Abigail[2] Warren, Richard[1]) b. Marshfield 2 Feb. 1712; d. bef. 22 Oct. 1765(2nd m.).

She m. Boston 19 Feb. 1735/6 WILLIAM TAYLOR, b. Jamaica, West Indies 18 May 1714; d. Milton 16 Feb. 1789 ae 75; son of John and Ann (Winslow) Taylor, a descendant of Pilgrim James Chilton. He m. (2) Boston 22 Oct. 1765 Sarah (Cheever) Savage by whom he had William and Thomas.

William Taylor was a Loyalist. He went to Halifax NS in 1776 and was proscribed and banished in 1778.

The will of William Taylor Esq. of Milton, dated 18 Dec. 1776, proved 14 April 1789, names wife Sarah; late son John; daughter Abigail; sons Joseph, William and Thomas and son-in-law Jonathan Amory. A codicil of 29 June 1788 indicates that son John had received his share and that son Joseph may be esteemed an alien. On 17 Oct. 1814 Thomas Taylor, trader of Boston, sought appointment of an administrator to replace William Taylor who died in 1809 without settling the estate of his father, William Taylor.

Children (TAYLOR) b. Boston:

i WILLIAM[6] b. 12 Oct. 1736
ii JOHN b. 25 April 1738
iii ABIGAIL b. 12 Dec. 1739
iv ELIZABETH b. 20 Aug. 1741; d. 16 Sept. 1743
v WINSLOW b. 1 March 1743; d. at sea Jan. 1772; prob. unm.
vi JOSEPH b. 16 March 1745; d. Boston Dec. 1816; unm.
vii JOSHUA b. 2 Aug. 1748; d. 15 Aug. 1748

References: BOSTON VR 24:227(b. Wm.), 235(b. John), 238(b. Abigail), 244(b. Eliz.), 250(b. Winslow), 258(b.

Joseph), 268(b. Joshua); 28:194(m.). MF 15:132-3. WINSLOW MEMORIAL 1:210(d. ch.). Suffolk Co. PR 88:145; 112:551(William Taylor). MILTON VR pp. 61(b. last 2 ch.), 178, 247(d. William, Sarah). BOSTON DEATHS 1700-1799, 2:887(d. Winslow).

752 KENELM WINSLOW[5] (Abigail Waterman[4], Sarah Snow[3], Abigail[2] Warren, Richard[1]) b. Marshfield 5 Nov. 1716; d. there 13 Aug. 1780 in 63rd yr.

He m. Barnstable 14 March 1754 ABIGAIL BOURNE, b. Barnstable 21 June 1729; d. Marshfield 21 Dec. 1761; dau. of Sylvanus and Mercy (Gorham) Bourne, a descendant of Pilgrim John Howland. The will of Silvanus Bourne of Sandwich dated 20 May 1763 names Kenelm Winslow, Joseph Winslow and Abigail Winslow, children of dau. Abigail Winslow, dec.

On 24 Aug. 1780 Kenelm Winslow and John Gallison, both of Marshfield, were named to administer the estate of Kenelm Winslow Esq., late of Marshfield. The estate was insolvent.

Children (WINSLOW) b. Marshfield:

i KENELM[6] b. 24 July 1756
ii ABIGAIL b. 28 June 1758
iii JOSEPH b. 12 Nov. 1760

References: MARSHFIELD VR p. 109(b. ch.), 390(deaths). MD 19:40-1(Silvanus Bourne will); 27:5(m.); 33:25(b. Abigail). WINSLOW MEMORIAL 1:210. Plymouth Co. PR 25:554; 27:47; 28:210(Kenelm Winslow).

753 JOSEPH WINSLOW[5] (Abigail Waterman[4], Sarah Snow[3], Abigail[2] Warren, Richard[1]) b. Marshfield 30 Oct. 1724; d. Boston 15 March 1777 ae 52y 4m 13d.

He m. (1) Boston 29 Jan. 1746/7 MARY BONNER, bp. Boston 3 May 1725; d. there 8 Aug. 1753 ae 29; dau. of John and Sarah (Belcher) Bonner.

He m. (2) int. Boston 11 Aug. 1757 MARGARET CAZNEAU, b. Boston 30 May 1733; d. Dorchester 15 Nov. 1820 ae 87; dau. of Isaac and Hannah (Johnson) Cazneau.

The inventory of the estate of Joseph Winslow was filed 31 Oct. 1777. On 31 Oct. 1777 Margaret Winslow, widow, was granted administration on the estate of her husband Joseph Winslow, brazier and ship chandler.

On 21 Nov. 1795 Margaret Winslow of Boston, widow, and other heirs of Isaac Cazneau of Boston, chaise maker, sold a tract on Scottow's Creek in Boston to Edward Power of Boston.

Children (WINSLOW) b. Boston; 2 by 1st wife:

i ABIGAIL[6] b. 20 Feb. 1750
ii SARAH b. 7 Dec. 1752

iii JOSEPH b. 6 Oct. 1766; d. March 1791; unm. No PR.

References: BOSTON VR 24:275(b. Abigail), 280(b. Sarah), 313 (b. Joseph); 28:267(1st m.); 30:25(int. 2nd m.). BOSTON NEWS OBITS 1:332(d. son Joseph). WINSLOW MEMORIAL 1:210-1(d. Joseph, Mary). Suffolk Co. PR 76:471(Joseph Winslow). Suffolk Co. LR 115:66(Margaret Winslow). NEHGR 142:136 (b. Margaret). Old South Church, Boston recs. 2:142(bp. Mary). Granary Burying Ground p. 251(d. both wives).

754 THOMAS WATERMAN[5] (Anthony Waterman[4], Sarah Snow[3], Abigail[2] Warren, Richard[1]) b. Marshfield 29 April 1710; d. there 27 Aug. 1774 in 65th yr.

He m. Marshfield 25 Jan. 1732 ABIGAIL THOMAS, b. Marshfield 5 April 1710; d. there 5 Jan. 1796 in 86th yr.; dau. of Israel and Bethia (Sherman) Thomas.

The will of Thomas Waterman of Marshfield dated 12 Feb. 1766, proved 17 Nov. 1774, names wife Abigail; children Thomas, Anthony, Joseph, Nathaniel, Abijah, Asa and John Waterman and Anna Hewit.

The will of Abigail Waterman of Marshfield, widow, dated 4 Jan. 1775, proved 7 March 1796, names sons Thomas, Joseph, Anthony, Abijah and Nathaniel Waterman; dau. Ann, wife of Joseph Hewit; sons Asa and John Waterman.

Children (WATERMAN) b. Marshfield:

i THOMAS[6] b. 16 Dec. 1733
ii ANTHONY b. 3 Dec. 1736
iii JOSEPH b. 29 Oct. 1738
iv ANN b. 6 Aug. 1740
v NATHANIEL b. 11 June 1742
vi ABIJAH b. 25 Dec. 1745
vii ASA b. 9 July 1748
viii JOHN b. 29 March 1750

References: MARSHFIELD VR pp. 29(b. Abig.), 47(b. Anthony), 50(b. Thomas), 108(d. Thomas), 140(m.), 168(b. Ann, Nath., Abijah, Asa), 169(b. John), 412(d. Abigail), 413 (d. Thomas). WATERMAN GEN 1:134-6. Plymouth Co. PR 21:642 (Thomas Waterman); 35:479-80(Abigail Waterman).

755 JOSEPH WATERMAN[5] (Anthony Waterman[4], Sarah Snow[3], Abigail[2] Warren, Richard[1]) b. Marshfield 3 Jan. 1711/2; d. after 8 Dec. 1778.

He m. (1) RUTH -----.

He prob. m. (2) New London CT 2 Nov. 1766 BATHSHEBA (-----) (SMITH) POWERS.

Joseph and Ruth Waterman were admitted into full communion with the New Concord Parish (then in Norwich CT) on 15 April 1739.

On 8 Dec. 1778 Joseph Waterman of New London conveyed to Bathsheba Smith of New London his right to a dwelling house and land where he lives. On the same date Bathsheba Smith leased the same to Joseph Waterman and wife Bathsheba.

On 8 Dec. 1778 Joseph Waterman obtained a judgment against John Smith.

No known children.

References: CT MARR 2:23, 27(2nd m.). WATERMAN GEN 1:136-8. New London CT LR 21:179(Joseph Waterman); 21:188(Bathsheba Smith); 21:187(judgement).

756 ZEBULON WATERMAN[5] (Anthony Waterman[4], Sarah Snow[3], Abigail[2] Warren, Richard[1]) b. Marshfield 6 Aug. 1713; d. East Haddam CT bef. 7 Jan. 1760.

He m. MARTHA -----, b. ca. 1714; d. Groton CT 3 July 1787 ae 73. She m. (2) aft. 3 March 1760 Walter Buddington.

On 22 May 1734 Joseph Waterman and Zebulon Waterman of Marshfield purchased a large tract of land in Norwich from Abigail Magoun and Abiah Eells.

On 4 Feb. 1739/40 Zebulon Waterman and wife Martha of Colchester sold 77 acres in Norwith to William Whiting.

On 7 Jan. 1760 Martha Waterman of East Haddam was appointed administratrix of the estate of Zebulon Waterman.

On 3 March 1760 Martha Waterman was appointed guardian of Ruth and Zebulon Waterman.

Children (WATERMAN) b. Colchester CT:

i ELIZABETH[6] bp. 26 Aug. 1739
ii MARY bp. 26 Aug. 1739
iii BILDAD bp. 9 Sept. 1739
iv ZEBULON bp. 21 June 1741
v LYDIA b. ca. 1743
vi RUTH b. ca. 1745 (based on age at d.)

References: Colchester First Church Records(bp. ch.). WATERMAN GEN 1:138-141. Colchester CT PR 3:37, #3104, #3106, #3107(Zebulon Waterman). Norwich CT LR 7:109(Joseph and Zebulon Waterman); 8:212(Zebulon Waterman).

757 ORPHAN WATERMAN[5] (Anthony Waterman[4], Sarah Snow[3], Abigail[2] Warren, Richard[1]) b. Marshfield 21 Aug. 1715; d. there 15 Feb. 1791 in 76th yr.

She m. (1) MICHAEL FORD, b. Marshfield 23 April 1710; d. there May 1764; son of James and Hannah (Dingley) Ford, a descendant of Pilgrim Richard Warren.

See #737 for an account of the Ford children.

She m. (2) Pembroke 18 Dec. 1775 AARON SOULE, b. Duxbury Dec. 1705; d. Pembroke 21 Jan 1783 ae 77y 1m; son of Aaron and Mary (Wadsworth) Soule, a descendant of Pilgrim George Soule.

No children by second marriage.

References: MARSHFIELD VR pp. 99(d. Orphan), 170(2nd m. int.). VR PEMBROKE pp. 348(2nd m.), 447(d. Aaron). MF 3:49.

758 LYDIA DOGGETT[5] (Bethiah Waterman[4], Sarah Snow[3], Abigail[2] Warren, Richard[1]) b. Marshfield 1712; d. Plainfield CT 8 March 1790 ae 76.

She m. Newbury 10 Oct. 1734 SAMUEL CLIFT, b. Marshfield 22 Oct. 1709; d. Preston CT 22 Aug. 1794 ae 85; son of William and Lydia (Wills) Clift.

On 16 June 1747 Samuel Clift of Marshfield, cordwainer, sold 80 acres in Marshfield where he dwelt to Seth Briant of Marshfield; wife Lydia and widowed mother Lydia Clift renounced dower.

On 3 June 1747 Richard Kimball of Norwich sold land in Norwich to Samuel Clift of Marshfield. On 30 Jan. 1758 Samuel Clift of Plainfield sold this land to Jeremiah Kinsman of Norwich.

On 29 March 1757 John Crery Esq. and Eleazer Fairbanks of Plainfield sold 190 acres in Plainfield to Samuel Cleft of Norwich. On 1 April 1761 Samuel Clefft of Plainfield sold 188 acres to Joseph Kimball Jr.

No probate found for Samuel Clift.

Children (CLIFT) first 8 b. Marshfield, rest b. Preston CT:

i RHODA[6] b. 29 April 1735; d. 5 Sept. 1737
ii AMOS b. 20 Sept. 1737
iii MARY b. 7 Oct. 1738
iv LEMUEL b. 20 April 1740; d. 14 Feb. 1741
v WATERMAN b. 28 Dec. 1741
vi BETHIA b. 21 Feb. 1744
vii WILLS b. 18 July 1745
viii DEBORAH b. 6 June 1749
ix JOSEPH b. 13 Sept. 1750
x LEMUEL b. 10 Oct. 1755

References: MARSHFIELD VR pp. 34(b. Sam.), 47(d. Rhoda), 168 (b. Rhoda, Amos, Mary; d. Lemuel). WATERMAN GEN 1:64(b. & d. ch.). VR NEWBURY 2:106(m.). Plymouth Co. LR 40:90 (Samuel Clift). Norwich CT LR 10:45(Richard Kimball); 16:36

(Samuel Clift). Plainfield CT LR 4:434(John Crery); 5:36(Samuel Clefft).

759 SARAH DOGGETT[5] (Bethiah Waterman[4], Sarah Snow[3], Abigail[2] Warren, Richard[1]) b. Marshfield Oct. 1716; d. there 22 Jan. 1794 in 78th yr.

She m. ca. 1736 EDWARD OAKMAN, b. ca. 1714; bp. Marshfield 28 Oct. 1716; d. there 28 May 1791 in 75th yr.; son of Tobias and Elizabeth (Doty) Oakman, a descendant of Pilgrim Edward Doty.

On 26 July 1791 widow Sarah Oakman and Edward Oakman, gentleman, were appointed to administer the estate of Edward Oakman of Marshfield, yeoman. In the 22 Oct. 1794 settlement, Amos Oakman was to get the estate and make payments to John Oakman, Samuel Oakman, Elizabeth Oakman, Alice Oakman, Bethia Stevens wife of William Stevens, Sarah the wife of Samuel Lathrop, and Abiah wife of Asa Rogers.

Children (OAKMAN) b. Marshfield:

i ELIZABETH[6] b. 20 Sept. 1737; unm. 22 Oct. 1794
ii BETHIAH b. 10 Oct. 1739
iii SARAH b. 12 Oct. 1741
iv JOHN b. 29 June 1743
v SAMUEL b. 15 Sept. 1745
vi JOSEPH b. 28 April 1749; d. near Portland Harbor ME in 1776; unm.
vii TOBIAS b. 13 March 1751
viii ALICE b. 10 June 1753; d. Marshfield 15 Oct. 1823 ae 70y 4m; unm.
ix ABIAH b. 26 April 1756
x AMOS b. 26 Jan. 1759

References: MD 9:168(d. Edward), 169(d. Sarah); 31:122(bp. Edward). MARSHFIELD VR pp. 100(b. ch.), 379(d. Edward, Sarah), 424(d. Alice). PN&Q 4:111. Plymouth Co. PR 33:333-4(Edward Oakman). MF 11:1:36-7. DOGGETT FAM p. 380.

760 BETHIAH DOGGETT[5] (Bethiah Waterman[4], Sarah Snow[3], Abigail[2] Warren, Richard[1]) b. Marshfield ca. 1718; living March 1785.

She m. Boston 27 Sept. 1749 ROBERT KINSMAN, bp. Ipswich 3 May 1713; d. Plainfield CT 16 Dec. 1788 in 76th yr.; son of Robert and Rebecca (Burley) Kinsman.

The will of Robert Kinsman of Plainfield dated March 1785, proved 9 March 1789, names wife Bethia; brother Jeremiah Kinsman.

References: WATERMAN GEN 1:65. BOSTON VR 28:251(m.). VR IPSWICH 1:223(bp. Robert). Old Plainfield CT Cemetery(d. Robert). Plainfield CT PR #1311(Robert Kinsman).

NOTE: It is unlikely they had a child Pelatiah as suggested in the 1876 KINSMAN GENEALOGY.

761 SAMUEL DOGGETT[5] (Bethiah Waterman[4], Sarah Snow[3], Abigail[2] Warren, Richard[1]) b. Marshfield ca. 1720; d. Boston 24 April 1781.

He m. Boston 21 June 1753 ESTHER FAIRFIELD, b. Wenham 5 Feb. 1729; d. Boston Jan. 1812; dau. of William and Elizabeth (White) Fairfield. She m. (2) Brookline 27 Oct. 1788 Benjamin White.

On 13 July 1780 Eather Doggett, wife of Capt. Samuel Doggett, sold all her rights in the estate on Hanover St. which she inherited from her father.

The will of Samuel Doggett of Boston, mariner, dated 23 April 1781, proved 8 May 1781, names wife Esther; youngest dau. Sarah; children Samuel and William Doggett and Elizabeth Miers wife of Marcus Miers.

Children (DOGGETT) b. Boston:

i BETHIAH[6] b. Feb. 1754; d.y.
ii SAMUEL b. 16 May 1755
iii WILLIAM b. 3 April 1757
iv ELIZABETH b. 22 May 1759
v SARAH b. 31 Dec. 1761; d.y.
vi SARAH b. 1 Oct. 1767

References: BOSTON VR 24:286(b. Sam.), 291(b. Wm.), 296(b. Eliz.), 301(b. Sarah); 30:48(m.). BOSTON NEWS OBITS 2:93(d. Sam.). Suffolk Co. PR 80:206(Samuel Doggett). DOGGETT FAM pp. 380-4. VR BROOKLINE p. 165(her 2nd m.). Suffolk Co. LR 131:228(Esther Doggett). COLOMBIAN CENTENNIAL of 4 Jan. 1812(d. Esther).

762 NOAH DOGGETT[5] (Bethiah Waterman[4], Sarah Snow[3], Abigail[2] Warren, Richard[1]) b. Marshfield ca. 1727; d. Boston 18 Oct. 1805 ae 77.

He m. (1) Boston 25 Oct. 1753 MARY CLARK, b. Boston 8 July 1733; d. there 8 March 1761; dau. of James and Rebecca (Newmarsh) Clark.

He m. (2) Boston 12 Oct. 1762 MARY ALLINE, b. Boston 25 May 1735; d. there 11 Aug. 1824 ae 89; dau. of Henry and Jane (Swett) Alline.

The will of Noah Doggett of Boston, shopkeeper, dated 10 April 1800, proved 16 Dec. 1805, names wife Mary; children Joseph, Bethiah, Henry, Noah, Samuel and Lydia.

Children (DOGGETT) b. Boston, 3 by first wife:

i JOSEPH[6] b. 16 Aug. 1754
ii BETHIAH b. 22 Aug. 1756
iii NOAH b. 1 April 1758; d.y.
iv AMOS b. 7 Jan. 1764; d.y.
v MARY b. 12 March 1766; d. 29 Oct. 1777
vi HENRY b. 15 Feb. 1767
vii JANE b. 27 Jan. 1769; d. 24 Sept. 1769
viii NOAH b. 1 Nov. 1770
ix SAMUEL b. 31 Aug. 1772
x LYDIA b. 14 Oct. 1775; d. Boston 7 Aug. 1815

References: BOSTON VR 24:284(b. Joseph), 288(b. Bethiah), 312 (b. Mary), 314(b. Henry), 318(b. Jane), 320 (b. Noah); 30:9(1st m.), 379(2nd m.). Suffolk Co. PR #22,501 (Noah Doggett). DOGGETT FAM pp. 384-8. COLOMBIAN CENTENNIAL of 19 Oct. 1805(d. Noah), issue of 14 Aug. 1824(d. Mary).

763 ZERVIAH THOMAS[5] (Lydia Waterman[4], Sarah Snow[3], Abigail[2] Warren, Richard[1]) b. Marshfield 3 Oct. 1715; d. Plainfield CT 23 Nov. 1808 ae 93.

She m. ca. 1743 JAMES BRADFORD, b. Plymouth 2 July 1717; d. Plainfield CT 10 Oct. 1801 ae 84; son of William and Hannah (Foster) Bradford, a descendant of Pilgrims William Bradford and Richard Warren. (See #978). He m. (1) Priscilla Spaulding.

On 12 May 1746 James Bradford of Plainfield CT sold to Samuel Foster land that belonged to his brother Zadock Bradford dec.

The will of James Bradford of Plainfield CT dated 17 May 1798, proved 5 Jan. 1802, names wife Keziah [sic]; sons Anthony and Samuel; oldest daughter Persillah Dorrance; and daughter Keziah Clift.

Children (BRADFORD) b. Plainfield CT:

i SAMUEL[6] b. ca. 1744
ii KEZIAH b. 15 Oct. 1747
iii ANTHONY b. 6 Sept. 1749
iv JAMES b. 20 Jan. 1751; d. 3 Dec. 1777 ae 25; unm.
v PRISCILLA b. 20 Dec. 1752
vi JOSIAH b. 15 Oct. 1754 (not in will)
vii HANNAH b. 8 Nov. 1756; d. 23 June 1778 ae 21; unm.
viii JOSEPH b. 30 Dec. 1758; d. 26 May 1759

References: THOMAS GEN p. 165. PLYMOUTH VR p. 56(b. James). BRADFORD DESC p. 53. Plainfield CT PR #230(James Bradford). Plymouth Co. LR 38:71(James Bradford). CSL Hale Cem. Rec., Plainfield CT p. 184(d. Priscilla, James, son James, Hannah). WATERMAN GEN 1:64-5, 627. Plainfield CT VR 1:20(b. Priscilla).

764 ANTHONY THOMAS[5] (Lydia Waterman[4], Sarah Snow[3], Abigail[2] Warren, Richard[1]) b. Marshfield 25 March 1719; d. there 14 July 1781 ae 62 yrs. 3 mos. 20 days.

He m. Marshfield 23 Jan. 1745/6 ABIGAIL ALDEN, b. Duxbury 27 Feb. 1727; d. Marshfield 24 July 1802 ae 75; dau. of John and Hannah (Briggs) Alden, a descendant of Pilgrim John Alden.

On 14 Nov. 1781 letters of administration were granted to Briggs Thomas and Waterman Thomas, both of Marshfield on the estate of Anthony Thomas of Marshfield, gentleman.

The will of Abigail Thomas of Marshfield, widow, dated 12 April 1802, proved 2 Aug. 1802, names eldest son Briggs Thomas; sons Waterman Thomas and Judah Thomas; grandsons John Anthony Thomas and Samuel Alden Thomas; granddaus. Sarah Sampson, Hannah Briggs Thomas; dau. [in-law] Abigail Thomas, wife of Briggs Thomas; granddaus. Allethea Thomas and Olive Thomas.

On 19 March 1787 Briggs Thomas of Marshfield, gent.; Waterman Thomas of Waldoboro, Lincoln Co.; and Judah Thomas of Marshfield, yeoman, all the children of Anthony Thomas late of Marshfield divided his land.

Children (THOMAS) b. Marshfield:

i JOHN[6] b. 6 June 1748; d. 11 Nov. 1748
ii BRIGGS b. 28 Oct. 1751
iii WATERMAN b. 4 March 1753
iv JUDAH b. 11 July 1758

References: THOMAS GEN p. 170. MARSHFIELD VR pp. 110(b. ch.; d. John), 160(m.), 388(d. Anthony), 420(d. Abigail). Plymouth Co. PR 27:95(Anthony Thomas); 38:147-9 (Abigail Thomas). Plymouth Co. LR 68:11(Briggs Thomas, etc.).

765 LYDIA THOMAS[5] (Lydia Waterman[4], Sarah Snow[3], Abigail[2] Warren, Richard[1]) bp. Marshfield 26 March 1721; d. there 9 April 1810 ae 89y 1m 2d.

She m. Marshfield 28 Feb. 1743 JOSEPH KENT, b. Marshfield 6 Dec. 1717; d. there 1 Jan. 1801 ae 83y 10d; son of John and Sarah (Smith) Kent.

The will of John Thomas of Marshfield dated 12 May 1764 names dau. Lidia, wife of Joseph Kent; grandson Thomas

Kent; granddau. Lidia Kent; grandson Nathaniel Kent; granddau. Abigail Kent and grandson John Kent and others.

On 9 July 1785 Joseph Kent of Marshfield, yeoman, and Lydia his wife sold part of the farm where they were living to sons John Kent and Nathaniel Kent, both of Marshfield, mariners; Abigail Kent was a witness.

No Plymouth Co. PR for Joseph Kent.

Children (KENT) b. Marshfield:

- i ANN[6] b. 28 Oct. 1744 (not named in grandfather's will)
- ii THOMAS b. 13 Oct. 1746. On 3 June 1776 Joseph Kent was appointed administrator of the estate of Thomas Kent late of Marshfield, mariner.
- iii LYDIA (named in grandfather's will)
- iv JOHN (named in grandfather's will)
- v NATHANIEL (named in grandfather's will)
- vi ABIGAIL b. 22 Dec. 1763
- vii ELIZABETH

References: MARSHFIELD VR pp. 38(b. Joseph), 74(b. Ann, Thomas), 159(m.), 388(deaths). Plymouth Co. LR 64:123(Joseph Kent). Plymouth Co. PR #12048(Thomas Kent); 20:35-7(John Thomas). GENEALOGIES OF THE DIFFERENT FAMILIES BEARING THE NAME KENT, L. Vernon Briggs, Boston, 1898, pp. 35-6(names of daughters).

766 JOHN THOMAS[5] (Lydia Waterman[4], Sarah Snow[3], Abigail[2] Warren, Richard[1].) b. Marshfield 9 Nov. 1724; d. Chambly, Quebec, Canada 2 June 1776 ae 52 yrs.

He m. int. Kingston 12 Sept. 1761 HANNAH THOMAS, b. Plymouth 20 June 1730; d. Kingston 1 April 1819 ae 88; dau. of Nathaniel and Hannah (Robinson) Thomas, a descendant of Pilgrim John Alden.

John Thomas was a surgeon and a Major General. His death record says he was Commander in Chief of the American Army in Canada.

The will of John Thomas Esq. of Kingston "being now at Chambler in the Province of Quebec," dated 31 May 1776, proved 15 Sept. 1776, names wife Hannah to have whole of the estate.

The will of Hannah Thomas of Kingston, widow, dated 28 April 1817, proved 5 July 1819, names dau. Hannah Willis; dau. in law Judith Thomas; son Nathaniel Thomas; grandchildren Bethiah Hayward Willis, Betsey Willis, Nathaniel Thomas Willis; Augustus Thomas, William Appleton Thomas and Hannah Thomas; son John Thomas.

Children (THOMAS) b. Kingston:

i HANNAH[6] b. 14 Nov. 1762
ii JOHN b. 17 Jan. 1766
iii NATHANIEL b. 23 June 1769; d. Kingston 1 Aug. 1846 ae 77y 1m 9d; unm.

References: VR KINGSTON pp. 143(b. Hannah, John), 144(b. Nathaniel), 289(int.), 385(deaths). THOMAS GEN pp. 170, 210-1, 252. MD 7:221(d. John, Hannah, Nathaniel). Plymouth Co. PR 24:194(John Thomas); 50:297-8(Hannah Thomas). PLYMOUTH VR p. 75(b. Hannah). DAR PATRIOT INDEX p. 674.

767 SARAH THOMAS[5] (Lydia Waterman[4], Sarah Snow[3], Abigail[2] Warren, Richard[1]) b. Marshfield 23 Nov. 1726; d. Lisbon CT 23 Sept. 1798.

She m. Marshfield 19 March 1752 JEREMIAH KINSMAN, b. Ipswich 28 Feb. 1719/20; d. Lisbon CT 24 June 1801; son of Robert and Rebecca (Burley) Kinsman.

Children (KINSMAN) b. Lebanon CT:

i JOHN[6] b. 7 May 1753
ii JOSEPH b. 15 Jan. 1755
iii JOANNA FANNING b. 19 July 1756
iv JEREMIAH b. 12 July 1759
v THOMAS b. 31 Aug. 1764; d. 12 Feb. 1766
vi SARAH (twin) b. 14 Dec. 1767
vii THOMAS (twin) b. 14 Dec. 1767

References: MARSHFIELD VR p. 162(m.). THOMAS GEN p. 165. Lisbon CT VR 1:91(m.; d. Sarah, Jeremiah; b.&d. ch.). WATERMAN GEN 1:65. VR IPSWICH 1:223(b.Jeremiah).

768 JAMES BARKER[5] (James[4], Alice Snow[3], Abigail[2] Warren, Richard[1]) b. rec. Abington 5 Feb. 1711; living 17 Sept. 1759.

He m. int. Scituate 1 Dec. 1750 MARY DWELLY, b. Scituate 18 May 1708; d. there 28 May 1752 in 45th yr.; dau. of John and Rachel (Buck) Dwelly.

On 17 Sept. 1759 James Barker of Scituate, Gentleman, sold land in Scituate to Ebenezer Thompson.

No Plymouth Co. PR for James Barker.

References: VR SCITUATE 1:141(b. Mary); 2:19(int.), 351(d. Mary). Plymouth Co. LR 46:32(James Barker).

769 ALICE BARKER[5] (James[4], Alice Snow[3], Abigail[2] Warren, Richard[1]) b. rec. Abington 3 June 1713; living 1 June 1752.

She m. Newport RI 25 April 1732 BENJAMIN BRENTON of Newport RI; b. Newport RI 16 Oct. 1710; living 27 Oct. 1763; son of Benjamin and Sarah (Collins) Brenton.

On 12 March 1732/3 Benjamin Brenton of Newport, goldsmith, sold land in South Kingstown to George Mumford; wife Alice also signed.

On 27 March 1740 Jahleel Brenton of Newport sold land to Benjamin Brenton of Newport, mariner, only son of Benjamin Brenton of Newport. On 22 Nov. 1746 he sold this land to Matthew Robinson; wife Alice also signed. On 1 June 1752 Benjamin and wife Alice signed a deed to correct boundaries of the last deed.

Benjmain Brenton of Newport signed a petition to the General Assembly 27 Oct. 1763.

No probate found for Benjmain Brenton.

Child (BRENTON):

i SARAH[6] d. Newport 9 June 1742 age 25 days

References: RIVR Newport 4:2:84(b. Benj.). RIVR 10:378(m.). RIVR (New Style) 11:50(d. Sarah). South Kingstown RI LE 3:359(Benjamin Brenton); 4:293(Jahleel Brenton); 5:337, 339(Benjamin Brenton).

770 DANIEL BARKER[5] (James[4], Alice Snow[3], Abigail[2] Warren, Richard[1]) b. rec. Abington 23 May 1714; d. bef. 23 May 1777 (adm.).

He m. Boston 23 June 1736 ELIZABETH BOSWORTH, b. Hull 27 Feb. 1716; d. Boston bef. 8 Aug. 1792 ae 77; dau. of Lemuel and Mary (Jones) Bosworth. On 8 Jan. 1749/50 Daniel Barker of Boston, blacksmith, was appointed administrator of the estate of his father-in-law Lemuel Bosworth of Hull.

On 17 Dec. 1754 Mary Bosworth, Daniel and Elizabeth Barker of Hull sold land in Hull to John Barnes Jr. and Cornelius Barnes of Hingham.

On 11 June 1761 Daniel and Elizabeth Barker of Boston sold 10 acres of Petox Island to Amos Binney.

On 4 June 1792 Elizabeth Barker, widow, Daniel Barker, blacksmith, and Hannah Barker, single woman, all of Boston, sold land on Fish St. owned by the heirs of Daniel Barker, dec., to Nathaniel Tidmarsh; Mary Barker, wife of Daniel released her dower.

Children (BARKER) b. Boston:

i DANIEL[6] b. 4 Aug. 1737; d. 12 Aug. 1737 ae 8d
ii HANNAH b. 31 Aug. 1738
iii ELIZABETH b. 8 Feb. 1741
iv ABIGAIL d. 17 Aug. 1747 ae 11m

v DANIEL b. ca. 1756 (based on age at d.)

References: BOSTON VR 24:228(b. Daniel), 232(b. Hannah), 242 (b. Elizabeth); 28:225(m.). VR HULL pp. 13(b. Elizabeth), 41(m.). Suffolk Co. LR 86:149(Mary Bosworth, etc.); 96:131(Daniel Barker); 174:146(Elizabeth Barker, etc.). BOSTON NEWS OBITS 1:17(d. Elizabeth). BOSWORTH GEN 3:307-9; 5:491. BOSTON DEATHS 1700-1799 1:50(d. son Daniel). INSCRIPTIONS AND RECORDS OF THE OLD CEMETERIES OF BOSTON, Robert J. Dunkle and Ann S. Lainhart, p. 530(d. first son Daniel, Abigail). Boston Deaths 1810-40(d. last son Daniel). Suffolk Co. PR 76:9(adm. Daniel Barker).

771 GEORGE BARKER[5] (James[4], Alice Snow[3], Abigail[2] Warren, Richard[1]) b. rec. Abington 16 May 1716.

Did he m. Scituate int. 17 Feb. 1737 LYDIA SAUNDERS?

References: VR SCITUATE 2:19(int.).

772 LYDIA BARKER[5] (James[4], Alice Snow[3], Abigail[2] Warren, Richard[1]) b. rec. Abington 8 April 1718; living 10 April 1779 (will).

She m. 1736 JOHN CROCKER, b. Barnstable Sept. 1709; d. bef. 22 Feb. 1790; son of John and Mary (Bacon) Crocker.

The will of John Crocker of Barnstable, yeoman, dated 10 April 1779, proved 22 Feb. 1790, names wife Lydia; daus. Elizabeth Baker wife of Ebenezer Baker, Bathsheba Kelly wife of David Kelly, Hannah Tobey wife of Nathan Tobey and Abigail Crocker; sons Joseph Crocker, Allen Crocker and John Crocker.

Children (CROCKER) b. Barnstable:

i ELIZABETH[6] b. 28 Feb. 1738
ii STEPHEN b. 8 Dec. 1740 (not in will)
iii JOSEPH b. 6 Feb. 1742
iv ALLYN b. 18 Feb. 1744/5
v BATHSHEBA b. 23 Jan. 1746
vi LYDIA b. 12 May 1749 (not in will)
vii DAVID b. ca. 1751 (not in will)
viii HANNAH b. 13 March 1753
ix JOHN b. 12 May 1755
x ABIGAIL b. Feb. 1758

References: BARNSTABLE FAMS 1:221-2(adds son David). MD 3:150(b. John); 31:149(b. 1st 7 ch.), 150(b. last 3 ch.). Barnstable Co. PR 24:67; 27:49(John Crocker).

773 ROBERT BARKER[5] (Caleb[4], Alice Snow[3], Abigail[2] Warren, Richard[1]) b. Scituate or Newport RI 27 March 1712; d. Hanover 9 Feb. 1796.

He m. Pembroke 24 Aug. 1737 HANNAH HOWLAND, b. Marshfield 23 Sept. 1713; d. Hanover 26 Dec. 1795; dau. of Thomas and Mary (-----) Howland.

Robert Barker Jr. and Hannah Barker were members of the Pembroke Friends Church 1 first mo. 1755.

No Plymouth Co. PR for Robert Barker.

Children (BARKER) b. Pembroke:

i THOMAS[6] b. 29 April 1738
ii ANN b. 21 Sept. 1739; d. 1744
iii ELIZABETH b. 25 Feb. 1743
iv HANNAH b. 10 Jan. 1745
v ROBERT bp. 1747; d. 16 Jan. 1753
vi MERCY bp. 1749; d. 28 Oct. 1749
vii GIDEON bp. 1754
viii ROBERT bp. 1756
ix JOSHUA

References: VR PEMBROKE p. 232(m.). BARKER GEN pp. 170-1. MD 39:25-6(Howland). HANOVER BY DWELLY pp. 20-1(b. & d. ch.). Pembroke Friends records. MARSHFIELD VR p. 77(b. Hannah).

774 JOHN BARKER[5] (Caleb[4], Alice Snow[3], Abigail[2] Warren, Richard[1]) b. Scituate 15 Aug. 1714; d. bef. 26 Feb. 1771 (adm.).

He m. Hanover 1 June 1737 GRACE TURNER.

John Barker was a member of the Pembroke Friend's Church 1 first mo. 1755.

On 9 June 1763 John Barker of Pownalborough [ME], blacksmith, sold 3 tracts in Hanover to Gideon Randall. On 15 April 1765 wife Grace Barker renounced dower to this land.

On 31 March 1762 the Kennebec Proprietors granted 100 acres in Pownalborough to John Barker of Pownalborough, blacksmith.

On 12 Sept. 1771 John Barker of Pownalborough sold 100 acres to son Carr Barker of Pownalborough, yeoman. On 10 May 1783 he sold 100 acres to son Caleb Barker of Pownalborough, yeoman.

Children (BARKER):

i JOHN[6] b. 1738
ii CARR b. ca. 1739 (based on age at d.)
iii CALEB b. 1749 (from his d. rec. in Dresden ME)

References: VR SCITUATE 2:19(int.). Pembroke Friend's records. Plymouth Co. Court of General Sessions 1730-49, p. 232(m.). Dresden ME VR 1771-1906, pp. 3(d. Carr), 30(d. Caleb). Plymouth Co. LR 48:226(John Barker); 50:17(Grace Barker). Lincoln Co. ME LR 2:69(Kennebec Proprietors); 8:148(to son Carr); 20:46(to son Caleb).

NOTE: No evidence found for a dau. Nancy as stated in BARKER GEN pp. 177-8.

775 GIDEON BARKER[5] (Caleb[4], Alice Snow[3], Abigail[2] Warren, Richard[1]) b. Scituate 22 Dec. 1723; d. 11 Jan. 1798.

He m. 1773 RACHEL HODGES, b. Norton 3 April 1755; d. Hanson 6 July 1849 ae 94y 3m 3d; dau. of Ephraim and Rachel (Cox) Hodges. The 18 June 1776 distribution of the estate of Ephraim Hodges includes Rachel, wife of Gideon Barker.

By 4 5th mo. 1774 Gideon Barker had married outside the Friend's Church and the church disowned him 3 8th mo. 1774.

Gideon Barker was 2-4-3 in the 1790 census of Hanover.

No Plymouth Co. PR or LR for Gideon Barker.

Children (BARKER) b. prob. Hanover (from BARKER GEN):

i CHARLES[6] b. 20 March 1774
ii DIADAMIA b. 10 Jan. 1776
iii CALEB b. 1 April 1779; d. 1797; unm.
iv ABIGAIL b. 6 Aug. 1782
v NATHANIEL HODGES b. 2 Feb. 1784
vi DANIEL b. 7 Aug. 1787
vii IRA b. 19 July 1790
viii THOMAS HOWLAND b. 19 Dec. 1795; d. 5 Feb. 1812; unm.

References: Pembroke Friends records. VR NORTON p. 78(bp. Rachel). VR HANSON p. 100(d. Rachel). BARKER GEN p. 178.

776 JOSHUA BARKER[5] (Caleb[4], Alice Snow[3], Abigail[2] Warren, Richard[1]) b. Scituate 17 July 1726; d. 19 Aug. 1754.

He m. ----- ----- and had 4 children.

No Plymouth Co. PR for Joshua Barker.

References: BARKER GEN.

777 CHARLES BARKER[5] (Caleb[4], Alice Snow[3], Abigail[2] Warren, Richard[1]) b. Scituate 5 Aug. 1729.

He m. ----- ----- and had 2 children.

Charles Barker was a member of the Pembroke Friend's Church 1 first mo. 1755.

No Plymouth Co. PR or LR for Charles Barker.

References: Pembroke Friend's records. BARKER GEN.

778 ROBERT HOWLAND[5] (Deborah Barker[4], Alice Snow[3], Abigail[2] Warren, Richard[1]) b. Duxbury 31 Aug. 1707; d. 1793.

He m. Duxbury 5 July 1733 MARGARET SPRAGUE, b. Marshfield 10 May 1713; living 21 May 1771 (ack. deed); dau. of Nathan and Margaret (-----) Sprague.

On 7 May 1771 Robert Howland and wife Margaret of Duxborough, yeoman, sold to Edward Stevens of Pembroke, land in Marshfield that Nathan Sprague gave to his daughter Margaret Howland. Prince Howland of Duxborough, son of Robert and Margaret, sold a way from the road to the meadow of Nathan Sprague.

No Plymouth Co. PR for Robert Howland.

Children (HOWLAND)*:

i URANIA[6] d.y.
ii MICHAEL d.y.
iii DEBORAH d. 1800 unm.
iv PRINCE (named in deed)
v ROBERT
vi ABIGAIL b. 3 March 1749

References: VR DUXBURY p. 266(m.). MARSHFIELD VR p. 80(b. Margaret). Plymouth Co. LR 56:170(Robert Howland).

*Children are from Aspinwall ms.

779 ALICE HOWLAND[5] (Deborah Barker[4], Alice Snow[3], Abigail[2] Warren, Richard[1]) b. Marshfield 30 Oct. 1709; d. Duxbury 12 Oct. 1785.

She m. Newbury 10 April 1730 HEZEKIAH KEEN, b. Duxbury 6 Aug. 1702; d. there 27 Dec. 1770 ae 68; son of Josiah and Lidia (Baker) Keen, a descendant of Pilgrim Richard Warren.

See #398 for an account of this family.

References: MD 28:1-6. VR DUXBURY pp. 101(b. Hezekiah), 390 (deaths). VR NEWBURY 2:241(m.).

780 ABIGAIL KEEN[5] (Deborah Barker[4], Alice Snow[3], Abigail[2] Warren, Richard[1]) b. bet. March 1720 and 7 Oct. 1722; d. Pembroke 2 Sept. 1790.

She m. Pembroke 6 Nov. 1746 PRINCE BARKER, b. Pembroke Feb. 1716/7; d. there 27 Jan. 1784; son of Isaac and Elizabeth (Howland) Barker.

The will of Prince Barker of Pembroke dated 2 Feb. 1776, proved 20 March 1784, names wife Abigail, sons Prince, Isaac and Benjamin; daus. Abigail and Deborah Barker.

Children (BARKER) b. Pembroke, except as noted:

i PRINCE[6] b. 6 Oct. 1747
ii ISAAC b. 1 May 1749
iii ABIGAIL b. Dartmouth 29 Jan. 1750/1; d. Pembroke 7 Jan. 1789; unm.
iv DEBORAH b. Dartmouth 29 Jan. 1753
v BENJAMIN b. 30 Sept. 1756

References: VR DARTMOUTH 1:35(b. Abigail), 36(b. Deborah). VR PEMBROKE pp. 23(b. Benjamin), 24(b. Isaac), 25(b. son Prince), 232(m.), 384(d. Abigail; dau. Abigail), 385(d. Prince). Plymouth Co. PR 29:112(Prince Barker).

781 BENJAMIN KEEN[5] (Deborah Barker[4], Alice Snow[3], Abigail[2] Warren, Richard[1]) b. Pembroke 2 Dec. 1724; d. there 11 May 1805.

He m. RACHEL -----, living 10 April 1764 (deed).

On 10 April 1764 Benjamin Keen and wife Rachel Keen of Pembroke sold all his share of his father's land to Abraham Booth.

No Plymouth Co. PR for Benjamin Keen.

References: VR PEMBROKE p. 421(d. Benj.). Plymouth Co. LR 49:122(Ben. Keen).

782 WILLIAM ESTES[5] (Alice Barker[4], Alice Snow[3], Abigail[2] Warren, Richard[1]) b. Pembroke 9 April 1713; d. Hanover 10 Dec. 1793 ae 80 yrs.

He m. int. 17 April 1736 ELIZABETH STETSON, bp. Hanover 3 March 1723; dau. of Elijah and Ruth (Chittenden) Stetson.

The will of William Estes of Hanover, yeoman, dated 6 Dec. 1793, proved 3 March 1794, names sons Matthew, Richard and William dec.; daus. Susannah Barker, Zilpha Estes & Sarah Estes; grandaus. Ruth Estes, Anna Robbins & Elizabeth Bates; grandson William Estes.

Children (ESTES) b. Hanover:

i SUSANNAH[6] (twin) b. 29 June 1737
ii ALICE (twin) b. 29 June 1737
iii WILLIAM b. 11 Feb. 1739
iv RUTH b. 9 Nov. 1741
v RICHARD b. 25 June 1745
vi ELIZABETH b. 10 Aug. 1747; d. 31 May 1750
vii ZILPHA b. 1 June 1750
viii MATHEW b. 17 Jan. 1754
ix ELIJAH b. 26 March 1757
x SARAH b. 20 Feb. 1761

References: HANOVER VR pp. 22(b. Susannah, Alice), 23(b. Wm. thru Mathew; d. Eliz.). HANOVER BY DWELLY p. 177 (b. Elijah, Sarah). ESTES GEN pp. 63-5.

783 SARAH ESTES[5] (Alice Barker[4], Alice Snow[3], Abigail[2] Warren, Richard[1]) b. Hanover 8 June 1733; d. Pembroke 20 June 1794 ae 68 [sic].

She m. THOMAS SYLVESTER, b. Hanover 19 Oct. 1723; d. there 1 Oct. 1760; son of Amos and Elizabeth (Henchman) Sylvester.

On 1 Dec. 1760 Sarah Sylvester was appointed administratrix of the estate of Thomas Sylvester.

Child (SYLVESTER):

i MATTHEW[6] bp. Hanover 19 Sept. 1760

References: HANOVER VR p. 9(b. Thomas). HANOVER BY BARRY p. 402(Sylvester family). NEHGR 86:128-9(d. Sarah). HANOVER FIRST CH pp. 137(bp. Matthew), 188(d. Thomas). Plymouth Co. PR 16:4; 19:74(Thomas Sylvester).

784 ROBERT ESTES[5] (Alice Barker[4], Alice Snow[3], Abigail[2] Warren, Richard[1]) b. Hanover 12 Jan. 1736; d. there 26 Nov. 1803.

He m. Sandwich 17 1st mo 1760 BEULAH WING, b. Sandwich 29 Jan. 1734/5; d. Hanover 20 Sept. 1833 ae 83 yrs.; dau. of Zacchues and Content (Swift) Wing.

On 16 Feb. 1791 Robert Estes of Hanover, yeoman, deeded land to son Zaccheus Estes, yeoman. On 29 May 1797 Robert Estes and wife Beulah; Timothy Robbins and John Hatch, gentleman, all of Hanover, sold land to Charles Bailey of Hanover.

On 16 Jan. 1804 Benjamin Estes of Hanover, yeoman, was named administrator of the estate of Robert Estes, late of Hanover dec.

Children (ESTES) b. Hanover:

i ZACCHEUS[6] b. 20 Dec. 1760
ii ROBERT b. 1 Feb. 1763; d. 3 Feb. 1763
iii ROBERT b. 20 April 1764; d. 11 May 1764
iv HANNAH b. 7 Aug. 1765
v ABIGAIL b. 8 June 1768; d. 1772
vi ALICE b. 27 March 1772
vii JOSEPH b. 9 Nov. 1774
viii BENJAMIN

References: HANOVER VR p. 31(b. 1st 5 ch.). HANOVER BY DWELLY pp. 177-8(b. & d. ch.; d. Beulah). ESTES GEN pp. 65-7. SANDWICH VR 1:80(b. Beulah); 2:1268(m.). Plymouth Co. PR 34:378(Robert Estes).

785 EBENEZER STETSON[5] (Lydia Barker[4], Alice Snow[3], Abigail[2] Warren, Richard[1]) b. Scituate 12 Dec. 1728; d. Antigua WI Oct. 1768.

He m. (1) Raynham 7 June 1753 HANNAH HALL, d. Dighton 6 April 1761.

He m. (2) 24 Feb. 1763 ANNA LEONARD, d. Bristol RI 2 April 1796; dau. of Zephaniah and Hannah (King) Leonard.

The 20 June 1782 deed shown in his father's account indicates that only Lydia, Ebenezer and Anna were alive at that date.

No Plymouth Co. PR for Ebenezer Stetson.

Children (STETSON) b. Dighton; 4 by 1st wife:

i HANNAH[6] b. 15 June 1754; apparently d.y.
ii THOMAS b. 17 June 1756*
iii LYDIA b. 9 June 1758
iv EBENEZER b. 9 (no month) 1761
v ANNE (twin) b. 15 Nov. 1763; d.y.
vi ZEPHANIAH (twin) b. 15 Nov. 1763; d.y.
vii ANNE LEONARD b. 31 July 1766**

References: Dighton VR p. 72(b. ch.; d. Hannah). STETSON DESC 1:85. RAYNHAM VR p. 19(m.).

*Aspinwall file says he d. on a prison ship ae 22.

**Her gravestone in Bucksport ME says she was born July 31, 1766 (BANGOR HISTORICAL MAGAZINE 3:52).

786 SNOW STETSON[5] (Lydia Barker[4], Alice Snow[3], Abigail[2] Warren, Richard[1]) b. March 1730; d. Barbados bef. 1 Nov. 1759.

He m. int. Dighton 6 Aug. 1757 ELIZABETH DUPREE "a French lady." She m. (2) Philip Trafforn.

On 1 Nov. 1759 Ebenezer Stetson of Dighton, shipwright, was appointed to administer the estate of Snow Stetson of Dighton. The inventory was dated 12 March 1764. The account of 20 Aug. 1764 mentions the funeral expense in Barbados. In 1764 Ebenezer Stetson was appointed guardian of children John and Snow.

Elizabeth Trafforn complained she had not received her widow's share and on 21 Jan. 1782 Snow Stetson complained to the probate judge that he had never received his share of his father's estate and his uncle (deceased) had embezzled it.

Children (STETSON) b. Dighton:

i JOHN[6] b. 15 Feb. 1758; d. ae 11 yrs.
ii SNOW b. 18 March 1759

References: Bristol Co. PR 16:420; 18:422-3; 19:132(Snow Stetson). Dighton VR pp. 94(b. ch.), 212(int.). STETSON DESC 1:85-6.

787 ZILPHA STETSON[5] (Lydia Barker[4], Alice Snow[3], Abigail[2] Warren, Richard[1]) d. bef. 10 April 1803.

She m. int. Scituate 5 May 1764 JOB CLAPP, b. Scituate 6 Nov. 1712; d. bet. 24 Jan. 1781 and 16 March 1781; son of Joseph and Hannah (Briggs) Clap. He m. (1) Pembroke 24 July 1758 Penelope Hatch by whom he had Sarah.

The will of Job Clapp of Scituate dated 24 Jan. 1781, proved 16 March 1781, names wife Zilpher and dau. Sarah Barnes.

See deed under her father's account. On 17 March 1784 Zilpha Clap sold to Michael Ford her share of her father's estate.

On 13 April 1803 Snow Stetson of Scituate, gentleman, was appointed to administer the estate of Zilpha Stetson.

Apparently no children.

References: VR PEMBROKE p. 254(his 1st m.). VR SCITUATE 1:73 (b. Job); 2:60(int.). Plymouth Co. PR 28:43-4(Job Clapp); 34:366; 38:338 (Zilpha Stetson). Plymouth Co. LR 62:184(Zilpha Clapp).

788 SAMUEL[5] WARREN (Samuel[4], Richard[3], Nathaniel[2], Richard[1]) b. Middleboro 9 Aug. 1707; living 28 Nov. 1770 (diary).

He m. Middleboro 13 June 1734 REBECCA DUNHAM, b. Plymouth 2 Feb. 1706; d. aft. 26 April 1769; dau. of Eleazer and Merriam (Phillips) Dunham.

On 26 April 1769 Samuel and Rebekah Warren of Middleborough received a bond from their son Jabez Warren for the whole of Samuel's homestead farm in Middleborough.

On 28 Nov. 1770 Samuel Warren and son Jabez were mentioned in the diary of Isaac Backus as moving to Oakham, but were delayed by a snowstorm.

On 9 July 1770 Jabez Warren of Middleborough bought 81 acres with mansion house and buildings at Oakham, Worcester Co. On 29 March 1773 Jabez Warren and wife Zilpah sold this land. Perhaps father Samuel Warren was with them.

No Worcester Co. PR for Samuel Warren.

Children (WARREN) b. Middleboro:

i BETTY[6] bp. 4 April 1741

ii JABEZ
iii poss. SAMUEL*
iv child d. Middleboro 18 Sept.1754.

References: MIDDLEBORO VR 1:61(m.). WARREN GEN p. 22. MF 5:123. BACKUS DIARY p. 786. Plymouth Co. LR 55:118(Samuel Warren). Middleboro First Ch. bps. p. 36(bp. Betty). Middleboro Mortality Recs - Addendum(d. child). Worcester Co. LR 67:37; 71:102(Jabez Warren). NEHGR 55:169. (PLYMOUTH) ANC LANDMARKS 2:317(Dunham). MD 5:53(b. Rebecca); 13:251(m.). PLYMOUTH VR p. 37(b. Rebecca).

*WARREN GEN p. 22 lists a son Samuel who m. 30 Oct. 1770 Bethia Snow. VR BRIDGEWATER 2:382 states that Samuel Warren Jr. of Middleborough married Bettie Snow 30 Oct. 1770.

789 CORNELIUS[5] WARREN (Samuel[4], Richard[3], Nathaniel[2], Richard[1]) b. Middleboro 12 June 1709; d. bef. 15 April 1752 (2nd m.).

He m. Plymouth 18 Jan. 1732/3 MERCY WARD, b. Plymouth 8 March 1708; d. aft. 20 Oct. 1770; dau. of Nathan and Elizabeth (Pope) Ward. She m. (2) Plymouth 15 April 1752 James Howard.

On 15 Feb. 1732/3 Cornelius Warren and his wife were warned out of Plymouth. On 7 June 1737 Cornelius, his wife and family were warned from Plymouth.

On 1 June 1739 Samuel Warren gave land in Middleboro to son Cornelius Warren.

On 6 June 1757 Elijah Clapp of Middleboro was appointed guardian of Benjamin Warren, minor son of Cornelius Warren, late of Middleboro.

On 20 Oct. 1770 widow Mercy Howard joined with her son Joseph Warren in a deed.

No Plymouth Co. PR for Cornelius Warren.

Children (WARREN) first 3 bp. Middleboro:

i JOSEPH[6] bp. 1 Sept. 1734
ii ELEANOR bp. 1 Aug. 1736
iii BENJAMIN bp. 9 Dec. 1738
iv poss. CORNELIUS*

References: MD 12:11(b. Mercy); 14:74(m.); 18:141(her 2nd m.). Middleboro First Ch. Bps. p. 34(bp. 3 ch.). WARREN GEN pp. 22-3(1770 deed, etc.). MF 5:124. PLYMOUTH CO CT RECS 2:179. Plymouth Co. LR 32:229(Samuel Warren). NEHGR 55:169. PLYMOUTH VR pp. 48(b. Mercy), 97(m.), 174(her 2nd m.). Plymouth Co. PR #21860 (Benjamin Warren).

*WARREN GEN p. 23 lists a son Cornelius who m. 1 March 1770 Patience Hoar. That marriage is in MIDDLEBORO VR 1:185 and it states "both of Middleboro."

790 JAMES[5] WARREN (Samuel[4], Richard[3], Nathaniel[2], Richard[1]) b. Middleboro 14 Feb. 1710/1; d. Tiverton RI 1790.

He m. int. Freetown 4 Sept. 1735 MARY TERRY, b. prob. Freetown ca. 1715; d. aft. 28 June 1768; dau. of Benjamin and Joanna (Spur) Terry, a descendant of Pilgrim Thomas Rogers.

On 4 Dec. 1788 James Warren of Westport sold land in Westport to sons Cornelius Warren of Westport and Gamaliel Warren of Tiverton RI; ack. at Newport RI 26 Dec. 1788.

Children (WARREN) first and last b. Freetown, others at Middleboro:

i SAMUEL[6] b. 29 Sept. 1737
ii MARY b. 6 Sept. 1739
iii CORNELIUS b. 29 July 1741
iv GAMALIEL bp. Middleboro 8 Jan. 1744
v JAMES b. 13 Nov. 1745

References: MD 15:122(b. Mary, Cornelius). WARREN GEN p. 23. FREETOWN VR(b. James, int.). MF 5:124-5; 19:187. Bristol Co. LR 67:382(James Warren). NEHGR 55:170. MIDDLEBORO VR 1:70(b. Mary, Cornelius). Middleboro First Ch. bps. p. 30 (bp. Gamaliel). DAR PATRIOT INDEX p. 718.

NOTE: WARREN GEN p. 23 says JAMES d. at what is now Fall River in 1790; his tombstone (created in 1800s) reads "settled in Tiverton now Fall River and died there about 1790, was buried on his farm and removed from thence by his great-grandson, Theodore Warren who erected this stone in his memory." Mary (Terry) Warren is "said to have died at Nine Partners, New York."

791 NATHAN[5] WARREN (Samuel[4], Richard[3], Nathaniel[2], Richard[1]) b. Middleboro 5 March 1712/3; d. there 15 Feb. 1784 in 71st yr.

He m. prob. by 1745 RACHEL -----, b. ca. 1719; d. Middleboro 15 Aug. 1788 ae 69 yrs.

Elder Isaac Backus, minister of the Baptist church in Titicut Parish, Middleboro, preached at Nathan Warren's house in 1754 and 1756, as well as conducting funeral services for the four children who died in a diphtheria epidemic in 1755.

On 24 March 1781 Nathan Warren of Middleboro, black smith, with wife Rachel releasing dower, sold 38 acres in Middleboro to son Nathan. This was land he received from his father Samuel Warren. Witnesses were Silvanus Warren and Zenas Warren. The same day Nathan Warren Jr. mortgaged the same property to Silvanus Warren of Middleboro, gentleman, as surety, Silvanus becoming bondsman for Nathan Jr. who agreed to take care of Nathan Warren Sr. and his wife for the rest of their lives.

No Plymouth Co. PR for Nathan Warren.

Children (WARREN) b. prob. Middleboro:

i child[6] d. 10 Nov. 1755
ii child d. 13 Nov. 1755
iii child d. 15 Nov. 1755
iv child d. 18 Nov. 1755
v NATHAN b. ca. 1757 (based on age at d.)
vi prob. RACHEL b. ca. 1761 (based on ae at d.)*

References: MIDDLEBORO DEATHS p. 219(d. Nathan, Rachel). WARREN GEN p. 24. MF 5:125-6. MD 15:105(d. Nathan). Middleboro Mortality Recs. Addendum(d. 4 ch.). BACKUS DIARY pp. 323, 391, 392, 419. Plymouth Co. LR 62:21(Nathan Warren).

*WARREN GEN p. 24 lists a dau. RACHEL who m. 9 Dec. 1784 Zenas Tinkham of Halifax. MIDDLEBORO VR 2:145 records the m. of Mr. Zenas Tinkham of Halifax and Miss Rachel Warren of Middleboro on 9 Dec. 1784.

792 JOANNA[5] WARREN (Samuel[4], Richard[3], Nathaniel[2], Richard[1]) b. Middleboro 25 March 1717; d. aft. 2 April 1764 (deed).

She m. Plympton 15 Oct. 1735 WILLIAM BARLOW, b. Sandwich 14 April 1713; d. aft. 20 Sept. 1781 (ack. deed); son of John and Elizabeth (Dillingham) Barlow.

On 2 April 1764 William Barlow, cordwainer, and Joanna his wife; William Barlow Jr.; Eliakim Barlow, blacksmith; and Patience Barlow, spinster, all of Middleborough, sold 30 acres in Middleborough to Abiel Leach Jr.

On 14 April 1764 William Barlow of Middleborough purchased land in Woodstock CT from Samuel Child Jr. On 20 Aug. 1772 William Barlow and son William Barlow Jr. sold their Woodstock CT land.

It is claimed that William Barlow was the first settler in Bromley [VT] in 1773.

On 15 May 1777 William Barlow of Bromley sold to Semuel Barlow of Bromley a tract in Bromley. John Barlow, Warren Barlow and Ebenezer Barlow were witnesses.

On 25 May 1778, ack. 20 Sept. 1781, William Barlow Sr. of Brumbly in the county of Charlotte NY [now Bennington Co. VT] sold 300 acres "on the west part of the 400 acres I live on."

No probate, death or cemetery record found for William Barlow.

Children (BARLOW) b. Middleboro:

i WILLIAM[6] b. 12 July 1738
ii ELIAKIM b. 17 March 1739/40
iii PATIENCE b. 3 Aug. 1742
iv ELEANOR b. 20 Oct. 1745
v JOHN b. 1 Dec. 1747
vi JOANNA b. 8 March 1748
vii SAMUEL b. 8 June 1750
viii WARREN b. 29 June 1752
ix MICAH b. 5 June 1756
x SARAH b. 25 May 1758

References: VR PLYMPTON p. 249(m.). MD 30:103(b. William). TAG 35:68-70. MF 5:126-7. MIDDLEBORO VR 1:24(b. William), 77(b. Elkiam, Patience), 132(b. Eleanor, John), 133(b. last 5 ch.). Plymouth Co. LR 49:119(William Barlow). Bennington Co. VT LR 1:298(William Barlow). Woodstock CT LR 3:421; 4:264 (William Barlow). VT GAZETTEER 1:208(first settler). TORREY'S MARRIAGES p. 42. MQ 43:114. SANDWICH VR 1:73(b. William). Bennington Co. VT Misc. Rec. B:214(1777 deed).

793 BENJAMIN[5] WARREN (Samuel[4], Richard[3], Nathaniel[2], Richard[1]) b. Middleboro 30 July 1720; d. there 11 Jan. 1802 ae 81.

He m. Middleboro 31 Dec. 1741 JEDIDIAH TUPPER, b. Sandwich 21 Aug. 1725; d. Middleboro 20 Oct. 1807 in 83rd yr.; dau. of Ichabod and Mary (-----) Tupper.

Benjamin and Jedidah Warren joined the Middleboro First Church 7 March 1731/2.

On 9 Feb. 1782 Benjamin Warren deeded his homestead in Middleboro to son Sylvanus Warren, wife Jedidah resigned her dower.

No Plymouth Co. PR for Benjamin Warren.

Children (WARREN) b. Middleboro:

i MEHITABLE[6] b. 15 Sept. 1743
ii SILVANUS b. 9 March 1746
iii JEDIDIAH b. 20 Feb. 1748
iv ICHABOD b. 13 May 1750
v LUCY bp. 18 Nov. 1753; d.y.
vi SILAS b. 18 Feb. 1756
vii ZENAS b. 22 March 1758
viii ANDREW b. 14 Nov. 1760
ix LUCY bp. 29 May 1763
x HANNAH (twin) bp. 26 May 1765
xi SUSANNAH (twin) bp. 26 May 1765
xii EUNICE bp. 21 May 1769

References: MD 15:219(m.). MIDDLEBORO DEATHS p. 219(d.Benj., Jedidiah). WARREN GEN pp. 24-5. MF 5:127-8. MIDDLEBORO VR 1:134(b. 1st 4 ch.), 135(b. Silas, Zenas, Andrew). Middleboro First Ch. Bps. pp. 44(bp. Lucy), 46(Lucy, Hannah, Susanna), 47(bp. Eunice). MIDDLEBORO FIRST CH pp. 91(joined ch.). SANDWICH VR 1:99(b. Jedidiah).

794 SARAH[5] WARREN (Samuel[4], Richard[3], Nathaniel[2], Richard[1]) b. Middleboro 9 Feb. 1721/2; d. prob. Middleborough bet 27 April 1779 and 17 Sept. 1783.

She m. Middleboro 24 June 1742 WILLIAM REED, b. Middleboro 18 July 1715; d. there 7 April 1776; son of William and Elizabeth (-----) Reed.

On 6 May 1776 administration on the estate of William Reed of Middleborough was granted to son William Reed 2nd. On 3 Sept. 1777 the dower was set off to the widow Sarah Reed.

The estate, deemed unsuitable for division was settled on son William Reed, he paying his siblings for their shares in 1777, 1779 and 1780. Receipts were received from Benjamin Reed, Elizabeth Reed, Elijah Reed, Robert Hoar (husband of Sarah), Abraham Peirce and wife Priscilla, all of Middleborough.

The will of Sarah Reed dated 27 April 1779, not recorded, names dau. Elizabeth Reed; other children. A citation was issued 17 Sept. 1783 for a 6 Oct. 1783 court hearing concerning the will to: Benjamin Reed, Sarah Hoars, wife of Robt. Hoars, heirs of Priscilla Pearce, wife of Abraham Pearce and all other heirs of Sarah Reed, dec.

Children (REED) b. Middleboro:

i PRISCILLA[6] b. 8 Dec. 1742
ii WILLIAM b. 24 Jan. 1744
iii BENJAMIN b. 29 Jan. 1746
iv SARAH b. 15 Jan. 1748
v ELIZABETH b. 4 May 1750; d.y.
vi ISRAEL b. 17 March 1752; n.f.r.
vii ELIJAH (signed receipt 11 Oct. 1780 when he must have been of age)
viii ELIZABETH b. 9 Sept. 1759
ix ABNER b. 12 Aug. 1764

References: MD 6:180(b. Wm.); 15:219(m.); 26:24(b. 1st 5 ch.), 25(b. Elijah, Elizabeth, Abner); 40:128-9(Reed fam.). MF 5:128-9. Plymouth Co. PR 23:108; 24:351-4; 29:51-2(William Reed); #16,704(unrecorded will of Sarah Reed and citation). Middleboro Mortality Recs(d. William). MIDDLEBORO VR 1:34(b. William), 73(m.), 162(b. ch. except Elijah).

795 JOSIAH^{5} WARREN (Samuel^{4}, Richard^{3}, Nathaniel^{2}, Richard^{1}) b. Middleboro 9 May 1724; d. prob. Middleboro bef. 4 June 1760.

He m. Middleboro 5 April 1747 JOANNA SPOONER, b. Middleboro 15 Aug. 1729; living 4 April 1763; dau. of Benjamin and Joanna (Tobey) Spooner.

On 4 June 1760 letters of administeration on the estate of Josiah Warren, late of Middleborough, husbandman, were granted to Micah Bryant. On 4 April 1763 an allowance for necessaries was made to the widow.

No Plymouth Co. PR for Joanna Warren.

Child (WARREN):

i poss. JOSIAH^{6} (no proof found)*

References: MD 7:243(b. Joanna); 16:109(m.). MF 5:129. Plymouth Co. PR 15:515; 16:398, 452(Josiah Warren). SPOONER DESC 1:63-4. MIDDLEBORO VR 1:41(b. Joanna), 89(m.).

*Bowman file for Warren shows Josiah Warren who m. Middleboro 29 March 1700 Susannah Makepiece (MD 30:12) as a possible child.

796 STEPHEN TORREY^{5} (Hope^{4} Warren, Richard^{3}, Nathaniel^{2}, Richard^{1}) b. Scituate Jan. 1710/1; living 5 April 1769 (ack. deed).

He m. Hanover 15 Aug. 1734 RACHEL BATES, b. Scituate 22 Feb. 1710; d. Hanover 14 Oct. 1778; dau. of Joseph Bates.

On 24 March 1769, ack. 5 April 1769, Stephen Torrey of Hanover, yeoman, sold a tract of land to Samuel Witherell.

No Plymouth Co. PR for Stephen Torrey.

Children (TORREY) bp. Hanover:

i STEPHEN^{6} bp. 10 Oct. 1742
ii RUTH bp. 10 Oct. 1742
iii DAVID bp. 21 April 1745
iv RACHEL bp. 1 April 1750
v ANNA bp. 7 June 1752

References: VR SCITUATE 1:29(b. Rachel). HANOVER FIRST CH 1:88 (m.), 124(bp. Stephen, Ruth), 126(bp. David), 129 (bp. Rachel), 131(bp. Anna), 194(d. Rachel). Plymouth Co. LR 60:135-6(Stephen Torrey).

797 RACHEL TORREY^{5} (Hope^{4} Warren, Richard^{3}, Nathaniel^{2}, Richard^{1}) b. Scituate 7 March 1712/3.

She m. Hanover 22 Feb. 1738/9 DENNIS CARRIE.

Nothing further could be found on this family.

References: HANOVER FIRST CH 1:89(m.).

798 ELIZABETH TORREY[5] (Hope[4] Warren, Richard[3], Nathaniel[2], Richard[1]) bp. Scituate 11 Aug. 1717; d. Hanover 2 April 1779.

She m. Hanover 10 May 1742 THOMAS TORREY, b. Marshfield 20 Oct. 1714; d. Hanover 6 Oct. 1778; son of Nathaniel and Hannah (Tilden) Torrey.

On 15 Dec. 1778 letters of administration on the estate of Thomas Torrey late of Hanover, yeoman, were granted to Seth Bates of Hanover. The estate was divided 2 May 1780 between eldest son Nathaniel and Warren Torrey, Samuel Torrey, Elizabeth Torrey and Sarah Torrey.

Children (TORREY) bp. Hanover:

i THOMAS[6] bp. 1 Dec. 1745 (not in division)
ii NATHANIEL bp. 24 May 1747
iii WARREN bp. 14 May 1749
iv ELIZABETH bp. 18 Aug. 1751
v SARAH bp. 12 Aug. 1753
vi LUCY bp. 5 Oct. 1755 (not in division)
vii dau. d. 19 Feb. 1758
viii SAMUEL bp. 24 Feb. 1760

References: HANOVER FIRST CH 1:90(m.), 127(bp. Thomas), 128 (bp. Nath.), 129(bp. Warren), 131(bp. Eliz.), 132(bp. Sarah), 134(bp. Lucy), 136(bp. Sam.), 188(d. dau.), 194(d. Thomas, Eliz.). MARSHFIELD VR p. 84(b. Thomas). Plymouth Co. PR 23:234; 25:490, 510(Thomas Torrey).

799 MARY MAY[5] (Anne[4] Warren, Richard[3], Nathaniel[2], Richard[1]) b. Plymouth 7 Feb. 1713; living 26 Nov. 1776 (deed).

She m. int. Plymouth 22 Sept. 1733 JOHN VALLER, d. bef. 17 April 1758 (adm.).

On 25 Dec. 1733 John Valler, husbandman, and wife Mary sold land given to Mary by her father John May on 19 Nov. 1733.

On 31 May 1749 John May Sr., yeoman of Plymouth, gave land to son John May Jr., wheelwright of Plymouth, and dau. Mary, wife of John Valler of Plymouth, husbandman.

On 17 April 1758 John May, wheelwright, was appointed administrator of the estate of John Vallier, husbandman, dec.

On 26 Nov. 1776 Mary Valler, widow, sold to son Simeon Valler of Plymouth, yeoman, land in Plymouth.

On 26 Nov. 1776 Mary Valler, widow and spinster of Plymouth, deeded to son Simeon Valler of Plymouth, yeoman, 1/2 of salt marsh.

Children (VALLER) b. Plymouth:

i SARAH[6] b. 29 Oct. 1734
ii ANN b. 24 Oct. 1736; d. 1 Aug. 1738
iii JOHN b. 1 Aug. 1739
iv SYLVANUS b. 21 Nov. 1742
v SILAS b. June 1744
vi ANNE b. 9 Sept. 1746
vii SIMEON b. 13 Dec. 1748
viii LOIS b. 15 Nov. 1752 o.s.

References: MD 15:111(b. ch.); 18:120(int.). Plymouth Co. PR 14:482, 510(John Valler). PLYMOUTH VR pp. 118(b.& d. ch.), 169(int.). Plymouth Co. LR 28:216(John Valler); 40:55 (John May); 64:15(Mary Valler).

800 JOHN MAY[5] (Anne[4] Warren, Richard[3], Nathaniel[2], Richard[1]) b. Plymouth 8 Dec. 1722; d. there 4 Sept. 1769 ae 46y 8m.

He m. Sandwich 11 Dec. 1745 BATHSHEBA BLACKWELL, b. Sandwich 9 Feb. 1725/6; d. Plymouth 20 May 1770 ae 45y 3m; dau. of Michael and Bathsheba (Bourne) Blackwell.

On 14 Oct. 1770 David Lothrop was appointed guardian of John May, minor son of John May. On the same date Thomas Wetherell was appointed guardian of Sarah May, minor daughter of John May.

The 7 Dec. 1773 division of the estate of John May went to only son John May and daughters Anna, wife of Thomas Witherell; Bathsheba, wife of Thomas Lathrop, and Sarah May.

Children (MAY) b. Plymouth:

i ANNA[6] b. 20 Feb. 1746/7
ii BATHSHEBA b. 19 Feb. 1748/9; d. 31 July 1753 in 5th yr.
iii JOHN d. 7 Aug. 1753 in 2nd yr.
iv BATHSHEBA b. 1754
v JOHN
vi SARAH b. Sept. 1759; d. 13 Sept. 1761 ae 2y 4d
vii WILLIAM b. 1762; d. 14 Aug. 1762 ae 13d
viii SARAH

References: NEHGR 117:297-8. Plymouth Co. PR 20:285(John May), 441(guardianships); 21:398-403(div.). MD 2:225(b. 1st 2 ch.). (PLYMOUTH) BURIAL HILL pp. 30(d. Bathsheba, John), 35(d. Sarah), 36(d. Wm.), 42(d. John, Bathsheba). SANDWICH VR 1:109(b. Bathsheba), 166(m.). PLYMOUTH VR p. 24(b. 1st 2 ch.).

801 NAOMI[5] WARREN (John[4], Richard[3], Nathaniel[2], Richard[1]) bp. Scituate 8 Sept. 1717; d. Middleboro 21 June 1795 ae 79y 4m 11d.

She m. Middleboro 6 June 1740 JEREMIAH TINKHAM, b. Middleboro 20 Feb. 1712/3; d. there 4 June 1790 in 77th yr.; son of Jeremiah and Joanna (Parlow) Tinkham, a descendant of Pilgrim Peter Brown.

The will of Jeremiah Tinkham of Middleboro, yeoman, dated 2 June 1790, proved 5 July 1790, names wife Naomi; son Jeremiah; son Elisha; sons James and Jesse; daus. Anna Warren, Abigail Tinkham and Huldah Tinkham; grandson Tiler Tinkham, son of Ebenezer Tinkham.

No Plymouth Co. PR for Naomi Tinkham.

Children (TINKHAM) b. Middleboro:

i JEREMIAH[6] b. 27 Oct. 1740
ii ELISHA b. 18 Aug. 1742
iii JOANNA b. 6 Dec. 1743; d. 2 June 1761 in 18th yr.
iv JAMES b. 8 May 1745
v ABIGAIL b. 25 Dec. 1746
vi ANNA b. 9 Oct. 1748
vii JESSE b. 25 July 1750
viii BENJAMIN b. 6 Jan. 1755; d. 23 Aug. 1775 ae 20y 7m 17d
ix HULDAH b. 8 Dec. 1756; d. Middleboro 25 May 1835 in 79th yr.; unm.
x EBENEZER b. 26 Aug. 1758

References: MD 3:84(b. Jeremiah); 15:100(d. Benj.), 101(d. Huldah, Jeremiah), 102(d. Naomi, Joanna), 220(b. 1st 3 ch.); 20:36(b. 6 ch.), 38(b. Eben.). MIDDLEBORO VR 1:76 (b. 1st 3 ch.), 127(b. 6 ch.), 129(b. Eben.). Plymouth Co. PR 31:218-221(Jeremiah Tinkham). MF 7:80-1.

802 JAMES[5] WARREN (John[4], Richard[3], Nathaniel[2], Richard[1]) bp. Scituate 3 Aug. 1718; d. Sharon CT 14 May 1788 ae 70 yrs. (g.s.).

He m. Sharon CT 15 July 1746 DEBORAH (FULLER) TYLER, b. Sharon CT 2 May 1725; d. there 31 Dec. 1794 ae 70 yrs.; dau. of Benjamin and Content (Fuller) Fuller, a descendant of Pilgrim Edward Fuller. She m. (1) Sharon CT 17 Jan. 1741/2 Gideon Tyler by whom she had Gideon.

The will of James Warren of Sharon dated 8 Dec. 1774, proved 10 July 1788, gave all to wife Deborah, except for 40 shillings to sister Naomi Tinkham.

No known children.

References: MF 4:119-20. NEHGR 57:248. Hillside Cemetery, Sharon CT(g.s. James, Deborah). SHARON CT CEMS p. 55(d. James, Deborah). Sharon CT PR 7:61-2(James Warren). Sharon CT VR LR 2:17(b. Deborah), LR 2:20(Deborah's 1st m.).

803 JOHN[5] WARREN (John[4], Richard[3], Nathaniel[2], Richard[1]) bp. Scituate 11 Sept. 1720; d. bef. 21 Jan. 1768 (father's will).

He m. Rochester 2 Jan. 1745/6 ELIZABETH LEWIS, b. Rochester 9 May 1721; dau. of Thomas and Mary (-----) Lewis.

No Plymouth Co. PR or LR for John Warren.

Children (WARREN) b. Rochester:

i JAMES[6] b. 14 May 1748
ii NAOMI b. 29 Dec. 1750
iii RICHARD b. 1 Nov. 1754
iv JOHN b. 21 April 1758

References: VR ROCHESTER 1:208(b. Elizabeth), 298(b. ch.); 2:311(m.).

804 NATHANIEL[5] WARREN (John[4], Richard[3], Nathaniel[2], Richard[1]) bp. Scituate 30 Sept. 1722; living 12 May 1789 (judgement).

He m. Sharon CT 10 Nov. 1748 JEMIMA FULLER, b. Colchester CT 15 Dec. 1731; living 27 May 1765 (deed); dau. of Benjamin and Content (Fuller) Fuller; a descendant of Pilgrim Edward Fuller.

On 1 July 1785 Nathaniel Warren formerly of New Lebanon [NY] conveyed land in the Kayaderosseras Patent [now in Saratoga Co. NY] to his brother James Warren.

On 10 Feb. 1789 Nathaniel Warren of Sharon quitclaimed to Judah Rowley and Isaiah Rowley all rights to the estate of brother James Warren of Sharon, dec.

On 12 May 1789, served 25 July 1789, Henry Vanskerk had a judgement against Nathaniel Warren at Litchfield CT.

No probate found for Nathaniel Warren and he was not in the 1790 census of CT or NY.

Children (WARREN) b. Sharon CT:

i JEMIMA[6] b. 6 May 1749
ii RACHEL b. 26 July 1751
iii NATHANIEL b. 29 March 1757
iv JOHN b. 2 June 1759
v JAMES b. 5 June 1761
vi CYNTHIA b. 18 Sept. 1763

References: Sharon CT VR LR 2:17(b. Jemima); 3:261(m.); 5:253 (b. ch.). MF 4:119-20. NEHGR 57:249. Sharon CT LR 9:528; 10:31(Nath. Warren).

805 ANNA[5] WARREN (John[4], Richard[3], Nathaniel[2], Richard[1]) bp. Scituate 28 July 1728; living 28 Feb. 1789 (deed).

She m. Sharon CT 10 Oct. 1751 JOSEPH DICKINSON, living 28 Feb. 1789.

On 23 Nov. 1747 Jonathan Elmer sold part of the iron works in Sharon to Thomas Dickinson and Joseph Dickinson.

On 28 Feb. 1789 Joseph Dickinson of Hebron, Washington Co. NY and wife Anna quitclaimed her interest in the land of her brother James Warren to Gideon Tyler.

No Washington Co. NY PR or LR for Joseph Dickinson.

References: Sharon CT VR LR 3:261(m.). Sharon CT LR 2:343 (Jonathan Elmer); 10:27(Joseph Dickinson).

806 NEHEMIAH[5] WARREN (John[4], Richard[3], Nathaniel[2], Richard[1]) b. Middleboro 14 Aug. 1731; d. Sharon CT bef. 3 Oct. 1785.

He m. Sharon CT 31 March 1754 ANNA FULLER, b. Sharon CT 23 Dec. 1738; dau. of Benjamin and Content (Fuller) Fuller, a descendant of Pilgrim Edward Fuller.

On 25 May 1765 Simeon Rowlee and wife Jane of Salisbury and Nehemiah Warren and wife Anna of Sharon sold to Abraham Mudge of Sharon land in Sharon on the right of Benjamin Fuller dec.

On 3 Oct. 1785 Simeon and Nehemiah sons of Nehemiah Warren late of Sharon made choice of guardian.

On 24 Jan. 1789 Simeon Warren of Salisbury CT deeded to Gideon Tyler all rights to estate of uncle James Warren. Nehemiah Warren of Sharon also deeded to Gideon Tyler all rights to the estate of James Warren, dec.

On 27 Feb. 1795 Jeduthan Gray of Great Barrington sold to Jehiel Rowley of Sharon his [wife's] interest in the estate of James Warren dec.; wife Anna also signed.

On 22 April 1795 Zophar Betts of Chenango NY sold to Jehiel Rowley of Sharon his [wife's] interest in the estate of James Warren dec.; wife Jane also signed.

No probate for Nehemiah Warren.

Children (WARREN):

i LOIS[6] b. 3 April 1755
ii EUNICE b. 7 March 1757
iii JAMES b. 30 Dec. 1758
iv ANNA b. ca. 1760 (based on age at d.)
v JANE
vi SIMEON b. 12 June 1767 (from gdn. papers)
vii NEHEMIAH b. 20 June 1769 (from gdn. papers)

References: Sharon CT VR LR 29:17(b. Anna); 3:262(m.), 320(b. James), 416(b. Lois, Eunice). MF 4:119-20. Sharon CT LR 5:422(Simeon Rowlee); 9:589(Simeon Warren); 10:216(Nehemiah Warren); 11:404(Jeduthan Gray); 12:504(Zophar Betts). NEHGR 57:249.

807 SARAH BUMPAS[5] (Joanna[4] Warren, Richard[3], Nathaniel[2], Richard[1]) b. Barnstable 5 April 1718.

She m. Barnstable 17 July 1740 SAMUEL LATHROP.

On 6 March 1759 Joseph Hamblen Jr. was appointed guardian of Samuel Lathrop of Barnstable, yeoman, who had been judged by the selectmen of the town to be non compos. On 2 July 1760 Joseph Hamblen was released from the guardianship as Samuel Lathrop was judged to be in his right mind.

No other Barnstable Co. PR for Samuel Lothrop.

References: MD 33:170(m.). Barnstable Co. PR 7:505; 12:90-9 (Samuel Lathrop).

808 JOANNA BUMPAS[5] (Joanna[4] Warren, Richard[3], Nathaniel[2], Richard[1]) b. Barnstable 15 May 1719; d. there May 1790 in 70th yr.

She m. (1) Barnstable 16 Nov. 1749 SAMUEL HAMBLIN, bp. E. Barnstable 7 Jan. 1722; d. bef. 3 Dec. 1755 (her 2nd m.); son of Ebenezer and Sarah (Lewis) Hamlin.

She m. (2) Barnstable 3 Dec. 1755 EBENEZER HAMBLIN, b. Barnstable 26 Nov. 1719; d. Freeport ME 10 April 1797 ae 79 (g.s.); son of Ebenezer and Thankful (Hamblin) Hamblin.

No Barnstable Co. PR for Samuel Hamblin.

Children (HAMBLIN) b. Barnstable, one by 1st husband, rest by 2nd husband:

- i REBECCA[6] b. 13 Sept. 1750
- ii JOANNA bp. 17 April 1757
- iii EBENEZER bp. 14 Dec. 1760; d. 18 July 1765 ae 4y 7m 9d

References: MD 6:138(b. Ebenezer); 31:9(1st m.; b. Rebecca), 10(2nd m.). BARNSTABLE FAMS 1:532(bp. Joanna, Ebenezer; d. Joanna). First Parish Church cemetary in Freeport ME(d. Ebenezer). Methodist Burying Ground rec., Barnstable(d. son Ebenezer).

809 JABEZ BUMPAS[5] (Joanna[4] Warren, Richard[3], Nathaniel[2], Richard[1]) b. Barnstable 28 June 1721.

He is apparently the "Jabas" Bumpas who witnessed the 5 April 1746 will of Job Bumpous of Johnston Co. NC and "Javis" Bumpas on the 25 Oct. 1754 Onslow Co. NC militia list.

He m. ELIZABETH ----- who d. bef. Nov. 1793.

The will of Jabez Bumpas dated 28 Oct. 1793, proved Nov. 1793, left all to wife for life and then to friend William Griffith.

The will of Elizabeth Bumpas dated 29 Oct. 1793, proved Nov. 1793, left all to William Griffith.

Apparently no children.

References: STATE REC. OF NC 22:340(militia list). NC Sec. of State Wills 877/56(Job Bumpous). Jones Co. Wills A191(Elizabeth Bumpas), 119(William Bumpas.).

810 THOMAS BUMPAS[5] (Joanna[4] Warren, Richard[3], Nathaniel[2], Richard[1]) b. Barnstable 20 March 1720/1; d. bef. 26 March 1784.

He m. Barnstable 2 Jan. 1747/8 MERCY STEWART.

The only Barnstable Co. probate for Thomas Bumpas is for Thomas Bumpas of Sandwich who had gone to their enemies 1 Aug. 1778. On 11 (blank) 1787 he was called "absentee" and on 14 Feb. 1787 he was called "absentee deceased."

There is also a 26 March 1784 letter of administration granted to William Shearman of Rochester on the estate of Mercy Bumpas, widow, late of Sandwich, dec.

References: MD 17:8(int.); 31:85(m.). Barnstable Co. PR 10:6, 7; 26:264, 484-5(Thomas Bumpas); 19:98(Mercy Bumpas).

811 BETHIAH BUMPAS[5] (Joanna[4] Warren, Richard[3], Nathaniel[2], Richard[1]) b. Barnstable 23 Aug. (1729).

She apparently m. Barnstable 26 Oct. 1748 SETH PHINNEY, b. Barnstable 27 June 1723; living 24 March 1758 (father's will); son of Benjamin and Martha (Crocker) Phinney, a descendant of Pilgrim Thomas Rogers.

No Barnstable Co. PR for Seth or Bethia Phinney.

Children (PHINNEY) b. Barnstable:

i ZILPHA[6] b. 30 Nov. 1749
ii son (twin) b. 10 March 1753; d. same day
iii son (twin) b. 10 March 1753; d. same day

References: MF 19:124. MD 11:132(b. Seth); 31:7(b.& d. ch.); 33:165(m.). FINNEY-PHINNEY p. 6.

812 LYDIA BLACKWELL[5] (John[4], Sarah[3] Warren, Nathaniel[2], Richard[1]) b. Sandwich 24 Oct. 1716.

She m. ca. 1737 MOSES CUSHING, b. Hingham 24 Aug. 1704; son of Daniel and Elizabeth (Thaxter) Cushing.

The deposition of Malachi Ellis ca. 1750 calls Moses Cushing son-in-law to Lydia Skiff.

No Suffolk or Plymouth Co. PR for Moses or Lydia Cushing.

Children (CUSHING) b. Hingham:

i LUCY[6] b. 22 March 1737/8
ii LYDIA b. 9 March 1739/40
iii CATHERINE b. 2 Feb. 1741/2
iv ELIZABETH (twin) b. 7 Nov. 1743; d. 19 Nov. 1743
v DEBORAH (twin) b. 7 Nov. 1743; d. 17 Nov. 1743
vi DEBORAH b. 23 March 1745/6
vii CELIA bp. 25 Dec. 1748
viii SARAH b. 9 March 1749/50
ix JOHN b. 13 June 1753

References: HINGHAM HIST 2:152, 155. NEHGR 117:184-5, 191 (evidence for mar.).

813 CORNELIUS JENNY[5] (Desire Blackwell[4], Sarah[3] Warren, Nathaniel[2], Richard[1]) b. Dartmouth 3 Nov. 1697; d. there 12 Oct. 1774 ae 77.

He m.(1) ELIZABETH -----, b. ca. 1697; d. Dartmouth 18 March 1743 ae 46.

He m. (2) Eastham 3 Dec. 1745 ELEANOR (COLE) YOUNG, b. Eastham 16 April 1711; d. Dartmouth 14 Feb. 1786 ae 74; dau. of Daniel and Sarah (-----) Cole. She m. (1) Harwich 29 July 1731 Henry Young.

The will of Cornelius Jenny of Dartmouth dated 3 Sept. 1771, proved 7 Nov. 1774, names wife Eleanor; sons Jethro, Levi, Benjamin, Cornelius, Timothy, Jehazel, Henry and Jabez Jenne; daus. Jean, Jemima, Deborah, Esther, Hannah and Rebecca.

Children (JENNY) b. Dartmouth, 13 by first wife:

i JABEZ[6] b. 22 Jan. 1722/3
ii JETHRO b. 18 Sept. 1724
iii SARAH b. 16 Sept. 1726 (not in will)
iv JEMIMAH b. 6 Aug. 1727
v REBECCA b. 6 Aug. 1729
vi CORNELIUS
vii HANNAH
viii ESTHER
ix JEAN
x DEBORAH
xi ELIZABETH (not in will)
xii JEHAZIEL
xiii BENJAMIN b. 1743
xiv WESTON b. 1746; d. 12 Aug. 1767 in 20th yr.
xv HENRY
xvi LEVI
xvii TIMOTHY
xviii ICHABOD (not in will)

References: VR DARTMOUTH 1:138(b. Jabez, Jethro, Jemimah), 139(b. Rebecca), 140(b. Sarah); 3:42(deaths). MD 5:197(b. Eleanor); 11:175(her 1st m.); 24:86(m.). HARWICH VR p. 43(Eleanor's 1st m.). Bristol Co. PR 23:365(Cornelius Jenny).

814 SARAH JENNY[5] (Desire Blackwell[4], Sarah[3] Warren, Nathaniel[2], Richard[1]) b. Dartmouth 28 May 1699; d. aft. 27 Oct. 1743.

She m. Dartmouth 19 April 1724 SIMPSON SPOONER, b. Dartmouth 12 Jan. 1699; d. bef. 18 May 1742; son of Isaac and Alice (-----) Spooner.

On 18 May 1742 Sarah Spooner of Dartmouth, widow, was appointed administratrix of the estate of Simpson Spooner. Sarah rendered an account on 27 Oct. 1743.

Children (SPOONER) b. Dartmouth:

i DEBORAH[6] b. 15 Nov. 1724
ii ELIZABETH b. 29 Dec. 1726; d. 20 Sept. 1728 ae 2y
iii BENJAMIN b. 25 June 1729
iv CORNELIUS b. 10 Dec. 1732
v GAMALIEL b. 15 March 1735/6
vi ELIZABETH b. 28 Feb. 1737/8

References: VR DARTMOUTH 1:262(b. Simpson), 259-60(b. ch.); 2:476(m.); 3:69(d. Elizabeth). Bristol Co. PR 10:161, 183-4, 380-1(Simpson Spooner).

815 RELIANCE JENNY[5] (Desire Blackwell[4], Sarah[3] Warren, Nathaniel[2], Richard[1]) b. Dartmouth 1 April 1701.

She m. Dartmouth ca. 1720 THOMAS POPE, b. Dartmouth 6 April 1695; d. there bet. 13 March 1761 and 25 May 1761 (inv.); son of Isaac and Alice (Freeman) Pope.

On 9 June 1761 Thomas Pell of Dartmouth was appointed administrator of the estate of Thomas Pope. The inventory was dated 25 May 1761.

Children (POPE) b. Dartmouth:

i JOANNA[6] b. 5 April 1721
ii AMAZIAH b. 31 Jan. 1722/3
iii ABIGAIL b. 15 Jan. 1724/5
iv RACHEL b. 1 Feb. 1726/7

References: VR DARTMOUTH 1:185(b. Thomas), 182-4(b. ch.); 2:365(m.). Bristol Co. PR 17:435-6; 18:6(Thomas

Pope). TORREY'S MARRIAGES p. 593(Pope). TAG 40:108-110(Alice Freeman).

816 IGNATIUS JENNEY[5] (Desire Blackwell[4], Sarah[3] Warren, Nathaniel[2], Richard[1]) b. Dartmouth 6 Feb. 1702/3; d. bet. 14 April 1763 and 1 Nov. 1763.

He m. Dartmouth 21 Jan. 1724/5 CATHERINE GREEN of Dartmouth; living 14 April 1763 (will).

The will of Ignatius Jenney of Dartmouth, gentleman, dated 14 April 1763, proved 1 Nov. 1763, names wife Catherine; sons Thomas, Samuel and Tucker; daus. Susanna, Reliance, Ruth, Mary, Eunice and Catherine. (No surnames but he mentions some daus. are married.)

Children (JENNEY) b. Dartmouth (named in will):

- i SUSANNA[6] b. 5 Dec. 1725
- ii THOMAS b. 11 July 1727
- iii SAMUEL
- iv RELIANCE
- v TUCKER
- vi RUTH
- vii MARY
- viii EUNICE
- ix CATHERINE

References: VR DARTMOUTH 1:140(b. Susanna, Thomas); 2:271(m.). Bristol Co. PR 18:265(Ignatius Jenney).

817 MARY JENNEY[5] (Desire Blackwell[4], Sarah[3] Warren, Nathaniel[2], Richard[1]) b. Dartmouth 20 April 1705.

She m. int. Dartmouth 27 April 1728 THOMAS WEST,* b. 23 Oct. 1702; d. Freetown 11 Feb. 1802 ae 100y 3m 18d.**

On 10 Jan. 1740 Jonathan Negus of Dartmouth sold 8 acres in Dartmouth to Thomas Weast, formerly of Tiverton and now of Dartmouth, cordwainer. On 15 July 1748 Thomas and wife Mary West sold this land to Benjamin Allen.

On 14 March 1788, acknowledged by Thomas alone, 26 Jan. 1795, Thomas West of Freetown, cordwainer, sold land in Dartmouth to Nathaniel Morton.

No probate found for Thomas West.

Children (WEST) b. Dartmouth:

- i SUSANNAH[6] b. 5 Sept. 1730
- ii RICHARD b. 1 Jan. 1733
- iii MARY b. 22 Aug. 1735
- iv PERNAL b. 28 April 1738
- v THOMAS b. 26 May 1742
- vi ELIZABETH b. 24 June 1750

References: VR DARTMOUTH 1:293-5(b. ch.). "Columbian Courier" of New Bedford, issue of 18 Feb. 1803(d. Thomas). Bristol Co. LR 31:53(Jonathan Negus); 42:309; 74:20(Thomas West).

*The mar. int. is in the original Dartmouth records but is not in the published VR DARTMOUTH.

**His obituary says he left 3 children, 30 grandchildren, 142 great grandchildren and 8 great great grandchildren.

818 CALEB JENNEY[5] (Desire Blackwell[4], Sarah[3] Warren, Nathaniel[2], Richard[1]) b. Dartmouth 20 June 1709; d. there 25 Aug. 1761 in 63rd yr. [sic].

He m. (1) Duxbury 6 April 1738 PATIENCE STANDISH, b. Duxbury 16 Aug. 1707; d. bef. 20 May 1746; dau. of Myles and Experience (Sherman) Standish, a descendant of Pilgrims Edward Doty and Myles Standish.

He m. (2) Middleboro 29 May 1746 SILENCE (FRENCH) HOUSE, d. Dartmouth bet. 12 March 1776 and 24 June 1776. She m. (1) Scituate 29 Feb. 1727 David House by whom she had Abel, John, Sarah, Susanna, Elizabeth and Patience.

On 6 Oct. 1761 Silence Jenney of Dartmouth was appointed administratrix of the estate of Caleb Jenney. On 1 Oct. 1765 Silence rendered an account.

The will of Silence Jenney of Dartmouth, widow, dated 12 March 1776, proved 24 June 1776, names sons Abel House, John House, Caleb Jenne; daus. Sarah Robbins, Susanna Badcock, Elizabeth Horlesey and Patience Taber; granddaus. Silence Badcock and Marcy Hammond; son-in-law Jeduthan Taber.

Children (JENNY) b. Dartmouth, two by each wife:

i RUBEN[6] b. 25 Aug. or Sept. 1739; d.y.
ii DESIRE b. 4 Dec. 1741
iii PATIENCE b. 28 March 1747
iv CALEB (under 14 yrs. 6 Oct. 1761, over 14 on 4 Oct. 1763)

References: VR DARTMOUTH 1:137-9(b. ch); 2:270(int. 2nd m.); 3:42(d. Caleb). VR DUXBURY pp. 170(b. Patience) 269(1st m.). VR SCITUATE 2:153(1st m.Silence). MQ 46:59. NGSQ 71:55. Bristol Co. PR 17:523, 559; 19:210(Caleb Jenney); 24:190(Silence Jenney). MF 14:33-4. MIDDLEBORO VR 1:103(2nd m.).

819 RUTH JENNEY[5] (Desire Blackwell[4], Sarah[3] Warren, Nathaniel[2], Richard[1]) b. Dartmouth 5 Sept. 1711; d. bef. 1 Dec. 1736 (2nd m.).

She m. 18 Jan. 1728/9 JEDUTHAN SPOONER, b. Dartmouth 10 April 1706; d. bet. 15 April 1740 and 19 Aug. 1740; son of John and Rosamond (Hammond) Spooner, a descendant of Pilgrim Francis Cooke. He m. (2) Dartmouth 1 Dec. 1736 Sarah Waste by whom he had Charity and a child.

The will of Jeduthan Spooner of Dartmouth, cordwainer, dated 15 April 1740, proved 19 Aug. 1740, names wife Sarah; daus. Ruth Spooner, Charity Spooner and child his wife "now goes with."

Child (SPOONER) b. Dartmouth:

i RUTH[6] (called granddau., under 10, in the 24 Jan. 1731/2 will of Lettis Jenne.

References: VR DARTMOUTH 2:473(his 2nd m.). Bristol Co. PR 9:470-1(Jeduthan Spooner). SPOONER DESC p. 71(b. Jeduthan).

820 SAMUEL JENNEY[5] (Desire Blackwell[4]), Sarah[3] Warren, Nathaniel[2], Richard[1]) b. Dartmouth 30 March 1714; d. there 21 Feb. 1784 in 70th yr.

He m. Dartmouth 30 Nov. 1746 PATIENCE HALL, b. ca. 1725; d. Dartmouth 16 Feb. 1802 in 78th yr.; prob. dau. of Benjamin and Patience (Cory) Hall.

The will of Samuel Jenne of Dartmouth, yeoman, dated 20 June 1777, proved 6 Oct. 1784, names wife Patience; sons Jonathan, Abishai and Edward; daughters Thankful, Eleanor, Patience Hall and Desire Jenne.

Children (JENNEY) b. Dartmouth:

i ELEANOR[6] b. 15 April 1747
ii JEPHTHA b. 3 Sept. 1749; d. 4 Aug. 1766 in 17th yr.
iii THANKFUL b. 10 April 1751
iv JONATHAN b. 3 Sept. 1753
v ABIASAI b. 1 Oct. 1755; d. at sea 12 Oct. 1780; unm.
vi REUBEN b. ca. 1759; d. 2 March 1777 in 18th yr.
vii PATIENCE HALL b. ca. 1761
viii EDWARD bp. 30 Oct. 1763; d. at sea 12 Oct. 1780; unm.
ix DESIRE bp. 30 June 1765

References: VR DARTMOUTH 1:137-40(b., bp. ch.); 2:273(m.); 3:42-3(deaths). Bristol Co. PR 28:161(Samuel Jenne).

NOTE: The published VR DARTMOUTH errs in stating that Seth Jenne was the grandfather of the first 5 children. The original records says he was Lettis Jenne.

821 ELIZABETH JENNY[5] (Desire Blackwell[4], Sarah[3] Warren, Nathaniel[2], Richard[1]) b. Dartmouth 16 June 1716; d. bef. 29 Nov. 1763 (int. 2nd m.).

She m. Dartmouth 13 Jan. 1736/7 SAMUEL HAWES, b. Edgartown 25 Feb. 1717/8; d. aft. 19 April 1776 (ack. deed); son of Benjamin and Dorcas (Smith) Hawes, a descendant of Pilgrim John Howland. He m. (2) int. Dartmouth 29 Nov. 1763 Mary Newton of Tiverton by whom he had Joseph, Deborah, Experience, Samuel and Dolle Newton.

On 15 May 1738 Samuel Hawes of Dartmouth, house carpenter, sold to his brother Benjamin Hawes of Edgartown, mariner, part of the dwelling in Edgartown which formerly belonged to their father Benjamin Haws.

On 9 Dec. 1763 Samuel Hawes of Dartmouth, house carpenter, gave half his homestead farm in Dartmouth to son Shobel Hawes of Dartmouth, laborer.

On 14 Sept. 1765 Samuel Haws, carpenter, and his brother Shubael Haws, both of Dartmouth, sold to Ephraim Pease and Abraham Prebel, land in Edgartown which was the houselot of their father Benjamin Haws, Esq., dec'd.

On 29 March 1766 Samuel Hawes of Dartmouth, housewright, sold land in Dartmouth to John Crandon; wife Mary also signed.

On 2 April 1776, ack. 19 April 1776, Samuel Hawes of Dartmouth, house carpenter, sold land in Dartmouth to Andrew Riche; wife Mary also signed.

No Bristol Co. PR for Samuel Hawes.

Children (HAWES) b. Dartmouth:

i SHUBEL[6] b. 7 July 1737
ii DORCAS b. 22 April 1739
iii JEDIDIAH b. 7 June 1744
iv ELIZABETH b. 7 July 1746
v BENJAMIN b. 1 Aug. 1753

References: VR DARTMOUTH 1:115(b. ch.); 2:237(m.; int. 2nd m.). VR EDGARTOWN p. 38(b. Sam.). Dukes Co. LR 6:272(Samuel Hawes); 9:525(Sam. & Shubal Haws). Bristol Co. LR 49:17; 50:512; 56:510(Samuel Hawes).

822 NATHANIEL JENNY[5] (Desire Blackwell[4], Sarah[3] Warren, Nathaniel[2], Richard[1]) b. Dartmouth 3 Oct. 1720; d. there 13 Jan. 1802 in 82nd yr.

He m. Dartmouth 15 Dec. 1743 MERCY MITCHELL, b. Chatham 4 May 1722; d. Dartmouth 6 Feb. 1802 in 79th yr.; dau.

of William and Sarah (Higgens) Mitchell, a descendant of Pilgrim Thomas Rogers.

Nathaniel Jenney was a private in the Revolutionary War.

The will of Nathaniel Jenney of New Bedford, yeoman, dated 2 Nov. 1793, proved 4 May 1802, names wife Mercy; sons Israel and Weston; daughters Sarah Kemton, Elizabeth Hathaway, Rebecca Jenne, Pernel Whitfield and Lydia Hammond.

Children (JENNEY) b. Dartmouth:

i SARAH^{6} b. 20 Jan. 1744
ii AGNES b. 20 Aug. 1747; d. 5 March 1763 in 16th yr.
iii ELIZABETH b. 17 Jan. 1749/50
iv REBECCA b. 29 April 1752
v PERNAL
vi ISRAEL
vii LYDIA
viii WESTON bp. 5 Aug. 1768

References: VR DARTMOUTH 1:137-40(b. & bp.ch.); 2:272(m.); 3:42-3(deaths). MD 4:184(b. Mercy). MF 19:147. Bristol Co. PR 39:88(Nathaniel Jenney). DAR PATRIOT INDEX p. 367.

823 PERNAL JENNY^{5} (Desire Blackwell^{4}, Sarah^{3} Warren, Nathaniel^{2}, Richard^{1}) b. Dartmouth 1 Sept. 1722; d. there 21 May 1784 in 60th yr.

She m. int. Dartmouth 10 Feb. 1745 WILLIAM MITCHELL, b. Chatham 31 June 1725 [sic]; d. Dartmouth 5 Feb. 1793 in 68th yr.; son of William and Sarah (Higgins) Mitchell, a descendant of Pilgrim Thomas Rogers.

The will of William Mitchel of New Bedford, yeoman, dated 23 Jan. 1793, proved 7 May 1793, names son David; daughter Ruth Studson; grandsons Seth Mitchell, William Mitchell, William Studson and Mitchell Studson and granddaughters Pernal and Elizabeth Studson.

Children (MITCHELL) b. Dartmouth:

i DAVID^{6} b. 20 Jan. 1748/9
ii RUTH b. 10 Oct. 1752

References: VR DARTMOUTH 1:162(b. David, Ruth); 2:320(int.); 3:49(deaths). MF 19:147-8. Bristol Co. PR 32:188 (William Mitchell). MD 4:185(b. William).

824 JEMIMA SPOONER^{5} (Alice Blackwell^{4}, Sarah^{3} Warren, Nathaniel^{2}, Richard^{1}) b. Dartmouth 7 Dec. 1700; d. there 1727.

She m. ca. 1723 GEORGE BADCOCK, b. Dartmouth 21 June 1692; d. there 7 March 1771 in 79th yr.; son of Return and Sarah (Denison) Badcock. He m. (2) Elizabeth ----- by whom he had George, Sarah and Jemima.

The will of George Badcock of Dartmouth, wheelwright, dated 31 Oct. 1765, proved 3 April 1771, names wife Elizabeth; sons John, Benjamin and George Badcock; daughters Sarah Bell and Jemima Badcock.

Children (BADCOCK):

i JOHN[6] b. 1724
ii BENJAMIN b. 16 June 1726

References: VR DARTMOUTH 1:32(b. George, Benjamin); 3:18(d. Jemima, George). TORREY'S MARRIAGES p. 29(Badcock). Bristol Co. PR 21:548-9(George Badcock). TAG 45:123(d. Jemima).

825 JEAN SPOONER[5] (Alice Blackwell[4], Sarah[3] Warren, Nathaniel[2], Richard[1]) b. Dartmouth 12 May 1703; d. bef. 15 Dec. 1728 (int. 3rd m.).

She m. Dartmouth 12 July 1727 JAMES WHITCOMB, b. Scituate 21 Aug. 1697; d. Warren 16 Nov. 1763; son of James and Mary (Parker) Whitcomb. He m. (1) Rochester 15 Aug. 1721 Mercy Winslow. He m. (3) int. 15 Dec. 1728 Mercy -----. He m. (4) Rochester 31 May 1731 Sarah Lincoln by whom he had James, Thomas, Sarah, Mercy, Scotaway, Elnathan and Nathan.

References: VR DARTMOUTH 2:536(m.). VR ROCHESTER 2:316(his 1st and 4th m.). VR SCITUATE 1:407(b. James). VR WARREN p. 196(d. James).

826 NATHANIEL SPOONER[5] (Alice Blackwell[4], Sarah[3] Warren, Nathaniel[2], Richard[1]) b. Dartmouth 21 April 1709; d. there 25 Nov. 1732 in 24th yr.

He m. Plympton 6 Nov. 1729 PHEBE CUSHMAN, b. Plymouth 14 March 1702/3; d. Kent CT 31 May 1790 ae 87; dau. of Isaac and Sarah (Gibbs) Cushman, a descendant of Pilgrims Isaac Allerton and Richard Warren. She m. (2) Tolland CT 2 June 1735 Barnabas Hatch (see #878).

The will of Nathaniel Spooner of Dartmouth dated 5 July 1732, bond posted 20 March 1732/3, names wife Phebe; brother Ebenezer Spooner; daus. Alice and Rebekah Spooner.

Children (SPOONER) b. Dartmouth:

i ALLIS[6] b. 23 Aug. 1730
ii REBEKAH b. 9 Jan. 1731/2

References: MD 2:226(b. Phebe). VR DARTMOUTH 1:258(b. Allis), 262(b. Rebekah); 3:69(d. Nathaniel). PLYMOUTH VR p. 25(b. Phebe). Bristol Co. PR alpha file(Nathaniel Spooner). MF 17:109. SPOONER DESC p. 73. VR PLYMPTON p. 399(m.).

827 SARAH SPOONER[5] (Alice Blackwell[4], Sarah[3] Warren, Nathaniel[2], Richard[1]) b. Dartmouth 18 Jan. 1712; d. Newport RI 26 June 1768.

She m. Newport RI 23 June 1735 JAMES PITMAN, b. ca. 1700; d. Newport RI 20 Nov. 1769; son of John and Mary (Saunders) Pitman.

The will of James Pitman of Newport, shipjoiner, dated 24 Sept. 1762, proved 4 Dec. 1769, names wife Sarah; sons James, William and Elijah; daughters Sarah, wife of James Fox, Rachel, wife of William Downing, and Susannah and Elizabeth Pitman.

Children (PITMAN) bp. Newport RI:

i SARAH[6] bp. 4 July 1736
ii RACHEL bp. 22 Jan. 1737/8
iii JAMES bp. 20 April 1740
iv SUSANNAH bp. 18 April 1742
v ELIZABETH bp. 29 April 1744; d. Newport RI 5 April 1769
vi WILLIAM bp. 26 Oct. 1746
vii ELIJAH bp. 5 March 1748/9

References: SPOONER DESC pp. 73-4(ch.). RIVR Newport 4:2:56(m. but no date). TAG 45:123. RIVR 8:450(bp. ch.), 472 (m.). RIVR (NS) 11:320(deaths). Newport TC & PR 16:103(James Pitman).

828 MARY SPOONER[5] (Alice Blackwell[4], Sarah[3] Warren, Nathaniel[2], Richard[1]) b. Dartmouth 8 Jan. 1713/4; d. bef. 18 June 1740 (2nd m.).

She m. Dartmouth 21 or 31 Dec. 1730 MARK HASKELL, b. Rochester 28 March 1708/9 [sic]; d. bef. 6 Sept. 1785; son of Roger and Joana (Swift) Haskell. He m. (2) Middleboro 18 June 1740 Abiah (Leonard) Nelson by whom he had Mariah, Roger, Elisha and Zebulon.

The will of Mark Haskell, late of Middleboro, yeoman, dated 10 Feb. 1770, proved 6 Sept. 1785, names wife Abiah; eldest son Nathaniel, second son Samuel, third son Micah, fourth son Roger, fifth son Elisha and sixth son Zebulon. He mentions land from his father Roger Haskell.

Children (HASKELL) b. Rochester:

i NATHANIEL[6] b. 26 Feb. 1731/2

ii SAMUEL b. 6 Feb. 1733/4
iii MICAH b. 20 Nov. 1735
iv JOANNA b. 11 Dec. 1737 (not in will)

References: VR DARTMOUTH 2:225(m.). VR ROCHESTER 1:162(b. Mark; b. ch.). MIDDLEBORO VR 1:63(2nd m.). Plymouth Co. PR 29:376-9(Mark Haskell).

829 ISAAC SPOONER[5] (Alice Blackwell[4], Sarah[3] Warren, Nathaniel[2], Richard[1]) b. Dartmouth 9 Jan. 1715/6; d. New Bedford 14 May 1800.

He m. Nantucket 15 Nov. 1743 RUTH GARDNER, b. Nantucket 12 May 1720; living 3 Sept. 1793 (deed); dau. of Jeremiah and Sarah (Coffin) Gardner.

On 8 March 1791 Isaac Spooner of New Bedford, yeoman, sold part of his homestead to Jeremiah Spooner of New Bedford, laborer. On 12 Aug. 1791 Isaac Spooner of New Bedford, husbandman, sold 7 acres of his homestead in New Bedford to Jeremiah Spooner of New Bedford, husbandman.

On 3 Sept. 1793 Isaac Spooner of New Bedford, yeoman, sold part of his homestead in New Bedford to Jonathan Cushman of New Bedford, mariner; wife Ruth also signed.

No probate found for Isaac Spooner.

Children (SPOONER) b. Dartmouth:

i GARDNER[6] b. 21 June 1745
ii SARAH b. 26 Nov. 1746
iii WILLIAM b. 24 April 1748
iv NATHANIEL b. 10 Sept. 1749
v WARD b. 21 April 1751
vi MARY b. 24 Feb. 1753
vii HEPZIBAH b. 18 Dec. 1754
viii JEREMIAH

References: VR DARTMOUTH 1:260-2(b. ch.). SPOONER DESC pp. 74-5). VR NANTUCKET 2:71(b. Ruth); 4:386(m.). VR NEW BEDFORD 3:159 (d. Isaac). Bristol Co. LR 70:10, 62; 72:358 (Isaac Spooner).

NOTE: No evidence found for daughters ELIZABETH b. 1760 and RUTH who d.y. as listed in SPOONER DESC.

830 ALICE SPOONER[5] (Alice Blackwell[4], Sarah[3] Warren, Nathaniel[2], Richard[1]) b. Dartmouth 27 March 1718; d. New Braintree bef. 18 May 1759 (adm.).

She m. Rochester 13 March 1736/7 ROGER HASKELL, b. Rochester 8 March 1710/11; d. Hardwick 21 Dec. 1750; son of John and Mehitable (Clark) Haskell.

On 8 Feb. 1750/1 widow Allis Haskell was named administratrix of the estate of Roger Haskell of Hardwick, husbandman.

On 18 May 1759 James Woods of New Braintree was named adminsitrator of the estate of Alice Haskell of New Braintree, widow. The 21 June 1768 distribution went to Roger Haskell, Rebecca Grainger, Hannah Haskell and Mehetabel Haskell.

Children (HASKELL) b. Hardwick:

i REBEKAH[6] b. 20 Nov. 1738; d.y.
ii MEHITABLE b. 17 Jan. 1740/1
iii REBEKAH b. 29 March 1743
iv ROGER b. 11 July 1746
v HANNAH b. 15 May 1750

References: VR HARDWICK pp. 53-4(b. ch.), 299(d. Roger). VR ROCHESTER 1:162(b. Roger); 2:163(m.). Worcester Co. PR 104:59 (Roger Haskell); 107:214(Alice Haskell); 10:130 (distribution).

831 WILLIAM SPOONER[5] (Alice Blackwell[4], Sarah[3] Warren, Nathaniel[2], Richard[1]) b. Dartmouth 29 Jan. 1719/20; d. 1796.

He m. Warren CT 8 Nov. 1750 RACHEL NOBLE, b. New Milford CT 3 July 1726; dau. of John and Abigail (Buck) Noble.

The will of William Spooner of Warren CT dated 8 May 1796, proved 22 Nov. 1796, names wife Sarah; son Nathaniel; daus. Rebecca Spooner, Sarah Johnson, Allis Phelps and Abigail Sanford; grandchildren Anson, Orancy and Ira Beeman; son William.

Children (SPOONER) b. Kent CT:

i WILLIAM[6] b. 8 May 1752
ii REBECCA b. 30 Oct. 1753
iii SARAH b. 27 Feb. 1755
iv RACHEL b. 8 July 1757
v ALICE b. 11 Oct. 1759
vi NATHANIEL b. 3 July 1761
vii NOBLE b. 18 July 1764; d. 17 Jan. 1774
viii ABIGAIL b. 8 Aug. 1766
ix RUTH b. 14 March 1771; d. 16 Aug. 1776
x JOHN NOBLE b. 24 Dec. 1773; d. 17 Aug. 1776

References: SPOONER DESC pp. 75-6. Litchfield CT PR #5439 (William Spooner). Kent CT VR LR 1:13(m.; b. Wm., Rebecca), 88(b.&d. other ch.).

832 EBENEZER SPOONER[5] (Alice Blackwell[4], Sarah[3] Warren, Nathaniel[2], Richard[1]) b. Dartmouth 29 May 1724; d. prob. Monkton VT in 1800.

He m. Rochester 29 Jan. 1745 SARAH ROBINSON, b. 9 Feb. 1720; d. Monkton VT 22 Feb. 1806; dau. of James and Patience (Ruggles) Robinson.

On 19 Aug. 1755 Ebenezer Spooner, wife Sarah and children Micah, Ebenezer, Sarah, Hannah and Alice were warned from Hardwick. In May 1758 Ebenezer Spooner, wife Sarah and children Micah, Ebenezer, Sarah, Alice, Hannah, Bethia and Elizabeth were warned from New Braintree.

In the 1790 census of Warren CT Ebenezer Spooner was 1-1-2.

Children (SPOONER):

- i SARAH[6] bp. Rochester 22 Feb. 1746
- ii MICAH bp. Rochester 25 May 1746; d. Ticonderoga NY in 1778 while serving in the Rev. War.
- iii DOROTHY bp. Hardwick 26 Feb. 1749
- iv EBENEZER bp. Hardwick 5 May 1751
- v HANNAH bp. Hardwick 21 Jan. 1753
- vi ALICE bp. Hardwick 15 Dec. 1754
- vii BETHIAH (twin) bp. Rochester 5 Sept. 1756
- viii ELIZABETH (twin) bp. Rochester 5 Sept. 1756
- ix poss. MARY (named in SPOONER DESC)
- x REBECCA b. 25 Jan. 1761
- xi PATIENCE b. 24 Feb. 1764

References: VR HARDWICK pp. 105-6(b. ch.). VR ROCHESTER 1:282-3(bp. 4 ch.). SPOONER DESC pp. 76-7(last 3 ch.). WORCESTER CO WARNINGS pp. 20(Hardwick), 44(New Braintree). Warren CT LR 3:89(1790 deed). TAG 45:123.

833 LYDIA PECKHAM[5] (Jane Blackwell[4], Sarah[3] Warren, Nathaniel[2], Richard[1]) b. Newport RI 19 March 1706; d. there bet. 14 Dec. 1760 and 21 Dec. 1760.

She m. ca. 1722 JOB CASWELL, b. Taunton; d. Newport RI 5 Nov. 1774; son of Thomas and Mary (Ramsden) Caswell, a descendant of Pilgrim Francis Eaton.

On 8 Feb. 1725 Job Caswell purchased a lot in Newport RI from the Proprietors of Easton's Point. On 20 Feb. 1748 Job and wife Lydia sold this to Antipas Hathaway.

Job Caswell was admitted a freeman at Newport RI 2 May 1727.

On 31 May 1749 Job Caswell purchased an acre of land and buildings in Middletown RI. Job Caswell of Newport, house carpenter, and wife Lydia sold this land 4 March 1757.

No probate found for Job Caswell.

Children (CASWELL) all b. prob. Newport RI:

i SARAH[6] b. ca. 1722
ii LYDIA b. ca. 1725
iii ISRAEL b. ca. 1727
iv MARY bp. 20 April 1729
v PHILIP bp. 28 Feb. 1730/1; d. bef. 6 June 1757; unm. when his father petitioned for administration of his estate.
vi JOB bp. 21 Jan. 1732/3; d.y.
vii JANE bp. 15 Dec. 1734
viii ELIZABETH bp. 28 Nov. 1736; d.y.
ix ELIZABETH bp. 4 June 1738; n.f.r.
x JOB bp. 5 Aug. 1739; d.y.
xi JOB bp. 26 Oct. 1740; d.y.
xii JOHN bp. 7 March 1741/2
xiii JOB bp. 16 Oct. 1743
xiv ABIGAIL bp. 9 Dec. 1744; n.f.r.

References: MD 38:125-8(acct. of family). RIVR 8:460(bp. last 11 ch.). Newport RI Town Council Records 12:106 (adm. of son Phillip). Newport Mercury, issue of 7 Nov. 1774 (d. Job). Middletown RI LE 1:119-20, 265-6(Job Caswell). NEHGR 62:287(d. Lydia). Newport RI Town Council Records, Land Evidences 6:552-4(bought land in 1725); 3:110(sold this land).

834 CALEB PECKHAM[5] (Jane Blackwell[4], Sarah[3] Warren, Nathaniel[2], Richard[1]) b. Newport RI 10 Jan. 1711/2; d. there 8 Jan. 1766 in 56th yr.

He m. Dartmouth 6 Feb. 1732/3 MARY SPOONER, living 1774 (census); dau. of John and Experience (Wing) Spooner.

Mary and Caleb Peckham were admitted as members of the Second Baptist Church at Newport RI 26 April 1741. Children Philip, Nathaniel, Elizabeth, Caleb and Thomas were baptized there 14 June 1741.

On 25 Dec. 1758 Job Bennett Jr. and wife Mary deeded part of a lot in Newport RI to Caleb Peckham of Newport, bricklayer.

The will of Caleb Peckham of Newport dated 4 May 1756, proved 3 Feb. 1766, allows wife Mary use of all his estate until his youngest child is 18. He does not name the children.

In the 1774 census of Newport RI Mary Peckham had 3 females over 16 and 2 females under 16.

No Bristol Co. PR for Caleb Peckham.

Children (PECKHAM) b. Newport RI*:

i PHILIP[6] b. 9 Feb. 1734/5
ii EUNICE b. ca.1735
iii NATHANIEL b. ca 1736

iv ELIZABETH bp. 14 June 1741
v CALEB bp. 14 June 1741
vi THOMAS bp. 14 June 1741
vii JOSHUA bp. 7 March 1742; d.y.
viii JOSHUA bp. 14 Feb. 1742/3
ix MARY bp. 21 July 1745
x DAVID b. 26 March 1748; d. 9 Dec. 1748 ae 8m 23d
xi JOHN b. 9 Sept. 1750
xii PETER b. 1753; d. 5 Jan. 1771
xiii BENJAMIN b. 26 Jan. 1757; d. 26 Aug. 1765 ae 8y 8m

References: SPOONER DESC p. 31(her parents). NEHGR 57:157-8 (list of ch.). VR DARTMOUTH 2:347(m.). PECKHAM GENEALOGY, Stephen F. Peckham, NY, 1922, pp. 266-7(b. & bp. ch.). Newport RI TC & PR 15:6(Caleb Peckham). Newport RI LE 11:133(Job Bennett). RI CENSUS 1774 p. 25. RIVR New Series 11:307(d. Caleb, David, Benjamin).

*Children are from Aspinwall file and NEHGR 57:157-8. None are in RIVR Newport.

835 JOHN PECKHAM[5] (Jane Blackwell[4], Sarah[3] Warren, Nathaniel[2], Richard[1]) b. Newport RI 11 Feb. 1714; d. Petersham 14 Aug. 1792.

He m. (1) Newport RI THANKFUL ELLIS, b. Sandwich 6 June 1711/12; d. 28 Aug. 1741; dau. of Malthias and Thankfull (Bassett) Ellis.

He m. (2) Bristol 22 April 1742 TABITHA (HOWLAND) CARY, b. Bristol 13 Jan. 1716; d. 4 Feb. 1793; dau. of Samuel and Abigail (Cary) Howland, a descendant of Pilgrim John Howland. She m. (1) Bristol 12 May 1734 Nathaniel Cary.

On 15 Feb. 1769 John Peckham of Bristol sold 20 acres in Bristol to Loring Peck; wife Tabitha also signed.

On 1 April 1769 Jonathan Danforth of Petersham sold 2 tracts in Petersham to John Peckham of Bristol, yeoman.

On 11 Feb. 1779 John Peckham, housewright, of Petersham sold 3 acres including dwelling house to Robert Peckham, gent. of Petersham. On 3 May 1780 John Peckham sold land in Petersham to William Peckham, nailer. On 8 April 1784 he sold 10 acres in Petersham to Josiah Peckham, wheelwright. On 21 May 1784 he sold 7 acres in Petersham to William Peckham, husbandman.

The will of John Peckham of Petersham, housewright, dated 26 July 1792, proved 6 Nov. 1792, names wife Tabitha; sons John, Robert, Samuel, William and Josiah Peckham; daughter Sally Davis; grandchildren Robert and Polly Peckham, children of son Robert Peckham and granddaughter Thankful Peckham.

Children (PECKHAM) 6 b. Newport RI, rest b. Bristol RI; first 3 by first wife:

i JOHN[6] b. 13 April 1737
ii EUNICE
iii WILLIAM b. 18 July 1741; d. 14 Sept. 1741
iv ROBERT b. 16 Jan. 1742/3
v ABIGAIL b. 4 Nov. 1744; d. 9 Dec. 1762 ae 18y
vi SAMUEL b. 19 March 1746
vii TABITHA b. 22 Jan. 1748; d. 14 Sept. 1750
viii WILLIAM b. 1 Feb. 1750/1
ix SALLY b. 15 Jan. 1753
x JOSIAH b. 10 Feb. 1756

References: RIVR Bristol 6:1:42(Tabitha's 1st m.), 42(2nd m.), 83(b. Tabitha), 98(b. last 7 ch.), 155(d. Abigail, dau. Tabitha). NEHGR 92:158(1st m.; b. ch.). SANDWICH VR 1:95(b. Thankful). Worcester Co. PR 24:303 (John Peckham). Worcester Co. LR 62:397(Jonathan Danforth); 81:368(to Robert); 101:63(to William); 103:220(to Josiah); 109:204(to William). Bristol RI LE 3:214(John Peckham).

836 JOSHUA PECKHAM[5] (Jane Blackwell[4], Sarah[3] Warren, Nathaniel[2], Richard[1]) b. Newport RI 20 July 1718; d. Middletown RI 31 Oct. 1741.

He m. Newport RI 29 Sept. 1739 RUTH PECKHAM, b. Newport RI 22 July 1719; dau. of Isaac and Barbara (Philips) Peckham.

Nothing useful found in Newport RI or Middletown RI deeds, probates or town records.

Child (PECKHAM) b. Middletown RI:

i SARAH[6] b. 24 Oct. 1741

References: RIVR Middletown 4:3:34(b. Sarah; d. Joshua). RIVR Newport 4:2:108(b. Ruth). NEHGR 92:158(m.).

837 DAVID PECKHAM[5] (Jane Blackwell[4], Sarah[3] Warren, Nathaniel[2], Richard[1]) b. Newport RI 28 July 1722; d. prob. Newport RI bef. 12 Sept. 1761.

He m. Rochester 27 Oct. 1743 DOROTHY ROBINSON, b. Rochester 10 March 1722/3; d. there 25 Sept. 1810 ae 88; dau. of James and Patience (Ruggles) Robinson. She m. (2) Rochester 26 Nov. 1749 Elnathan Haskell.

On 12 Sept. 1761 David Peckham, minor son of David Peckham, late of Newport, bricklayer, dec. chose Timothy Ruggles of Rochester as his guardian.

Child (PECKHAM) b. Rochester:

i DAVID[6] b. 28 Aug. 1744

References: VR ROCHESTER 1:232(b. David), 252(b. Dorothy); 2:165(her 2nd m.), 235(m.), 392(d. Dorothy). NEHGR 92:158(Peckham). Plymouth Co. PR 18:43 (gdnship.).

838 SARAH BLACKWELL[5] (Caleb[4], Sarah[3] Warren, Nathaniel[2], Richard[1]) b. Rochester ca. 1714; d. there 25 June 1761 in 47th yr.

She m. Rochester 31 Dec. 1747 GEORGE NYE, b. Middleboro ca. 1717; d. New Braintree 28 Feb. 1805; son of Ichabod and Elizabeth (Bonum) Nye. He apparently m. (2) Rochester 17 Oct. 1762 Rebekah Marshall.

On 6 April 1763 Thomas White of New Braintree and wife Sarah sold land in New Braintree to George Nye of New Braintree.

On 6 Dec. 1788 George Nye of New Braintree, yeoman, gave his son John Nye of New Braintree land in Plympton which "fell to him" from his grandfather George Bonum and his aunt Anne Barnes. On the same day he gave son Philip Nye of New Braintree, yeoman, his homestead and other land in New Braintree.

George Nye was 1-0-1 in the 1790 census of New Braintree.

Children (NYE) bp. Rochester:

i JOHN[6] bp. 4 Dec. 1748
ii PHILIP bp. 24 Feb. 1750/1
iii CALEB bp. 24 Aug. 1755; prob. d.y.

References: VR ROCHESTER 1:223(bp. Caleb), 225(bp. John), 226 (bp. Philip); 2:226(both m.), 416(d. Sarah). NEHGR 117:192-3. Plymouth Co. PR 72:52(George Nye). VR NEW BRAINTREE p. 149(d. George). Worcester Co. LR 53:217(Thomas White); 157:531(George Nye).

839 BETHIA BLACKWELL[5] (Caleb[4], Sarah[3] Warren, Nathaniel[2]. Richard[1]) b. Rochester 31 Dec. 1722; d. there 24 Oct. 1767.

She m. Rochester 22 Nov. 1744 ICHABOD NYE, bp. Middleboro 2 Nov. 1719; d. Rochester 14 Oct. 1770; son of Ichabod and Elizabeth (Bonum) Nye. He m. (2) int. Rochester 17 April 1768 Mary Spooner.

The will of Ichabod Nye of Rochester, yeoman, dated 13 Sept. 1770, proved 2 May 1771, names wife Mary; sons Jonathan, George Bonum, Ichabod and Ebenezer; daughter Bethia.

Children (NYE) b. Rochester:

i CALEB[6] b. 2 Nov. 1745; d. Sept. 1754
ii JONATHAN b. 22 May 1748
iii GEORGE BONUM b. 15 Nov. 1750
iv SETH b. 17 June 1755; d. Sept. 1755
v ICHABOD b. 20 July 1756; d. 9 June 1776
vi BETHIA b. 16 Feb. 1759
vii EBENEZER b. 20 July 1761

References: VR ROCHESTER 1:223-6(b. ch.); 2:227(m.; int. 2nd m.), 415-6(deaths). NEHGR 117:193. Plymouth Co. PR 20:520-4(Ichabod Nye). Middleboro First Ch. Bp. p. 8(bp. Ichabod).

840 ALICE BLACKWELL[5] (Caleb[4], Sarah[3] Warren, Nathaniel[2], Richard[1]) b. Rochester 19 May 1725; d. there 23 Sept. 1800 in 78th yr.

She m. Rochester 14 Sept. 1749 NICHOLAS CRAPO, b. Rochester 5 Dec. 1721; d. there 3 Oct. 1793 in 73rd yr.; son of Peter and Penelope (White) Crapo, a descendant of Pilgrim William White.

On 31 Oct. 1752 Nicholas Crapo of Rochester, husbandman, sold land to his "father" Caleb Blackwell. The deed mentions his father Peter Crapo.

The will of Nicholas Crapo of Rochester dated 26 Sept. 1793, proved 20 Nov. 1793, names wife Alice; sons Nicholas and Philip; daus. Alice wife of William Crapo, Bethia Crapo and Rebecca Crapo.

Children (CRAPO) b. Rochester:

i BETHIAH[6] bp. 14 June 1752; d.y.
ii BETHIAH b. 3 Nov. 1753; d. Rochester 24 Nov. 1828 ae 75y 9d; unm.
iii ALICE b. 12 Aug. 1756
iv MICAH bp. 28 Oct. 1759 (not in will)
v REBECCA b. 25 Sept. 1761
vi NICHOLAS b. March 1765
vii PHILIP b. 30 Nov. 1767

References: VR ROCHESTER 1:94-6(b.& bp. ch.); 2:95(m.), 368 (deaths). NEHGR 117:193. Plymouth Co. PR 33:480(Nicholas Crapo). MF 13:59. Plymouth Co. LR 42:167 (Nicholas Crapo).

841 SETH BLACKWELL[5] (Caleb[4], Sarah[3] Warren, Nathaniel[2], Richard[1]) b. Rochester 1 Nov. 1729; d. there bef. 23 Oct. 1812.

He m. Rochester 25 Dec. 1753 RUTH STURTEVANT.

The inventory of the estate of Seth Blackwell was dated 23 Oct. 1812. The estate was insolvent.

Children (BLACKWELL) b. Rochester:

i JANE[6] b. 31 March 1755
ii ELIZABETH b. 26 March 1760; d. 12 Dec. 1835 ae 75; unm.
iii CALEB b. 9 March 1764
iv JOHN b. 1 Sept. 1766
v SETH b. 28 Nov. 1768
vi MICAH b. 3 Dec. 1770

References: VR ROCHESTER 1:39(b. ch.); 2:40(m.); 349(d. Elizabeth). Plymouth Co. PR 44:371-2; 45:78-9(Seth Blackwell). NEHGR 117:299-300.

842 HANNAH BLACKWELL[5] (Nathaniel[4], Sarah[3] Warren, Nathaniel[2], Richard[1]) b. Tiverton 21 Feb. 1718/9; d. 22 Feb. 1795.

She m. Dartmouth 29 June 1747 NATHANIEL SPOONER, b. Dartmouth 10 Sept. 1716; d. New Bedford 6 March 1799; son of William and Mercy (Delano) Spooner.

On 23 Oct. 1762 Nathaniel Spooner of Dartmouth, yeoman, and wife Hannah and Mary Blackwell of Dartmouth sold to Ezra Winslow of Dartmouth land in Freetown that had belonged to their father Nathaniel Blackwell, dec.

Nathaniel Spooner was 1-0-2 in the 1790 census of New Bedford.

The will of Nathaniel Spooner of New Bedford dated 23 Dec. 1796, proved 7 May 1799, names sons Nathaniel, Philip and Micah.

Children (SPOONER) b. Dartmouth:

i WILLIAM[6] b. 13 July 1750; d. 30 July 1750
ii NATHANIEL b. 6 Dec. 1751
iii MICAH b. 22 May 1754
iv PHILIP b. 14 Aug. 1756

References: VR DARTMOUTH 1:261(b. Nathaniel; son Nathaniel, Micah, Philip), 262(b. William); 2:475(m.); 3:70(d. William). SPOONER DESC pp. 82-3. VR NEW BEDFORD p. 70(d. Nathaniel). Bristol Co. PR 36:91(Nathaniel Spooner). Bristol Co. LR 47:198 (Nathaniel Spooner). DELANO GEN (1999) pp. 25-6.

843 NATHANIEL BLACKWELL[5] (Nathaniel[4], Sarah[3] Warren, Nathaniel[2], Richard[1]) b. Dartmouth 8 Jan. 1724/5; d. Freetown bef. 26 Aug. 1756 (father's will).

He m. Wareham 4 Feb. 1747/8 LYDIA LANDERS, b. ca. 1724; d. Wareham 4 April 1789 ae 66; dau. of Nathan Landers. The will of Nathan Landers of Wareham dated 20 Dec. 1764 names dau. Lidia Blackwell.

On 17 Jan. 1794 Elisha Burgess of Wareham, yeoman, and wife Desire and Joanna Blackwell of Wareham sold to Humphry Hathaway land left to them in the will of their grandfather Nathaniel Blackwell.

No PR for found Nathaniel Blackwell.

Children (BLACKWELL) named in grandfather's will:

i DESIRE[6] b. ca. 1748
ii JOANNA b. ca. 1755; d. Wareham 23 July 1795 ae 40; unm.

References: NEHGR 117:194. WAREHAM CH RECS pp. 54(d. Lydia), 56(d. Joanna), 73(m.). Plymouth Co. PR 19:209 (Nathan Landers). Bristol Co. LR 72:327(Elisha Burgess, etc.). WAREHAM VR p. 74(m.).

844 JOHN BLACKWELL[5] (Nathaniel[4], Sarah[3] Warren, Nathaniel[2], Richard[1]) b. Dartmouth 14 Dec. 1727; living 16 Aug. 1794 (deed).

He m. Little Compton RI 27 Oct. 1748 PARTHENIA SHAW,* b. Little Compton 19 March 1725/6; d. Dartmouth 6 Oct. 1787 ae 61; dau. of Israel and Abigail (Palmer) Shaw. The will of Abigail Shaw dated 8 March 1776 names dau. Parthenia Blackwell.

On 20 May 1752 Nathaniel Blackwell of Dartmouth, blacksmith, gave one acre in Dartmouth to son John Blackwell of Dartmouth, blacksmith.

On 16 Aug. 1794 John Blackwell and John Blackwell Jr., both of New Bedford, blacksmiths, sold land given them by their father and grandfather Nathaniel Blackwell to Humphry Hathaway of New Bedford.

No Bristol Co. PR for John Blackwell.

Children (BLACKWELL):

i NATHANIEL[6] b. ca. 1749
ii JOHN b. ca. 1751

References: VR DARTMOUTH 3:20(d. Parthenia - she is called Bethany). RIVR Little Compton 4:6:8(m.), 158 (b. Parthenia). Little Compton RI PR 3:198(Abigail Shaw). NEHGR 117:194. Bristol Co. LR 39:274(Nathaniel Blackwell); 73:100 (John Blackwell).

*Parthenia is called Phebe in mar. rec., Bethany in one deed and Bethiah in another deed.

845 ELIZABETH BURGE[5] (Mercy Lombard[4], Jane[3] Warren, Nathaniel[2], Richard[1]) b. Plymouth 25 Jan. 1702; living 22 May 1745.

She m. Falmouth 13 Dec. 1725 SAMUEL DEXTER, d. bef. 5 Nov. 1739 (inv.).

The inventory of the estate of Samuel Dexter of Falmouth is dated 5 Nov. 1739. On 22 May 1745 Elizabeth Dexter, administratrix of the estate of Samuel Dexter, gentleman, swore to the inventory.

Children (DEXTER) b. Falmouth:

i HANNAH[6] b. 17 Sept. 1726
ii MARY b. 3 June 1728
iii BARZILLAI b. 8 Oct. 1730
iv ELIZABETH b. 22 Oct. 1732
v ASA b. 23 April 1735; d. 1 Nov. 1735
vi MERCY b. 9 Sept. 1736
vii THANKFULL b. 29 Jan. 1738

References: MD 18:145(int.). Barnstable Co. PR 12:388, 399 (Samuel Dexter). VR FALMOUTH pp. 35-6(b. ch.), 154(m.), 231(d. Asa).

NOTE: Did she m. (2) Falmouth 6 June 1745 Joseph Jenkins of Edgartown?

846 SAMUEL BURGE[5] (Mercy Lombard[4], Jane[3] Warren, Nathaniel[2], Richard[1]) b. Plymouth 8 March 1703; d. Wareham 26 Oct. 1772.

He m. (1) Sandwich 30 March 1732 JEDIDAH GIBBS, b. Sandwich 30 Oct. 1707; d. Wareham 19 May 1749; dau. of Benjamin and Anne (Tupper) Gibbs.

He m. (2) Wareham 7 Nov. 1754 DEBORAH BESSE.

The will of Samuel Burge of Wareham, yeoman, dated 10 March 1772, proved 2 Nov. 1772, names wife Deborah; sons Jabez, James, Samuel and Benjamin; sons Elisha, Theophilus and David; daus. Mary, Abigail, Jedediah, Deborah and Thankful. On 7 July 1793 the court appointed Elisha Burge executor of the estate of his late father Samuel Burge, Jabez having died before completing his executorship.

Children (BURGE) 10 by 1st wife; 4 by 2nd; b. Wareham:

i JABEZ[6] b. 25 April 1733
ii NATHANIEL b. 22 Jan. 1734/5 (not in will)
iii JAMES b. 25 Oct. 1736
iv MARY b. 26 Dec. 1738

v infant d. Aug. 1740
vi ABIGAIL b. 21 Dec. 1741
vii ELISHA b. 11 Jan. 1744
viii JEDIDAH (twin) b. 10 June 1747
ix SAMUEL (twin) b. 10 June 1747
x BENJAMIN bp. 25 June 1749
xi THEOPHILUS b. 11 Dec. 1757; bp. 26 Feb. 1758
xii DEBORAH (twin) b. 18 July 1760; bp. 24 Aug. 1760
xiii DAVID (twin) b. 18 July 1760; bp. 24 Aug. 1760
xiv THANKFUL b. 4 Dec. 1762; bp. 3 Oct. 1762

References: NEHGR 123:63-5. SANDWICH VR 1:54(b. Jedidah), 137(m.). WAREHAM FIRST CH pp. 12(bp. Benj.), 60(bp. Theo.), 61(bp. Deborah, David, Thankful), 73(2nd m.). Plymouth Co. PR 21:186; 27:527(Samuel Burge). WAREHAM VR pp. 18-9(b. ch.; d. Jedediah), 86(2nd m.).

847 THANKFUL BURGE[5] (Mercy Lombard[4], Jane[3] Warren, Nathaniel[2], Richard[1]) b. Plymouth 19 Oct. 1704; d. Rochester 13 Nov. 1794 in 91st yr.

She m. int. Plymouth 27 Dec. 1729 CORNELIUS BRIGGS, b. Rochester 16 Nov. 1705; d. there 17 June 1764 in 59th yr.; son of John and Ruth (Barrows) Briggs.

The will of Cornelius Briggs of Rochester dated 5 Aug. 1763, proved 11 July 1764, names wife Thankfull; sons Nathaniel, John and Zepheniah.

No Plymouth Co. PR for Thankful Briggs.

Children (BRIGGS) b. Rochester:

i JOHN[6] b. 22 Nov. 1730
ii RUTH b. 12 May 1732; d. 11 July 1732
iii NATHANIEL b. 21 July 1733
iv RUTH b. 25 May 1735; d. 29 Dec. 1735 ae 7m 4d
v SUSANNA b. 20 June 1737; d. 6 May 1750
vi ELISHA b. 8 March 1738/9; d. 14 March 1745
vii ZEPHANIAH b. 29 Dec. 1742

References: VR ROCHESTER 1:47-59(b. ch.), 60(b. Cornelius); 2:354-6(deaths). JOHN BRIGGS OF SANDWICH MA, Edna Anne Hannibal, Palo Alto CA, 1962, pp. 9-10. Plymouth Co. PR 19:102(Cornelius Briggs). PLYMOUTH VR p. 170(int.).

848 EBENEZER BURGE[5] (Mercy Lombard[4], Jane[3] Warren, Nathaniel[2], Richard[1]) b. Plymouth 28 Nov. 1707; d. Wareham 11 Dec. 1768.

He m. Sandwich 18 Nov. 1739 ZERVIAH NYE, b. Sandwich 1 July 1706; d. 13 Nov. 1787 ae 81 yrs.; dau. of Jonathan and Patience (-----) Nye.

On 9 March 1762 Ebenezer Burge of Wareham, gentleman, sold part of a lot to Noah Fearing.

No Plymouth Co. PR for Ebenezer Burge.

Children (BURGESS) b. Wareham;

i PATIENCE[6] b. 24 Oct. 1740; bp. 24 May 1741
ii EBENEZER b. 14 June 1743; bp. 31 July 1743
iii BERZILLA b. 18 Dec. 1745; bp. 8 Jan. 1745/6
iv PRINCE b. 13 May 1749

References: SANDWICH VR 1:67(b. Zerviah), 153(m.). MD 30:67(b. Zerviah). WAREHAM FIRST CH pp. 9(bp. Patience), 10(bp. Eben., Berzilla). Plymouth Co. LR 53:220(Ebenezer Burge). WAREHAM VR p. 18(b. ch.).

849 BENJAMIN BURGE[5] (Mercy Lombard[4], Jane[3] Warren, Nathaniel[2], Richard[1]) b. Plymouth 9 July 1709; d. Dartmouth 18 Sept. 1748 in 40th yr.

He m. ca. 1735 MERCY -----, b. ca. 1710; d. Dartmouth 4 July 1746 in 36th yr.

The will of Benjamin Burges of Dartmouth "Practitioner of Phisicks" dated 17 May 1748, proved 4 Oct. 1748, names sons Seth, Benjamin, Silas and Thomas Burges (all under 21).

On 1 Aug. 1751 Seth Burge, minor son of Benjamin Burge, late of Dartmouth, dec. chose Ebenezer Burge of Wareham as his guardian. On 5 Aug. 1751 Ebenezer Burge was appointed guardian to minor sons of Benjamin Burge: Silas, Benjamin and Thomas.

On 27 April 1761 Seth Burge of Rochester sold to brother Benjamin Burge his share of land in Wareham which came to him from his grandfather Ebenezer Burge of Wareham dec. and other land.

Children (BURGE) last 3 b. Dartmouth:

i SETH[6] b. 22 May 1736
ii BENJAMIN b. 21 Jan. 1738/9
iii SILAS b. 20 Feb. 1730/1 [sic; should be 1740/1]
iv THOMAS bp. Dartmouth 18 Sept. 1743

References: VR DARTMOUTH 1:52(b. & bp. ch.); 3:22(d. Benjamin, Mercy). Bristol Co. PR 11:570-1(Benjamin Burgis). Plymouth Co. PR 12:260-2(gdns.). Plymouth Co. LR 48:220(Seth Burge).

850 HANNAH LOMBARD[5] (Benjamin[4], Jane[3] Warren, Nathaniel[2], Richard[1]) b. Barnstable 8 Sept. 1714; living 16 April 1767.

She m. 30 Jan. 1735 BENJAMIN THACHER; d. bet. 16 April 1767 and 9 Aug. 1768.

The will of Benjamin Thacher of Harwich, yeoman, dated 16 April 1767, proved 9 Aug. 1768, names wife Hannah; sons Jonathan, Samuel and Benjamin; daus. Sarah Foster, Hannah, Lydia Foster, Jane and Temperance.

Children (THACHER) all but first b. Harwich:

i BENJAMIN[6] b. Yarmouth 11 Feb. 1737/8
ii SARAH b. 1 Dec. 1741
iii LIDIA b. 9 May 1743; d. 30 May 1743
iv LIDIA b. 10 Sept. 1744
v JONATHAN b. 18 April 1746; d. June 1746
vi JANE b. 30 July 1747
vii JONATHAN b. 22 Jan. 1748
viii TEMPERANCE b. 9 April 1750; d.y.
ix SAMUEL b. 17 Jan. 1752
x TEMPERANCE b. 27 July 1754

References: MD 34:19(int.). YARMOUTH VR 1:43(b. son Benj.), 174(int.). HARWICH VR pp. 79(b. 1st 4 ch.), 80 (b. rest ch.). Barnstable Co. PR 17:355-6(Benjamin Thacher).

851 JABEZ GOODSPEED[5] (Hope Lombard[4], Jane[3] Warren, Nathaniel[2], Richard[1]) b. Barnstable 26 Jan. 1707/8; d. Sandwich 4 Jan. 1778.

He m. (1) int. Barnstable 7 July 1733 RELIANCE TOBEY, b. Sandwich March 1695; d. bef. 21 Oct. 1749 (2nd m.); dau. of John and Jane (-----) Tobey.

He m. (2) int. Barnstable 21 Oct. 1749 ELIZABETH ADAMS, b. Barnstable 10 Oct. 1728; d. bef. 4 Aug. 1761 (3rd m.); dau. of Thomas and Sarah (Phinney) Adams.

He m. (3) Barnstable 4 Aug. 1761 MARGARET BASSET, living 13 Jan. 1778.

The will of Jabez Goodspeed of Barnstable dated 31 Oct. 1777, proved 13 Jan. 1778, names wife Margaret; eldest son Jabez; youngest son Nathan; son Elisha; three daughters (unnamed); dau. Jean.

On 13 Jan. 1778 Margaret Goodspeed of Barnstable was appointed guardian of her minor son Nathan Goodspeed.

Children (GOODSPEED) b. Barnstable, 4 by first wife; 3 by 2nd wife; last by Margaret:

i JABEZ[6] b. 31 July 1737
ii JANE b. 21 March 1739
iii HEMAN b. 4 Sept. 1743
iv BENJAMIN b. 26 May 1745
v ELISHA b. 1752; bp. 31 Jan. 1753
vi SARAH bp. 2 April 1755
vii dau. b. 1758

viii NATHAN b. ca. 1764 (named in will)

References: GOODSPEED FAMILY p. 110. MD 19:156(3rd m.); 31:82 (int. 2nd m.); 32:52(b. Elizabeth); 33:25(b. 1st 4 ch.); 34:19(int. 1st m.). Barnstable Co. PR 20:340-1 (Jabez Goodspeed); 18:24(gdn.). SANDWICH VR 1:53(b. Reliance); 2:1621(d. Jabez). BARNSTABLE FAMS pp. 403-4(bp. Elisha, Sarah).

NOTE: SANDWICH VR 1:143 lists the mar. of EBENEZER Goodspeed and Reliance Toby on 29 Aug. 1733. This is probably the mar. of JABEZ Goodspeed and Reliance.

852 JAMES GOODSPEED[5] (Hope Lombard[4], Jane[3] Warren, Nathaniel[2], Richard[1]) b. Barnstable 30 June 1711.

He m. Barnstable 13 Nov. 1739 ELIZABETH FULLER.

No Barnstable Co. PR for James or Elizabeth Goodspeed.

Children (GOODSPEED) first 4 b. Barnstable:

i MARTHA[6] b. 31 July 1741
ii MARY b. 14 June 1743
iii DAVID b. 20 Aug. 1745
iv HANNAH b. 14 March 1747
v DESIRE bp. 21 July 1751
vi ABNER bp. 7 July 1754
vii TEMPERANCE b. 5 Sept. 1756; d.y.
viii TEMPERANCE b. 19 July 1759

References: MD 31:141(b. 1st 4 ch.); 33:128(m.). BARNSTABLE FAMS 1:404(last 4 ch.).

853 PATIENCE GOODSPEED[5] (Hope Lombard[4], Jane[3] Warren, Nathaniel[2], Richard[1]) b. Barnstable 25 March 1718.

She m. Barnstable 30 July 1753 EBENEZER CANNON; son of Timothy and Elizabeth (----) (Hamblin) Cannon. He m. (1) int. Barnstable 31 May 1735 Mercy Blossom by whom he had Ebenezer, Ruth, Nathan, Joanna, Joseph and Timothy.

No Barnstable or Plymouth Co. PR for Ebenezer Cannon.

Children (CANNON):

i MERCY[6] bp. 30 June 1754
ii EBENEZER bp. 30 June 1756
iii IRA bp. 12 Oct. 1760
iv ZIBA bp. Aug. 1762

References: MD 31:10(m.); 34:17(his 1st m. int.). TAG 63:242-3(Blossom). BARNSTABLE FAMS 1:250-1.

854 JONATHAN GOODSPEED[5] (Hope Lombard[4], Jane[3] Warren, Nathaniel[2], Richard[1]) b. Barnstable 23 April 1720; d. bet. 23 July 1776 and 18 Dec. 1776.

He m. Easton 10 Nov. 1743 ABIGAIL KEYZER, b. Bridgewater 17 Sept. 1723; living 23 July 1776 (will); dau. of George and Elizabeth (-----) Keyzer.

The will of Jonathan Goodspeed of Easton, husbandman, dated 23 July 1776, proved 18 Dec. 1776, names wife Abigail; daughters Patience Southworth, Abiah, Abigail, Lydia, Sarah and Mollie Goodspeed.

Children (GOODSPEED) b. Easton:

i NATHAN[6] b. 16 Dec. 1744; d. 7 July 1747
ii JONATHAN b. 12 Aug. 1747 (not in will)
iii PATIENCE b. 4 April 1750
iv ABIAH b. 13 Oct. 1752
v ABIGAIL b. 28 June 1755
vi LYDIA b. 12 Oct. 1758
vii SARAH b. 12 June 1761
viii SOLOMON b. 27 Aug. 1763; d. 4 Feb. 1768
ix MOLLIE b. 11 Feb. 1769

References: VR BRIDGEWATER 1:194(b. Abigail). Bristol Co. PR 24:302(Jonathan Goodspeed). MD 46:32(m.); 47:147 (b.&d. ch.).

855 MARY GREEN[5] (William[4], Elizabeth[3] Warren, Nathaniel[2], Richard[1]) b. Plymouth 8 March 1710; d. bef. 16 March 1756 (father's est.).

She m. Scituate 24 May 1736 BARNABAS BARKER, d. bef. 21 April 1763; son of Joshua Barker. He m. (1) Scituate 13 April 1719 Hannah Turner by whom he had Barnabas, Sarah, Barnabas, Hannah, Thomas, Desire, Abigail, Mary, John, Lydia, David and Ziporah.

The 16 March 1756 settlement of her father's estate names her children as Mercy, Joshua, Lucy, Content, Bersheba and Zipporah Barker.

The will of Barnabas Barker of Scituate, yeoman, dated 4 Nov. 1757, proved 21 April 1763, names sons Barnabas, Thomas, John, David and Joshua; daus. Sarah Neal, Hannah Briggs, Desire Bell (?), Lydia, Mercy, Content, Barsheba, Zipporah, Mary and Abigail Bell. The 16 July 1763 division went to Mary, Abigail, Lisha, Marcy, Lucy, Content, Barsheba and Zipporah and sons Thomas, John and David.

Children (BARKER) b. Scituate:

i WILLIAM[6] bp. 1 May 1737; d.y.

ii MERCY bp. 7 May 1738
iii JOSHUA bp. 16 Nov. 1740
iv LUCE bp. 26 June 1743; d.y.
v LUCE bp. 7 Oct. 1744
vi CONTENT bp. 5 April 1747
vii BERSHEBA bp. 15 April 1750
viii ZIPPORAH bp. 22 Oct. 1752

References: VR SCITUATE 1:21-3(bp. ch.); 2:18(both m.). Plymouth Co. PR 16:425(Barnabas Barker).

NOTE: She did not m. Thomas Smith as suggested in NEHGR 57:19. She is called Mary Barker, dec. in her father's will.

NOTE: MARY GREEN is called MARY NEAL in the VR SCITUATE rec. of her mar.

856 WARREN GREEN[5] (William[4], Elizabeth[3] Warren, Nathaniel[2], Richard[1]) b. Barnstable 9 June 1712; d. Jan. 1785 (Bible rec.).

He m. Eastham 14 March 1733/4 MARY PAINE, d. 1783 (Bible rec.); dau. of John Paine, a descendant of Pilgrim Stephen Hopkins.

On 26 April 1740 Samuel Pelton of Middletown sold land in Middletown to Warren Green of Eastham, Barnstable Co.

On 5 April 1741 Warren Green and wife Mary were admitted to the Haddam Neck Congregational Church.

On 5 Jan. 1767 Warren Green of Middletown gave part of a house John Green had lived in to Rachel Green of Middletown, widow of son John Green of Middletown, deceased.

No probate found for Warren Green.

Children (GREEN) last 2 b. Middle Haddam CT:

i DESIRE[6] b. Eastham 14 Jan. 1734/5
ii MARY b. 16 May 1736 (family records)
iii JOHN b. ca. 1738
iv ELIZABETH b. Middletown CT 8 June 1741; bp. 5 July 1742
v BATHSHEBA b. Middletown CT 23 Oct. 1743
vi SARAH b. Middletown CT 22 Sept. 1745
vii WARREN b. Middletown CT 3 Aug. 1747
viii BENJAMIN bp. 2 July 1749
xi HANNAH bp. 6 Oct. 1751

References: MD 17:141(m.; b. Desire). NEHGR 57:19. Middletown CT VR 2:113(b. Eliz., Bathsheba, Sarah, Warren.) Middletown CT LR 9:378(Samuel Pelton); 19:479(to Rachel Green). Haddam Neck Congregational Church recs. 1:5(bp. 6 youngest ch.), 23(adm. church). MF 6:204-5.

NOTE: Dau. MARY was accepted by the Mayflower Soc. but she is not listed in GREEN GEN.

857 DESIRE GREEN[5] (William[4], Elizabeth[3] Warren, Nathaniel[2], Richard[1]) b. Barnstable 24 Oct. 1718.

She m. (1) int. Eastham and Barnstable 8 March 1739/40 SAMUEL PAINE. The m. may not have occurred as she is still Desire Green in the 2nd m.

She m. (2) Barnstable 24 July 1746 NATHANIEL HINKLEY, b. Barnstable 30 June 1698; son of Benjamin and Sarah (Cobb) Hinkley.

No Bristol or Plymouth Co. PR for Samuel Paine or Nathaniel or Desire Hinkley.

Children (HINKLEY) b. Barnstable:

i BENJAMIN[6] b. 23 May 1747
ii NATHANIEL b. 15 March 1748
iii SARAH b. 29 June 1751

References: MD 6:99(b. Nathaniel); 29:10(1st m. int.); 31:83 (b. ch.); 33:165(2nd m.), 168(1st m. int.).

858 WILLIAM GREEN[5] (William[4], Elizabeth[3] Warren, Nathaniel[2], Richard[1]) b. Barnstable 17 July 1721; d. Middletown CT 15 Aug. 1775 ae 52.

He m. (1) Middletown CT 28 July 1750 MERCY KNOWLES, b. ca. 1730; d. Middletown CT 24 June 1768 ae 38; dau. of Cornelius and Elizabeth (Remick) Knowles.

He m. (2) Middletown CT 25 Jan. 1770 ELIZABETH YOUNG, b. Eastham 26 Aug. 1733; d. Middletown CT 24 Feb. 1778; dau. of Robert and Elizabeth (Pepper) Young.

The will of William Green dated 25 July 1775, proved 4 Sept. 1775, names wife Elizabeth; dau. Eunice; and sons William and Enoch Green.

Children (GREEN) b. Middle Haddam CT; 2 by each wife:

i MARCY[6] b. 12 July 1751; d. 12 Aug. 1752
ii EUNICE b. 7 Jan. 1753
iii WILLIAM b. 8 March 1771
iv ENOCH b. 18 May 1772

References: NEHGR 57:19. Middletown CT VR 2:238(d. Wm., Marcy, Eliz.; 1st & 2nd m.; b. ch.). MD 15:72(b. Eliz.).

859 SARAH GREEN[5] (William[4], Elizabeth[3] Warren, Nathaniel[2], Richard[1]) b. Barnstable 27 Dec. 1723; d. Rindge NH 20 Feb. 1797.

She m. Scituate ca. 1750 BARNABAS BARKER, b. Scituate 23 April 1723; d. Rindge NH 13 March 1797 ae 73; son of Barnabas and Hannah (Turner) Barker (see #855).

On 17 Nov. 1779 Barnabas Barker of Scituate, yeoman, sold his homestead in Scituate to James Torrey and George Torrey; wife Sarah also signed.

On 17 Feb. 1780 Thomas Sackville Tufton of Groton sold 250 acres in Rindge [NH] to Barnabas Barker of Scituate.

On 21 May 1792 Barnabas Barker of Rindge, yeoman, sold his land in Rindge to John and David Barker of Rindge, reserving 1/3 of the land for the lives of himself and his wife Sarah.

No probate found for Barnabas Barker.

Children (BARKER) b. Scituate:

i JOHN[6] bp. 23 Feb. 1752
ii MARY bp. 7 April 1754
iii BARNABAS bp. 19 Sept. 1756
iv DAVID b. ca. 1759 (based on age at d.)
v WILLIAM b. ca. 1762 (based on age at d.)
vi LEMUEL b. 26 July 1765 (family record)

References: VR SCITUATE 1:21-2(bp. ch.), 21(b. Barnabas); 2:18(m.). HIST OF TOWN OF RINDGE NH 1736-1874 by Star, 1875. NEHGR 60:178(bp. John), 179(bp. Mary), 181(bp. Barnabas). Plymouth Co. LR 60:103(Barnabas Barker). Cheshire Co. NH LR 6:4(Thomas Tufton); 85:13(Barnabas Barker).

860 JOHN GREEN[5] (William[4], Elizabeth[3] Warren, Nathaniel[2], Richard[1]) b. Barnstable 12 April 1726.

He m. Middletown CT 2 May 1745 ELIZABETH TRYON, bp. Middletown CT 7 Feb. 1724/5; living 6 May 1763(deed); dau. of Abel and Abiel (Birdsey) Tryon. The 1 Feb. 1762 distribution of the estate of Abel Tryon of Middletown names dau. Elizabeth Green.

On 1 Feb. 1763 John Green and wife Elizabeth sold to Benjamin Bevin her share of some land of her father Abel Tyron. On 16 May 1763 they sold to Benjamin Bevin their share of the house lot of her father Abel Tryon.

No probate found for John or Elizabeth Green.

Children (GREEN) b. Middletown CT:

i LUCIA (or LUCY)[6] bp. 9 March 1745/6
ii JOHN bp. 8 Nov. 1747; prob. d.y.
iii ELIZABETH bp. 26 Nov. 1749

References: Middletown CT VR 2:61(m.; b. Eliz., John, Lucia). First Church of Middletown CT 1:46(bp. wife

Elizabeth), 78(bp. Lucia), 80(bp. John), 82(bp. Elizabeth). Middletown CT PR 2:174(Abel Tryon). Middletown CT LR 19:20; 20:143(John Green).

861 JAMES GREEN[5] (William[4], Elizabeth[3] Warren, Nathaniel[2], Richard[1]) b. Barnstable 19 Sept. 1728; d. bef. 25 March 1809.

He m. E. Haddam CT 13 Feb. 1754 RUTH MARSHALL, b. Freetown 1 April 1737; d. E. Haddam 27 Nov. 1816; dau. of John and Elizabeth (Winslow) Marshall.

The will of James Green of East Haddam dated 10 Nov. 1805, proved 25 March 1809, names wife Ruth; dau. Hannah Pirson; dau. Nancy Spencer; sons Benjamin, Richard, Oliver and Timothy.

Children (GREEN) b. E. Haddam CT:

i HANNAH[6] b. 14 March 1755
ii RUTH b. 12 May 1756; d. 21 Jan. 1791
iii JAMES b. 8 April 1758; d. at sea 1784
iv WILLIAM b. 26 Aug. 1760 (not in will)
v BENJAMIN b. 31 Aug. 1762
vi RICHARD b. 10 March 1765
vii ANN (or NANCY) b. 13 Feb. 1768
viii TIMOTHY b. 31 Aug. 1771; d. 19 March 1775
ix OLIVER b. 16 Aug. 1773
x TIMOTHY b. 3 July 1776
xi WILSON b. 10 July 1780; d. at sea 1801

References: NEHGR 57:20-1. Colchester CT PR #1512(James Green). East Haddam CT LR 5:268(m.; b. Hannah, Ruth). East Haddam CT VR(b. other ch.); 2:27(d. Timothy).

862 ALICE SWIFT[5] (Abigail Gibbs[4], Alice[3] Warren, Nathaniel[2], Richard[1]) b. Sandwich 23 July 1698; d. Colchester CT 15 Jan. 1783 ae 84.

She m. Sandwich 2 Nov. 1721 JAMES CROCKER, b. Barnstable 3 Sept. 1699; d. Colchester CT 7 Nov. 1785 ae 86; son of Jonathan and Hannah (Howland) Crocker, a descendant of Pilgrim John Howland.

No CT PR for James Crocker.

Children (CROCKER) first 2 b. Barnstable, rest b. Colchester CT:

i SIMEON[6] b. 22 March 1722
ii ABIGAIL b. 19 Sept. 1724
iii HANNAH b. 17 Jan. 1726
iv LEVI b. 11 May 1728
v JONATHAN b. 16 March 1730
vi JAMES b. 20 April 1732

vii THANKFUL b. 27 Jan. 1733/4
viii LYDIA b. 14 Jan. 1735/6
ix EPHRAIM b. 21 Sept. 1739

References: MD 3:150(b. James); 32:155(b. 1st 2 ch). Colchester CT VR TPR:109(b. James); 1:126(b. Lydia); L3:7(b. Hannah, Levi, Jonathan). SANDWICH VR 1:119(m.).

863 SUSANNAH SWIFT[5] (Abigail Gibbs[4], Alice[3] Warren, Nathaniel[2], Richard[1]) b. Sandwich 6 Oct. 1699; d. Colchester CT 4 Jan. 1745 in 46th yr.

She m. Sandwich 11 Dec. 1730 JOSEPH ISHAM, b. Barnstable 1704/5; d. Colchester 20 Jan. 1798 ae 93 yrs.; son of John and Jane (Parker) Isham. He m. (2) Norwich CT 27 May 1773 Temperance (Edgerton) Calkin.

On 21 April 1740 Gershom Bulkeley sold land in Colchester to Joseph Isham of Colchester.

On 17 Sept. 1765 Joseph Isham of Colchester sold land to son John Isham Jr. On 3 Jan. 1776 he sold land to Joseph Isham Jr. On 24 March 1789 he sold all his land in Colchester to John Isham Jr.

No probate for Joseph Isham.

Children (ISHAM) b. Colchester CT:

i ABIGAIL[6] b. 21 May 1732
ii JANE b. 2 Feb. 1734
iii JOSEPH b. 15 Oct. 1735
iv SUSANNAH b. 14 Feb. 1737/8
v JIRAH b. 10 Sept. 1740; d. 30 Sept. 1747
vi JOHN b. 7 May 1742

References: SANDWICH VR 1:136(m.). ISHAMS IN ENGLAND AND AMERICA, Homer W. Brainard, Rutland VT, 1938, pp. 124-7. Colchester CT VR TPR:111(b. Abigail), 112(b. Jane, Joseph); 1:126(b.&d. Jirah; b. John); LR 3:467(b. Susannah). MD 6:140(b. Joseph). Colchester CT LR 4:83(Gershom Bulkeley); 8:538(to John); 9:196(to Joseph); 12:29(to John).

864 JABEZ SWIFT[5] (Abigail Gibbs[4], Alice[3] Warren, Nathaniel[2], Richard[1]) b. Sandwich 16 March 1700/1; d. Kent CT 2 Nov. 1767.

He m. Sandwich 9 Oct. 1729 ABIGAIL POPE, b. Sandwich 2 Aug. 1710; d. Kent CT 2 Sept. 1776 ae 66; dau. of Seth and Hannah (Bourne) Pope.

The will of Jabez Swift of Kent CT dated 30 Jan. 1767, sworn 16 Nov. 1767, names wife Abigail; son Elisha; daus. Hannah and Birshea; sons Hemen, Jabez, Jirah, Job and Seth; dau. Patience. The division of 6 Aug. 1770, names sons Elisha, Heman, Jabez, Jirah, Job and Seth; daus. Abigail Chamberlin, Hannah Bird, Barshua Crocker and Patience Swift.

Children (SWIFT) b. Kent CT:

i ELISHA[6] b. 16 May 1731
ii HEMAN b. 14 Oct. 1733
iii JABEZ b. 14 May 1736
iv JIRAH b. 20 Aug. 1738
v ABIGAIL b. 1 Dec. 1740
vi JOB b. 15 June 1743
vii HANNAH b. 31 Aug. 1745
viii BARSHUA b. 28 July 1747
ix SETH b. 30 Oct. 1749
x PATIENCE bp. 1755
xi SETH (named in will)

References: SANDWICH VR 1:49(b. Abigail), 136(m.). Sharon CT PR #3189(Jabez Swift). Kent CT VR LR 1:145(d. Jabez); LR 1:12(b. Hannah, Seth), 16(b. Elisha, Heman, Jabez, Jirah, Abigail, Job, Barshua). CAPE COD LIBRARY 1:255. Good Hill Cemetery, Kent CT p. 46(d. Jabez, Abigail).

865 ZEPHANIAH SWIFT[5] (Abigail Gibbs[4], Alice[3] Warren, Nathaniel[2], Richard[1]) b. Sandwich 6 March 1702/3; d. Wilmington VT 9 May 1781 in 78th yr. (g.s.).

He m. Sandwich 30 Sept. 1725 LYDIA CHIPMAN, b. Barnstable 9 June 1708; d. Wilmington VT 23 June 1790 in 82nd yr. (g.s.); dau. of John and Mary (Skeff) Chipman, a descendant of Pilgrims John Howland and Richard Warren (see #702).

At the March 1734/5 Plymouth Court Zephaniah Swift of Tiverton, husbandman, "alias Rochester, Innholder" sued Benjamin Chandler for debt.

He was of Lebanon CT in 1739; Groton CT 1743; Lebanon CT in 1746 where he sold 100 acres of land in 1764.

The will of Zephaniah Swift of Wilmington VT dated 13 April 1781, sworn 10 July 1781, names wife; sons Perez and Chipman; daughters Alse, Mary and Lydia; grandsons Perez, Zephaniah Young, Zephaniah Swift and Zephaniah, son of Chipman.

Children (SWIFT):

i PEREZ[6] b. Sandwich 14 Feb. 1725/6
ii LYDIA b. Plymouth 13 Sept. 1728
iii ALICE b. Plymouth 25 April 1731
iv MARY (named in will)
v SILAS (not mentioned in father's will)
vi CHIPMAN bp. Lebanon CT 8 July 1750

References: SANDWICH VR 1:121(b. Perez), 126(m.). MD 14:239(b. Lydia, Alice); 29:71(b. Lydia). CAPE COD LIBRARY 1:255-6. PLYMOUTH VR p. 104(b. Lydia, Alice). PLYMOUTH CO CT

RECS 5:541. CAPE COD LIBRARY 1:255-6. Windham Co. VT, Marlboro Dist. PR 1:1(Zephaniah Swift).

866 WILLIAM SWIFT[5] (Abigail Gibbs[4], Alice[3] Warren, Nathaniel[2], Richard[1]) b. Sandwich 5 July 1705; d. bet. 2 Oct. 1748 and 20 Dec. 1748.

He m. (1) int. Plymouth 30 March 1733 KEZIA RIDER, b. Plymouth 1 March 1713/4; d. Sandwich 23 March 1735/6; dau. of Samuel and Ann (Eldred) Rider.

He m. (2) ca. 1740 ABIGAIL BURGESS.

The will of William Swift of Sandwich, yeoman, dated 2 Oct. 1748, proved 20 Dec. 1748, names eldest daus. Ann and Keziah; former wife Keziah; wife Abigail; daus. Abigail and Mary.

Children (SWIFT) b. Sandwich, two by Kezia:

i ANNE[6] b. 18 Jan. 1733/4
ii KEZIAH b. 22 Jan. 1735/6
iii STEPHEN b. 5 June 1741 (not in father's will)
iv JACOB b. 16 Oct. 1742 (not in father's will)
v ABIGAIL b. 24 April 1744
vi MARY b. 23 June 1746

References: MD 12:11(b. Kezia); 17:134(int. 1st m.); 29:27 (d. Kezia). SANDWICH VR 1:36(d. Keziah), 118(b. ch.). Barnstable Co. PR 8:344-6(William Swift). PLYMOUTH VR pp. 48(b. Keziah), 161(int.). CAPE COD LIBRARY 1:256(name of 2nd wife).

867 NATHANIEL SWIFT[5] (Abigail Gibbs[4], Alice[3] Warren, Nathaniel[2], Richard[1]) b. Sandwich 14 March 1707/8; d. Warren CT 13 March 1790 ae 83.

He m. Sandwich 14 Sept. 1730 ABIAH TUPPER, b. Sandwich 1 Nov. 1713; d. Kent CT 4 April 1782 ae 70; dau. of Eliakin and Joanna (Gibbs) Tupper.

On 4 Jan. 1749/50 Daniel Owen of Easton sold 50 acres in Kent to Nathaniel Swift of Kent.

No probate record for Nathaniel Swift and no deeds to children.

Children (SWIFT) last 5 b. Kent CT:

i INNOMINATUS[6] b. April 1731; d. ae 3d
ii RUFUS b. Plymouth 24 Nov. 1731; d.y.
iii JOANNA b. Rochester 17 July 1737; d.y.
iv MOSES b. 2 Aug. 1743
v ABIGAIL b. 12 Nov. 1746
vi NATHANIEL b. 18 Sept. 1749
vii ISAAC b. 27 Feb. 1753

viii RUFUS b. 3 Oct. 1756; d. 16 Dec. 1760

References: MD 15:42(b. Rufus). VR ROCHESTER 1:289(b. Joanna). SANDWICH VR 1:88(b. Abia), 136(m.). PLYMOUTH VR p. 113(b. 1st Rufus). CSL Cem. Rec. 622-1 p. 14(d. Nathaniel, Abiah). Kent CT LR 1:8(b. Moses), 46(b. Abigail, Nathaniel, Isaac). Kent CT LR 1:516(Daniel Owen). CAPE COD LIBRARY, 1:256-7.

868 JIRAH SWIFT[5] (Abigail Gibbs[4], Alice[3] Warren, Nathaniel[2], Richard[1]) b. Sandwich 23 Nov. 1709; d. Dartmouth 16 March 1782 in 74th yr.

He m. Dartmouth 9 Oct. 1730 DEBORAH HATHAWAY, b. Dartmouth 10 July 1713; d. there 17 Jan. 1794 in 82nd yr.; dau. of Jonathan and Susannah (Pope) Hathaway, a descendant of Pilgrim Francis Cooke.

The will of Jireh Swift of Dartmouth dated 23 Dec. 1776, proved 7 May 1782, names wife Deborah; grandsons John and David sons of son Jonathan; granddau. Abigail Haskell; sons Jirah, Silas and Paul; daus. Susanna, Lois and Deborah.

Children (SWIFT) b. Dartmouth:

i JONATHAN[6] b. 12 Dec. 1730
ii SUSANNAH b. 21 Feb. 1734
iii LOIS b. 4 Sept. 1737
iv JIRAH b. 31 May 1741
v SILAS b. 2 March 1745
vi DEBORAH b. 7 July 1748
vii PAUL b. ca. 1753 (based on age at d.), (named in will)

References: VR DARTMOUTH 1:110(b. Deborah), 265-6(b. ch.); 2:483(m. - his wife called Abigail); 3:71(d. Jirah, Deborah, Paul). Bristol Co. PR 27:79-83(Jireh Swift). MF 12:316-7.

869 JOB SWIFT[5] (Abigail Gibbs[4], Alice[3] Warren, Nathaniel[2], Richard[1]) b. Sandwich 3 Oct. 1711; d. Sharon 14 Feb. 1801.

He m. Sandwich 20 Jan. 1733/4 SARAH BLACKWELL, b. Sandwich 6 Feb. 1713; d. Sharon 2 April 1772; dau. of Joshua and Sarah (Ellis) Blackwell. The will of Joshua Blackwell of Sandwich dated 2 April 1751 names dau. Sarah Swift.

The will of Job Swift of Sharon, yeoman, dated 20 Dec. 1790, never proved, names eldest son Joshua Swift; second son Job Swift; eldest dau. Lusannah Price; second dau. Sarah Johnson; third dau. Temperance Manly; fourth dau. Abigail Lewis; fifth dau. Unity Randall; grandsons Jirah Swift, Zipha Swift, Azal Swift and Wyeth Swift; dau.-in-law Elizabeth Swift, wife of Job Swift.

Children (SWIFT):

i LUSANNAH[6]
ii SARAH
iii TEMPERANCE
iv ABIGAIL
v PATIENCE bp. Sharon 1743; d. 12 Feb. 1768
vi JOSHUA b. Stoughton 28 Aug. 1744
vii JOB b. Stoughton 3 Sept. 1746
viii JIREH b. Stoughton 4 June 1748 (not in will)
ix CHARITY bp. 11 Nov. 1750; d. 13 Nov. 1754
x UNITY b. Stoughton 13 Sept. 1752
xi PHILIP b. 1 Sept. 1754; d. 17 Oct. 1754

References: SANDWICH VR 1:80(b. Sarah), 142(m.). STOUGHTON VR p. 86(b. Joshua, Job, Jireh, Unity). Sharon First Ch. Rec.(bp. Patience, Joshua, Job, Jirah, Charity, Unity and Philip). NEHGR 117:295-6. Barnstable Co. PR 9:70 (Joshua Blackwell). Unrecorded will of Job Swift from an application to the Mayflower Society. CAPE COD LIBRARY 1:257-8(d. Job). MD 48:35-7.

870 SILAS SWIFT[5] (Abigail Gibbs[4], Alice[3] Warren, Nathaniel[2], Richard[1]) b. Sandwich 2 Aug. 1713; d. Lebanon CT 24 Sept. 1794 ae 81.

He m. Lebanon CT 16 Oct. 1735 ABIGAIL TUPPER, b. Sandwich 13 Aug. 1717; d. Lebanon CT 15 Feb. 1811 ae 94; dau. of Eliakim and Joanna (Gibbs) Tupper.

On 12 Feb. 1786 Silas Swift of Lebanon sold 30 acres to William Swift 3d of Lebanon.

No probate for Silas or Abigail Swift.

Children (SWIFT) last 7 b. Lebanon CT:

i ELIAS[6] b. Rochester 10 June 1736
ii LYDIA b. May 1740; d.y.
iii CHARLES b. 16 March 1742
iv ABIGAIL b. 19 July 1745
v SUSANNA b. 28 July 1747
vi SILAS b. 17 Nov. 1749
vii WILLIAM b. 14 Dec. 1751
viii DARIUS b. 28 Nov. 1757
ix ROXILLANA b. 8 Oct. 1761

References: VR ROCHESTER 1:289(b. Elias). Lebanon CT VR 1:289 (m.; b. Charles, Abigail, Susanna, Silas, William, Darius, Roxillana). SANDWICH VR 1:88(b. Abigail). Lebanon CT First Ch. Rec. 5:159(d. Silas, Abigail). Lebanon CT LR 15:291(Silas Swift).

871 ABIGAIL SWIFT[5] (Abigail Gibbs[4], Alice[3] Warren, Nathaniel[2], Richard[1]) b. Sandwich 26 July 1715; d. Rochester 31 Jan. 1796 in 81st yr.

She m. int. Plymouth 21 Dec. 1736; int. Rochester 25 Dec. 1736 ANTIPAS HAMMOND, b. Rochester 16 July 1704; d. there 29 March 1773; son of Benjamin and Elizabeth (-----) Hammond.

The will of Antipas Hammond of Rochester, yeoman, dated 27 Feb. 1773, proved 7 June 1773, names wife Abigail; only dau. Elizabeth; sons Joseph, Benjamin, Jireh and Hunnewell.

On 7 April 1778 Honnewell Hammond, Joseph Hammond, Benjamin Hammond, yeomen, and Job Haskell, cordwainer, and his wife Elizabeth, all of Rochester sold their rights to land left to them in their father's will and from the estate of brother Jirah Hammond, dec.

No Plymouth Co. PR for Abigail Hammond.

Children (HAMMOND) b. Rochester:

i JIREH[6] b. 5 Dec. 1737
ii HUNNEWELL b. 9 Aug. 1740
iii ABIGAIL b. 24 March 1742 (not in will)
iv JOSEPH b. 5 Sept. 1747
v ELIZABETH b. 18 Jan. 1752
vi BENJAMIN b. 5 April 1756

References: VR ROCHESTER 1:144(b. Antipas), 143-5(b. ch.); 2:148(int.), 365(d. Abigail, Antipas). Plymouth Co. PR 21:266-7(Antipas Hammond). PLYMOUTH VR p. 164(int.). Plymouth Co. LR 64:248(Honnewell Hammond, etc.).

872 ISAAC SWIFT[5] (Abigail Gibbs[4], Alice[3] Warren, Nathaniel[2], Richard[1]) b. Sandwich 3 May 1720; d. Bridgewater 22 Nov. 1811 in 97th yr.

He m. Bridgewater 26 Jan. 1748/9 SUSANNA (KEITH) AMES, b. Bridgewater 2 Sept. 1714; d. there 23 May 1795 in 81st yr.; dau. of Samuel and Bethiah (Forbes) Keith. She m. (1) Bridgewater 27 Dec. 1737 Solomon Ames by whom she had Simeon, Solomon and Jotham.

On 3 March 1789 Isaac Swift of Bridgewater, yeoman, and wife Susanna sold Ephraim Sprague part of home and farm where he lived. On 21 Aug. 1789 they sold land in Bridgewater to Isaac Lazell Jr.

No Plymouth Co. PR for Isaac Swift.

Children (SWIFT) b. Bridgewater:

i JIRAH[6] b. 18 Dec. 1749
ii WILLIAM b. 5 June 1752

iii SUSANNA b. 8 April 1754
iv MARY b. 5 Jan. 1759

References: VR BRIDGEWATER 1:192(b. Susanna), 310(b. ch.); 2:34(her 1st m.), 360(m.), 562(d. Isaac), 563(d. Susanna). Plymouth Co. LR 68:237; 74:158(Isaac).

873 ROWLAND SWIFT[5] (Abigail Gibbs[4], Alice[3] Warren, Nathaniel[2], Richard[1]) b. Sandwich 24 March 1721/2; d. Lebanon CT 13 Feb. 1795 ae 72.

He m. Wareham 5 Dec. 1745 MARY DEXTER, b. Falmouth 3 June 1728; d. Lebanon CT 19 Oct. 1798 ae 70; dau. of Samuel and Elizabeth (Burge) Dexter, a descendant of Pilgrim Richard Warren (see #845ii).

On 10 Aug. 1763, ack. 14 Sept. 1768, Rowland Swift of Wareham, gentleman, and wife Mary sold housing, lands, etc. in Wareham to Josiah Swift of Sandwich.

The will of Roland Swift of Lebanon CT dated 8 April 1785, exhibited 9 March 1795, names wife Mary; son Barzillai; dau. Abigail; son Roland; son Zepheniah; dau. Mary; son William and dau. Thankful; son-in-law Lathrop Davis.

Children (SWIFT) b. Wareham:

i BARZILLAI[6] b. 9 Jan. 1747
ii ABIGAIL b. 3 Feb. 1749; d. 9 Feb. 1749
iii ABIGAIL b. 8 July 1751
iv ROWLAND b. 10 Dec. 1753; drowned
v JIREH b. 6 Dec. 1755; drowned at sea unm.
vi ZEPHANIAH b. 27 Feb. 1759
vii MARY b. 1 March 1761
viii WILLIAM b. 8 Jan. 1764
ix THANKFUL b. 14 Oct. 1766

References: WAREHAM FIRST CH p. 73(m.). Plymouth Co. LR 54:243(Rowland Swift). VR FALMOUTH p. 35(b. Mary). CAPE COD LIBRARY 1:259-60. Windham CT PR 13:411(Roland Swift). WAREHAM VR pp. 54(b. 1st 3 ch.; d. Abigail), 55(b. Jireh), 56(b. Rowland, Mary), 57(b. Zephaniah, William, Thankful), 156(m.). CSL Hale Cem. Rec. Lebanon p. 113(d. Rowland, Mercy).

874 EXPERIENCE GIBBS[5] (Thomas[4], Alice[3] Warren, Nathaniel[2], Richard[1]) b. Sandwich 17 Aug. 1714; d. Liverpool NS 8 May 1777.

She m. Sandwich 16 Jan. 1734/5 NATHAN TUPPER, b. Sandwich 28 June 1709; d. Liverpool NS 4 April 1784; son of Medad and Hannah (-----) Tupper.

On 13 Feb. 1760 Nathan Tupper of Rochester, mariner, and wife Experience sold land in Rochester to Ivory Henry.

On 9 July 1777 Nathan Tupper of Liverpool, Esq., sold land in Liverpool to Medad Tupper of Liverpool, yeoman.

On 12 July 1779 Nathan Tupper of Liverpool, Esq., sold land in Liverpool to Nathan Tupper Jr.

The will of Nathan Tupper dated 12 July 1774, proved 3 May 1784, names wife Experience; sons Nathan and Medad; daughters Joanna, wife of William Murray; Abigail, wife of Elkanah Mitchell; Experience, wife of Ebenezer [unreadable]; Martha, wife of Howes Stuart; Hannah, wife of Nathaniel Freeman and Elizabeth, unmarried.

Nathan Tupper moved to Liverpool NS in 1760.

Children (TUPPER) all but first b. Rochester:

i JOANNA[6] b. Sandwich 1 Nov. 1735
ii ABIGAIL b. 20 March 1737
iii EXPERIENCE b. 11 Feb. 1739
iv NATHAN b. 25 Jan. 1741; d. 1748
v MARTHA b. 5 April 1744
vi MEDAD b. 25 April 1746
vii HANNAH b. 8 March 1749
viii MARY b. 12 May 1751; "died in the second year of her age."
ix MARY b. 24 Nov. 1753; d. Liverpool NS 14 July 1772
x ELIZABETH b. 20 Oct. 1755
xi NATHAN b. 7 April 1757

References: VR ROCHESTER 1:296(b.&bp. ch.). SANDWICH VR 1:81 (b. Nathan), 95(b. Joanna), 144(m.). NEHGR 126:162(b. ch.; d. Nathan, Mary; move to Liverpool). Diary of Simeon Perkins (d. Nathan, Experience). Queens Co. NS Wills 1:97(Nathan Tupper). Plymouth Co. LR 49:230(Nathan Tupper). Queens Co. NS LR 2:1(to Medad); 2:50(to Nathan). Liverpool NS VR p. 36(b.&d. ch.; d. Nathan).

875 ELIZABETH GIBBS[5] (Thomas[4], Alice[3] Warren, Nathaniel[2], Richard[1]) b. Sandwich 8 April 1717.

She m. int. Rochester 18 Sept. 1736 SAMUEL MUXAM, b. Rochester; d. bef. 17 July 1755; son of Samuel and Hannah (Perry) Muxam.

On 17 July 1755 Ezra Muxum of Middleborough was appointed administrator of the estate of Samuel Muxum of Rochester, yeoman.

On 15 June 1762 the estate was divided between Elizabeth Muxum, widow of Samuel; eldest son Nathan; children Hannah, David, Elizabeth, Caleb, Samuel & Ezra Muxum.

Children (MUXAM) b. Rochester except last:

i HANNAH[6] b. 2 July 1737
ii NATHAN b. 2 Oct. 1739
iii DAVID b. 30 Sept. 1741
iv ELIZABETH b. 19 Jan. 1743
v CALEB b. 9 June 1746
vi SAMUEL b. 12 Sept. 1748
vii EZRA bp. Wareham 9 June 1751

References: VR ROCHESTER 1:211(b. ch.); 2:223(int.). WAREHAM FIRST CH p. 13(bp. Ezra). Plymouth Co. PR 13:487; 16:328(Samuel Muxum).

876 JOANNA GIBBS[5] (Thomas[4], Alice[3] Warren, Nathaniel[2], Richard[1]) b. Sandwich 16 July 1719; living 7 May 1768.

She m. (1) Sandwich 11 Nov. 1742 MEDAD TUPPER, b. Sandwich 2 April 1718; drowned New London CT ca. 1743; son of Medad and Hannah (-----) Tupper.

She m. (2) Plymouth 17 May 1744 JAMES SHURTLEFF, d. bef. 2 April 1767.

On 14 March 1748 James Shurtleff of Plymouth, cordwainer, and wife Joanna, sold part of his homestead to Joseph Shurtleff.

On 2 April 1767 Joanna Shurtleff, widow, was appointed administratrix of the estate of James Shurtleff, cordwainer, dec. On 7 May 1768 Joanna received her dower.

Child (TUPPER):

i MEDAD[6] b. ca. 1743

Child (SHURTLEFF) b. Plymouth:

ii JAMES b. 21 July 1745

References: NEHGR 123:132. MD 13:116(b. James); 14:166(2nd m.). Plymouth Co. LR 40:10(James Shurtleff). Plymouth Co. PR 17:181; 19:489; 20:9, 112, 209(James Shurtleff). PLYMOUTH VR pp. 69(b. James), 103(2nd m.). SANDWICH VR 1:82(b. Medad), 134(m.).

877 SOLOMON GIBBS[5] (Thomas[4], Alice[3] Warren, Nathaniel[2], Richard[1]) b. Sandwich 30 Jan. 1729/30; d. there 27 March 1796 ae 66.

He m. Sandwich 8 March 1753 HANNAH GIBBS, b. Wareham 18 June 1735; d. there 26 Sept. 1811 ae 77; dau. of Micah and Sarah (Sanders) Gibbs.

Solomon Gibbs was 4-1-4 in the 1790 census of Sandwich.

No Barnstable Co. PR for Solomon or Hannah Gibbs.

Children (GIBBS) b. Sandwich:

i THOMAS[6] b. 29 Dec. 1753; d. 14 Dec. 1754
ii THOMAS b. 25 Oct. 1755
iii DOROTHY b. 27 Dec. 1757
iv MACAI (son) b. 10 Feb. 1760
v SARAH b. 19 March 1762
vi WARREN b. 15 May 1764
vii LYDIA b. 2 Jan. 1767
viii DAVID (twin) b. 1 June 1769
ix JONATHAN (twin) b. 1 June 1769
x EUNICE b. 19 Feb. 1772; d. 17 May 1806 ae 35
xi HANNAH b. 11 Sept. 1774
xii MICAH b. 19 May 1779

References: SANDWICH VR 1:174(d. Thomas), 186(m.), 188(b. Thomas), 226(b. rest of ch.); 2:1435(d. Solomon), 1440(d. Eunice), 1444(d. Hannah). NEHGR 123:205-6. WAREHAM VR p. 31(b. Hannah).

878 PHEBE CUSHMAN[5] (Sarah Gibbs[4], Alice[3] Warren, Nathaniel[2], Richard[1]) b. Plymouth 14 March 1702/3, d. Kent CT 31 May 1790 ae 87.

She m. (1) Plympton 6 Nov. 1729 NATHANIEL SPOONER, b. Dartmouth 21 April 1709; d. there 25 Nov. 1732 in 29th yr.; son of William and Alice (Warren) (Blackwell) Spooner, a descendant of Pilgrim Richard Warren (see #826).

She m. (2) Tolland CT 2 June 1735 BARNABAS HATCH, b. Falmouth 29 Nov. 1703/4; d. Kent CT 25 Oct. 1781 ae 78; son of Joseph and Amey (Allen) Hatch. He m. (1) Duxbury 7 June 1728 Abigail Lassell by whom he had Thomas, James and Lidiah.

The will of Nathaniel Spooner of Dartmouth dated 5 July 1732, proved 20 March 1732/3, names wife Phebe; brother Ebenezer Spooner; daus. Allis and Rebekah Spooner.

The will of Barnabas Hatch of Kent dated 28 Nov. 1778, proved 29 Oct. 1781, names wife Phebe; dau. Abigail wife of William Chamberlain; dau. Elizabeth wife of Ebenezer Hatch; son Nathaniel; daus. of son Thomas Hatch late of Kent: Phebe, Abigail, Sarah, Abi and Lydia; grandsons Barnabas Jr. and his brother Lassell Hatch and grandson James Hatch.

Children (SPOONER) b. Dartmouth:

i ALLIS[6] b. 23 Aug. 1730
ii REBEKAH b. 9 Jan. 1731/2

Children (HATCH) first 2 b. Tolland CT; last 2 b. Kent CT:

iii NATHANIEL b. 26 March 1736
iv PHEBE b. 19 April 1739; d.y.
v ABIGAIL b. 9 Nov. 1742
vi PHEBE b. 3 Feb. 1743/4; d. 3 Feb. 1743/4
vii ELIZABETH b. 24 Feb. 1744/5

References: VR DARTMOUTH 1:258(b. Alice), 261(b. Nathaniel), 262(b. Rebekah); 3:69(d. Nathaniel). Tolland CT VR 1:92(b. Nath., Phebe; d. Phebe). Kent CT LR 1:9(b. Abigail, Elizabeth); VR 1:58(d. Barnabas). Sharon CT PR #1547(Barnabas Hatch). Bristol Co. PR, alpha. file(Nathaniel Spooner). VR PLYMPTON p. 399(1st m.). VR FALMOUTH p. 63(b. Barnabas). VR DUXBURY p. 262(1st m.Barnabas).

879 ALICE CUSHMAN[5] (Sarah Gibbs[4], Alice[3] Warren, Nathaniel[2], Richard[1]) b. Plymouth 26 June 1706; d. Plympton 13 Aug. 1724 in 20th yr.

She m. Plympton 19 Dec. 1723 JONATHAN BOSWORTH, b. Plympton 16 Feb. 1701; d. Halifax 24 Jan. 1741 in 41st yr.; son of David and Marcy (Sturtevant) Bosworth. He m. (2) Plympton 30 Sept. 1725 Ruth Tilson by whom he had Jabez.

On 3 March 1741 Ruth Bosworth was appointed administratrix of the estate of her husband Jonathan Bosworth.

Child (BOSWORTH) b. Plympton:

i child[6] d. 13 Aug. 1724; ae 3 days

References: VR PLYMPTON pp. 261(both m.), 446(d. Alice & ch.). MD 9:152(d. Jonathan). Plymouth Co. PR 8:475, 536; 9:489(Jonathan Bosworth).

880 REBEKAH CUSHMAN[5] (Sarah Gibbs[4], Alice[3] Warren, Nathaniel[2], Richard[1]) b. Plympton 14 Oct. 1707; d. there 21 Aug. 1727 ae 19y 10m 6d.

She m. Plympton 8 Dec. 1726 JABEZ NEWLAND, b. ca. 1706; d. Plympton 7 April 1787 in 81st yr.; son of Jeremiah and Susannah (Harris) Newland. He m. (2) Plympton 23 Sept. 1728 Sarah Standish.

The will of Jabez Newland dated 20 Jan. 1781, proved 7 May 1787, names heirs of sister Keturah Pearce; wife Sarah; and Jabez Newland Cushman.

Child (NEWLAND) b. Plympton:

i infant[6] d.y.

References: VR PLYMPTON pp. 353(both m.), 496(d. Jabez, Rebekah). Plymouth Co. PR 30:141(Jabez Newland). MF 17:110.

881 SARAH CUSHMAN[5] (Sarah Gibbs[4], Alice[3] Warren, Nathaniel[2], Richard[1]) b. Plympton 2 Dec. 1709.

She m. Sandwich 6 Dec. 1726 JOHN GIBBS, b. Plymouth 16 Feb. 1699; d. aft. 11 March 1778; son of John and Hester (Swift) Gibbs.

On 8 Sept. 1729 John Gibbs of Lebanon bought land in Lebanon CT from Caleb Loomis.

On 2 June 1733 John Gibbs of Lebanon, yeoman, and wife Sarah sold land that was her father Isaac Cushman Jrs. of Plympton to Nathaniel Cushman of Plympton.

On 23 Oct. 1758 John Gibbs of Lebanon gave son John Gibbs Jr. of Lebanon 40 acres of his farm. On 16 June 1761 John Gibbs Jr. sold the land back to his father.

On 28 May 1773 John Gibbs of Lebanon sold Isaac Gibbs of Lebanon half of his farm in Lebanon.

On 11 March 1778 John and Isaac Gibbs of Lebanon sold 100 acres in Lebanon to Thomas Tyrril.

No CT PR for John Gibbs.

Children (GIBBS) b. Lebanon CT, except first:

i REBEKAH[6] b. Sandwich 7 Dec. 1727
ii ESTHER b. 5 Sept. 1730
iii SARAH b. 14 Oct. 1732; d. 26 Oct. 1735
iv SARAH b. 26 Jan. 1736
v JOHN b. 16 April 1737
vi FEAR b. 6 Aug. 1743
vii LOIS b. 22 April 1748
viii ISAAC b. 26 April 1752

References: NEHGR 123:136-7. MD 3:12(b. John). Lebanon CT VR 1:23(b. ch.). SANDWICH VR 1:128(m.), 134(b. Rebecca). PLYMOUTH VR p. 27(b. John). Lebanon CT LR 4:236(Caleb Loomis). Plymouth Co. LR 28:160(John Gibbs). MF 17:110-1. Lebanon CT LR 9:395(to John Jr.); 12:419(to Isaac); 12:515 (John & Isaac Gibbs).

882 NATHANIEL CUSHMAN[5] (Sarah Gibbs[4], Alice[3] Warren, Nathaniel[2], Richard[1]) b. Plympton 28 May 1712; d. Montague 25 Oct. 1793 ae 82.

He m. (1) int. Plympton 29 Sept. 1733 SARAH COOMER, b. Plympton 28 Feb. 1713; d. Columbia CT 14 April 1753 ae 40; dau. of William and Joanna (-----) Coomer.

He m. (2) Lebanon CT 23 Aug. 1753 TEMPERANCE (DAMON) SIMS, b. Scituate 19 March 1718; d. 27 Feb. 1774 ae 54; dau. of John and Temperance (Nye) Damon. She m. (1) Lebanon CT 6

Sept. 1739 George Sims by whom she had Mercy, Sarah and William. The will of John Damon of Lebanon CT dated 27 March 1742 names wife Temperance; dau. Temperance Sims and others.

On 16 April 1741 Nathaniel Cushman of Plympton, tanner, sold his homestead in Plympton to William Churchill. Sarah Cushman, wife of Nathaniel, gave up her right to dower.

He moved to Lebanon CT ca. 1741 and to Bernardston between 1774 and 1785.

No Hampshire Co. PR for Nathaniel Cushman.

Children (CUSHMAN) first 4 b. Plympton, next 5 b. Lebanon CT by Sarah; last 4 by Temperance b. Lebanon CT:

i ISAAC[6] b. 20 Oct. 1734
ii SARAH b. 12 Nov. 1736
iii NATHANIEL b. 2 Sept. 1738
iv CONSIDER b. 16 July 1740
v SIMEON b. 14 Feb. 1742/3
vi WILLIAM b. 29 Jan. 1744/5
vii AMBROSE b. 27 July 1748
viii POLYCARPUS b. 15 Nov. 1750
ix ARTEMAS b. 28 July 1752
x REBECCA b. 30 May 1754
xi TEMPERANCE b. 28 Nov. 1755
xii ABIGAIL b. 22 March (or April) 1757; d.y.
xiii MERCY b. 10 Feb. 1760; d. 24 Feb. 1760
xiv JOAB b. 27 Feb. 1761

References: VR PLYMPTON pp. 83-7(b. 1st 4 ch.), 302(int.). VR SCITUATE 1:127(b. Temperance). Lebanon CT VR 1:48(b. Abigail), 51(b. Simeon thru Temperance), 284(1st m. of Temperance). Windham Co. CT PR 3:104-5 (John Damon). MONTAGUE VR p. 133(d. Nathaniel). CUSHMAN GEN pp. 134-5, 154-8. Plymouth Co. LR 34:94(Nathaniel Cushman). SMALL DESC 2:751. MF 17:111-2.

883 PHEBE GIBBS[5] (Warren[4], Alice[3] Warren, Nathaniel[2], Richard[1]) b. Little Compton 11 Nov. 1714.

She m. Little Compton 20 Dec. 1738 OLIVER PRICE, b. Little Compton 1 Sept. 1713; d. bef. 2 May 1759; son of John and Martha (Graves) Price.

Phebe Price was a member of the Amicable Congregational Church in Tiverton as of 3 May 1747.

On 2 May 1759 Thomas Kempton of Dartmouth was appointed guardian of Oliver and Simeon Price, children of Oliver Price of Tiverton, dec.

Children (PRICE) b. Little Compton:

i BENJAMIN[6] b. 1737

ii PHEBE b. 6 Dec. 1739
iii ISAAC b. 25 Aug. 1741
iv OLIVER b. 21 June 1743
v SIMEON b. 6 March 1745

References: NEHGR 123:133. RIVR Little Compton 4:6:40(m.), 150(b. Oliver, ch.). LITTLE COMPTON FAMS pp. 508-9. RIVR 8:60(Phebe member). Bristol Co. PR 126:72(gdn.).

884 NATHANIEL WARREN GIBBS^{5} (Warren^{4}, Alice^{3} Warren, Nathaniel^{2}, Richard^{1}) b. Little Compton 13 Jan. 1715/6.

He m. Little Compton RI 3 July 1745 ELIZABETH TABOR.

No probate or deeds found for Nathaniel Warren Gibbs.

Child (GIBBS) b. Little Compton RI:

i MERCY^{6} b. 24 Feb. 1748

References: NEHGR 123:133. RIVR Little Compton 4:6:27(m.), 116(b. Mercy).

885 DEBORAH GIBBS^{5} (Warren^{4}, Alice^{3} Warren, Nathaniel^{2}, Richard^{1}) b. Little Compton 19 Dec. 1717.

She m. Little Compton March 1743 WILLIAM PRICE, b. Little Compton 12 Jan. 1707/8; son of John and Martha (Graves) Price. He m. (1) Little Compton 24 Dec. 1731 Susanna Salisbury by whom he had Nathaniel, John and Joseph.

She apparently had an illegitimate child by Thomas Taber. (See MD 40:153).

No probate or land records found for William Price.

Children (PRICE) b. Little Compton RI:

i JOB^{6} bp. Little Compton 3 March 1742/3 "of Deborah"
ii SUSANNA b. 2 Dec. 1743
iii WILLIAM b. 13 April 1745
iv SETH b. 23 Oct. 1746
v MARY b. 24 Dec. 1747
vi WARREN b. 26 Dec. 1749
vii DEBORAH b. 3 Nov. 1751

References: NEHGR 123:133(Gibbs Gen.). Bristol Co. Sessions Court 1739-1746, p. 321(illeg. child). RIVR Little Compton 4:6:49(m., his 1st m.), 150(b. William; b. ch. by both wives), 116(b. Mercy). LITTLE COMPTON FAMS pp. 508-9. RIVR 8:15(bp. Job).

886 THOMAS GIBBS^{5} (Warren^{4}, Alice^{3} Warren, Nathaniel^{2}, Richard^{1}) b. Little Compton 15 June 1721.

He m. Little Compton RI 23 Oct. 1745 TEMPERANCE PEARCE, b. Little Compton 20 Jan. 1723/4; living 23 Nov. 1763(father's will); dau. of George and Deborah (Searl) Pearce. The will of George Pearce dated 23 Nov. 1763 names dau. Temperance Seabury. She m. (2) Little Compton RI 1 Aug. 1756 Ichabod Seabury.

No probate found for Thomas Gibbs.

Child (GIBBS) b. Little Compton RI:

i ALICE[6] b. 26 July 1747

References: NEHGR 123:133. RIVR Little Compton 4:6:28(m.; her 2nd m.), 116(b. Alice), 145(b. Temperance). LITTLE COMPTON FAMS p. 275. Little Compton RI TC & PR 2:8(George Pearce).

887 JABEZ GIBBS[5] (Warren[4], Alice[3] Warren, Nathaniel[2], Richard[1]) b. Little Compton 10 May 1725; d. there March 1758.

He m. ca. 1747 MARY GIFFORD, b. ca. 1728; dau. of John and Comfort (Hart) Gifford, a descendant of Pilgrim Francis Cooke. She m. (2) Tiverton RI 14 Oct. 1759 Eleazer Reed. The will of John Gifford of Little Compton dated 14 Dec. 1788 names daughter Mary Read, dec.; grandson John Gibbs; granddau. Mary Taber dau. of his dau. Mary Read, dec.

On 3 June 1755 Jabez Gibbs of Little Compton, blacksmith, and John Gifford agreed where Gifford would pay Jabez Gibbs' debts in exchange for real estate except his debt to his father Warren Gibbs.

On 4 April 1758 Mary Gibbs, widow, was appointed administratrix of the estate of Jabez Gibbs.

Children (GIBBS) b. Little Compton RI:

i JOHN[6] b. 21 May 1748
ii ELIZABETH b. 13 Aug. 1750 (not in grandfather's will)
iii MARY b. 22 March 1752

References: NEHGR 123:206. RIVR Little Compton 4:6:116(b. ch.). Little Compton RI TC & PR 1:228, 236, 265(Jabez Gibbs); 4:88(John Gifford). MF 12:469-70. Little Compton RI LE 1:331(John Gibbs). LITTLE COMPTON FAMS p. 275. RIVR Tiverton 4:7:43(her 2nd m.).

888 SARAH GIBBS[5] (Cornelius[4], Alice[3] Warren, Nathaniel[2], Richard[1]) b. Sandwich 8 May 1717.

She m. Chilmark 30 Aug. 1738 JOHN TILTON, b. Chilmark 24 March 1705/6; d. there bet. 1 April 1783 and 4 Aug. 1783; son of John and Sarah (Mayhew) Tilton.

The will of John Tilton of Chilmark, yeoman, dated 1 April 1783, proved 4 Aug. 1783, names sons Silas, John, Cornelius and Ebenezer; daughters Mary Norton, Jane wife of John Tilton Jr., Sarah and Eunice Tilton.

Children (TILTON) b. Chilmark:

i CORNELIUS[6] b. ca. 1739
ii SILAS b. ca. 1740
iii JANE b. 1 Dec. 1741
iv SARAH b. ca. 1743
v JOHN b. 11 June 1746
vi MARY b. ca. 1748
vii EUNICE b. ca. 1750
viii EBENEZER b. ca. 1753

References: NEHGR 123:133-4. VR CHILMARK pp. 32(b. John), 32-3(b. ch.), 76(m.). MARTHA'S VINEYARD BY BANKS 3:471, 473. Dukes Co. PR 7:65(John Tilton).

889 SUSANNAH GIBBS[5] (Cornelius[4], Alice[3] Warren, Nathaniel[2], Richard[1]) b. Plympton 5 July 1723; living 7 April 1783.

She m. Easton 6 Nov. 1755 ICHABOD CHURCHILL, b. Plympton 24 Sept. 1722; d. there 24 Aug. 1808 ae 85y 10m 13d; son of William and Ruth (Bryant) Churchill. He m. (1) Plympton 14 Nov. 1742 Rebecca Curtis by whom he had Ebenezer, Joanah, Deborah, Ichabod and Rebecca.

On 7 April 1783 Ichabod Churchill of Plympton, yeoman, and wife Susanna, sold land in Plympton to Elkanah Cushman.

On 1 March 1784 it was petitioned to declare Ichabod Churchill of Plympton, yeoman, non compos mentis. On the same date Isaac Churchill was appointed guardian of Ichabod Churchill who was declared non compos mentis.

No Plymouth Co. PR for Susanna Churchill.

Children (CHURCHILL) b. Plympton:

i THOMAS[6] b. 7 March 1756
ii SARAH b. 9 May 1758; d. Plympton 27 July 1848 ae 90; unm. No PR.
iii WILLIAM b. 18 Feb. 1761
iv EUNES b. 20 Jan. 1765

References: NEHGR 123:134. VR PLYMPTON pp. 58(b. Ichabod), 60(b. Eunes), 62(b. Thomas, Sarah, William), 280(m.), 461(d. Ichabod), 463(d. Sarah). Plymouth Co. LR 63:43-4(Ichabod Churchill). Plymouth Co. PR 29:103, 485; 26:485(non compos mentis).

890 NATHAN GIBBS[5] (Cornelius[4], Alice[3] Warren, Nathaniel[2], Richard[1]) b. Sandwich 22 April 1729; d. bef. 7 May 1792.

He m. Norton 1 April 1756 HANNAH WILLIS of Easton.

On 11 April 1774 Nathaniel Perry sold land in Easton to Nathan Gibbs of Easton. On 13 March 1774 Thomas and Lydia Tisdale sold land in Easton to Nathan Gibbs. On 7 May 1792 Cornelius Gibbs and Warren Gibbs of Easton sold their share of the above land to their brother Nathan Gibbs of Easton, furnaceman.

No probate for Nathan Gibbs.

Children (GIBBS):

- i NATHAN[6] b. Easton 6 Feb. 1757
- ii THOMAS b. ca. 1759; prob. d. bef. the 7 May 1792 deed.
- iii CORNELIUS b. ca. 1761
- iv WARREN b. ca. 1763

References: NEHGR 123:206-7. Easton TR(b. son Nathan). VR NORTON p. 239(m.). Bristol Co. LR 71:469(Cornelius and Warren).

891 EUNICE GIBBS[5] (Cornelius[4], Alice[3] Warren, Nathaniel[2], Richard[1]) b. Sandwich 14 Sept. 1732; living 9 July 1783 (ack. deed).

She m. Easton 15 Nov. 1757 SAMUEL DANFORTH, b. Taunton 29 Aug. 1731; d. Mansfield 10 Feb. 1808 ae abt. 78 yrs.; son of Samuel and Bethiah (Crossman) Danforth.

On 28 June 1783 Samuel Danforth of Mansfield, clothier, sold land in Mansfield to Thomas Shaw; wife Eunice ack. 2 July 1783.

On 24 Dec. 1779 Samuel Danforth of Mansfield, clothier, sold to David Arnold all rights to a tract of land inherited from his father Samuel Danforth of Taunton.

No probate for Samuel Danforth.

Children (DANFORTH):

- i THOMAS[6] b.ca. 1760 (based on age at d.)
- ii SAMUEL b. ca. 1762
- iii EUNICE b. ca. 1764 (based on age at d.)
- iv HANNAH b. ca. 1766 (based on age at d.)

References: NEHGR 123:134. VR TAUNTON 2:135(m.). VR MANSFIELD p. 187(d. Samuel). Bristol Co. LR 61:349; 64:165 (Samuel Danforth). DANFORTH GENEALOGY, John Joseph May, Boston, 1902, p. 49(list of ch.).

892 SARAH DELANO[5] (Jonathan[4], Mercy[3] Warren, Nathaniel[2], Richard[1]) b. Dartmouth 18 March 1705; d. Tolland CT 22 Oct. 1752 in 48th yr.

She m. Tolland CT 4 Nov. 1724 SAMUEL WEST, b. Stonington CT 10 April 1700; d. Tolland CT 3 Feb. 1779 in 79th yr.; son of Francis and Marcy (Minor) West. He m. (2) Tolland CT 26 Nov. 1754 Abigail (Baker) Lothrop by whom he had Ann and Ruth.

The will of Samuel West of Tolland dated 7 Jan. 1778, names wife Abigail; dau. Prudence Lothrup; dau. Sarah Redington; son Samuel West executor; son Abner West; dau. Joanna Smith; son Elisha; dau. Ruth. The inventory was dated 1 April 1779. Distribution was made on 28 June 1781.

Children (WEST) b. Tolland CT:

i PRUDENCE[6] b. 5 Sept. 1726
ii SARAH b. 21 March 1728/9
iii SAMUEL b. 30 March 1732
iv ABIGAIL b. 22 July 1734; d. 5 Nov. 1752
v ABNER b. 1 May 1737
vi JOANNA b. 6 Dec. 1739
vii ELIJAH b. 14 Sept. 1742
viii ANN b. 16 Sept. 1745; d. 13 Feb. 1750

References: Stonington CT VR 1:93(b. Samuel). Tolland CT VR 1:60(m.; b.&d. ch.; d. Sarah), 80(d. Samuel; his 2nd m.); 2:17(2nd m.). NEHGR 72:122(d. Sarah). DELANO GEN (1999) pp. 97-98. STONINGTON CT HIST p. 627.

893 JANE DELANO[5] (Jonathan[4], Mercy[3] Warren, Nathaniel[2], Richard[1]) b. Dartmouth 16 Dec. 1706; d. Tolland CT 18 May 1798 in 92nd yr.

She m. Tolland CT 19 May 1725 JOSEPH WEST, b. Stonington CT 1 Oct. 1701; d. Tolland CT 27 Jan. 1764 ae 62; son of Francis and Marcy (Minor) West.

The will of Joseph West of Tolland dated 18 Jan. 1764, proved 5 May 1764, names wife Jane; sons Rufus, Joseph, Andrew and Jabez; daus. Mercy Grant, Jean Stanly, Bathsheba; granddau. Deborah Morgan.

Children (WEST) b. Tolland CT:

i MERCY[6] b. 20 April 1726
ii JOSEPH b. 2 Nov. 1728
iii JANE b. 21 Aug. 1732
iv RUFUS b. 1 Oct. 1735
v DEBORAH b. 30 Jan. 1737
vi BATHSHEBA b. 9 July 1741
vii ANDREW (named in will)

viii EPHRAIM b. 5 Dec. 1747; d. 17 Sept. 1760
ix JABEZ b. 30 Jan. 1750/1

References: Stafford CT PR #2324(Joseph West). Stonington CT VR 1:93(b. Joseph). Tolland CT VR 1:60(b. ch.), 64(m.), 98(d. Jane). DELANO GEN (1999) pp. 114-5.

894 JABEZ DELANO[5] (Jonathan[4], Mercy[3] Warren, Nathaniel[2], Richard[1]) b. Dartmouth 12 Jan. 1708; d. 22 Jan. 1752 ae 43.

He m. Windham CT 22 Feb. 1730/1 PRUDENCE HIBBARD, b. 3 Feb. 1711/2; d. aft. 8 June 1752 (will); dau. of Ebenezer and Margaret (Morgan) Hibbard. The 6 Nov. 1752 division of the estate of Ebenezer Hebberd of Windham names dau. Prudence Delano.

The will of Jabez Delano of Tolland dated 8 June 1752, sworn 7 July 1752, names wife Prudence; son Jonathan; dau. Clarenda Lothrop; daus. Margaret, Sarah, Prudence and Amey Delano.

Children (DELANO) b. Tolland CT except as noted:

i CLARINDA[6] b. 26 Dec. 1731
ii MARGARET b. ca. 1733 (named in will)
iii JONATHAN b. Coventry CT 23 Nov. 1735
iv SARAH b. 22 May 1739
v PRUDENCE b. 25 Feb. 1740
vi AMEY b. 7 April 1742
vii son b. 6 May 1744; d. ae 1 day

References: Stafford CT PR #1571(Jabez Delano). Tolland CT VR 1:84(m.; b. ch. except Marg. & Jonathan). Coventry CT VR D:35(b. Jonathan). NEHGR 71:367(b. Prudence; div. of her father's estate). MD 47:76(will).

895 NATHAN DELANO[5] (Jonathan[4], Mercy[3] Warren, Nathaniel[2], Richard[1]) b. Dartmouth 1 March 1710/1; d. Walpole NH by 1774.

He m. Tolland CT 6 April 1731 RUTH LASSELL, b. Windham CT 12 May 1711; d. aft. 1774; dau. of Thomas and Mary (Allen) Lasell.

On 13 Feb. 1745 Nathan Delano and wife were dismissed from the Congregational Church in Kent CT to Mr. Knibloe's church in Amenia NY.

On 11 June 1769 Nathan Delano and wife Ruth were members of the Sharon CT church.

Nathan Delano moved to Walpole NH after 11 June 1769.

A 1774 Walpole NH probate record records the agreement of the heirs of Nathan Delano of Walpole: widow Ruth; eldest sons Abish, John; daughters Ruth, Olive and Sarah.

Children (DELANO) b. rec. Tolland CT, except Sarah. However, some were born in other towns:

i JOHN[6] b. 3 Dec. 1731
ii JABEZ b. 10 Feb. 1733; d. Coventry CT 31 Jan. 1755
iii NATHAN b. 18 Sept. 1736; d. 14 March 1738
iv NATHAN b. 5 Jan. 1738/9
v RUTH b. 14 May 1743; bp. Kent CT 1743
vi ABISHA b. 23 May 1746
vii OLIVE b. 21 Aug. 1749; d. 26 Jan. 1750
viii OLIVE b. 1 Jan. 1751/2
ix SARAH b. Dover NH 22 Sept. 1755

References: Tolland CT VR 1:76(b. Sarah; d. Jabez), 86(m.; b. & d. ch.). Windham CT VR 1:17(b. Ruth). WALPOLE NH HIST p. 78. SHARON CH REC 1:4(dismissal). DELANO GEN (1999) pp. 100-1. Coventry CT VR 1:76(d. Jabez).

896 AMY DELANO[5] (Jonathan[4], Mercy[3] Warren, Nathaniel[2], Richard[1]) b. Dartmouth 11 Aug. 1713.

She m. Tolland CT 25 Oct. 1732 CHRISTOPHER WEST, bp. Stonington CT 19 June 1709; son of Francis and Mercy (Minor) West.

On 2 June 1731 Amasa West and Christopher West, both of Tolland, agreed to a division of land left to them in the will of their father Francis West.

On 23 March 1750 Christopher West of Tolland sold land in Tolland to Richard Carlton.

On 15 July 1752 Christopher West of Coventry sold land in Coventry to Jabez Edgerton.

On 22 Sept. 1756 John Sackett of Dover [NY] sold land in the Oblong to Christopher West of Dover. On 19 May 1757 Christopher West of Dover, yeoman, sold the same to Nathan Barlow.

No probate found for Christopher West in Dutchess Co. NY or in Berkshire Co.

Children (WEST) b. Tolland CT except as noted:

i PRISCILLA[6] b. 26 Aug. 1733
ii PRINCE b. 30 Oct. 1735
iii JONATHAN b. 30 Dec. 1737
iv JERUSHA b. 27 April 1740
v MINOR b. 9 Jan. 1742/3
vi LOIS b. Coventry CT 5 Aug. 1745
vii LYDIA b. Coventry CT 24 Nov. 1747
viii MARY b. 25 May 1750
ix SARAH b. Dover NY 22 Sept. 1755
x SUBMIT b. "in York Gov." 29 April 1757

References: Tolland CT VR 1:67(m.), 94(b. first 5 ch. & Mary). Coventry CT VR D:120(b. Lois, Lydia). Salisbury CT VR 1:170(b. Sarah, Submit). NEHGR 60:144, 147(West). First Church, Stonington CT Rec. 1:96(bp. Christopher). Tolland CT LR 3:289(Amasa West); 5:272(Christopher West). Coventry CT LR 4:97(Christopher West). Dutchess Co. NY LR 4:133(John Sackett); 4:135(Christopher West).

NOTE: The Coventry VR calls the mother Ann.

897 JONATHAN DELANO[5] (Jonathan[4], Mercy[3] Warren, Nathaniel[2], Richard[1]) b. Dartmouth 2 Dec. 1715; d. Tolland CT after 31 May 1758.

He m. Coventry CT 2 Nov. 1743 SUSANNA WEST, b. Lebanon CT 17 Jan. 1719; living 31 May 1758 (will); dau. of Ebenezer and Susanna (Wales) West.

On 10 Feb. 1746/7 Jonathan Delano of Coventry gave son Jonathan Delano of Coventry 25 acres in Coventry.

On 31 March 1750 Jonathan Delano of Tolland sold his father Jonathan Delano of Coventry 111 acres in Tolland.

The will of Jonathan Delano Jr. of Tolland dated 31 May 1758, proved 2 Feb. 1759, names wife Susannah; daughters Mary, Susanah and Elizabeth Delano.

Children (DELANO) 1st 3 b. Coventry CT by first wife; rest b. Tolland CT by 2nd wife:

i MARY[6] b. 18 Sept. 1744
ii SUSANNA b. 15 Feb. 1745
iii ELIZABETH b. 31 Oct. 1747

References: Coventry CT VR D:35(b. ch.), 37(m.). Coventry CT LR 3:520(Jonathan Delano). Tolland CT LR 4:327 (Jonathan Delano). Hartford CT PR #1572(Jonathan Delano Jr.). DELANO GEN (1999) p. 102.

NOTE: SUSANNA (WEST) DELANO prob. m. (2) 15 June 1763 Silas Owen. (NEHGR 83:44).

898 BARNABAS DELANO[5] (Jonathan[4], Mercy[3] Warren, Nathaniel[2], Richard[1]) b. Dartmouth 11 April 1718; d. Alstead NH 10 Nov. 1791 (TR says 1792).

He m. (1) Kent CT 4 May 1742 RUTH PACK (or PECK), b. Tolland CT 21 Dec. 1723; d. Alstead NH 1 Aug. 1777 ae 54; dau. of Joseph and Margaret (-----) Pack.

He m. (2) bef. 18 March 1786 MEHITABEL (CHAMBERLAIN) BENTON, b. Colchester CT 9 April 1725; living 16 Nov. 1792; dau. of Daniel and Elizabeth (Brown) Chamberlain. She m. (1)

Tolland CT 25 April 1751 Elijah Benton by whom she had Abijah and William.

Barnabas Delano was selectman in Norwich VT 8 March 1763 and 13 March 1764 and town clerk 1765-6. On 9 Dec. 1776 Barnabas Delano of Walpole NH was a Representative to the General Assembly.

On 29 Oct. 1765 Barnabas Delano of Tolland gave his home farm in Tolland to son Gideon Delano.

On 1 Sept. 1774 Jonathan Wheeler of Keene sold land in Alstead NH to Barnabas and Gideon Delano of Alstead, husbandmen.

On 25 April 1777 Barnabas Delano of Walpole and Gideon Delano of Alstead, husbandmen, sold 50 acres in Alstead to Eli Snow.

On 16 Nov. 1792 Mehitable Delano of Alstead, widow, sold her life interests under the will of her husband Mr. Barnabas Delano in certain land in Alstead to Gideon Delano of Alstead.

Child (DELANO) b. Tolland CT:

i GIDEON[6] b. 27 Nov. 1742

References: DELANO GEN p. 363(d. Barnabas). CT MARR 5:19(m.). Tolland CT VR 1:8(b. Ruth), 86(b. Gideon). NORWICH HIST p. 69. WALPOLE NH HIST 2:11. DELANO GEN (1999) pp. 102-3. Alstead NH TR 1:459(d. Ruth), 574(d. Barnabas). Cheshire Co. NH PR 2:40(Barnabas Delano). Tolland CT VR 1:94(Mehitable's 1st m.). Colchester CT VR 1:446(b. Mehitable). Norwich CT TR 1:1(selectman). Tolland CT LR 6:14(Barnabas Delano). Cheshire Co. NH LR 1:144(Jonathan Wheeler); 21:412(Barnabas and Gideon Delano); 22:225(Mehitable Delano).

899 SILVANUS DELANO[5] (Jonathan[4], Mercy[3] Warren, Nathaniel[2], Richard[1]) b. Dartmouth 17 May 1720; d. Tolland CT 11 July 1796 in 77th yr.

He m. (1) Tolland CT 3 July 1744 ELIZABETH (ABBOTT) PECK; b. Tolland CT 31 Dec. 1721; d. there 17 Dec. 1782; dau. of John and Elizabeth (Berge) Abbott. She m. (1) Joseph Peck.

He m. (2) Tolland CT 10 July 1783 MRS. ABIGAIL LADD.

The will of Silvanus Delano of Tolland dated 18 June 1794, proved 31 Oct. 1796, names wife Abigail; heir Elizabeth Eaton wife of Solomon Eaton "what was her own mothers"; 6 surviving children and heirs of sons Silvanus and Barnabas, dec. Distribution was made to Abigail Rellick and widow on 13 April 1797 and again on 7 Sept. 1801.

Children (DELANO) b. Tolland CT:

i SILVANUS[6] b. 20 April 1745

ii JOSEPH b. 17 Aug. 1746; d. ae 2d
iii AMOS b. 2 Aug. 1747
iv SARAH b. 28 May 1749; d. 29 Aug. 1750
v NATHANIEL b. 27 May 1751
vi BARNABAS b. 6 May 1753
vii ELIZABETH b. 12 March 1755
viii AARON b. 13 Nov. 1756
ix SARAH b. 5 Aug. 1758; d. 30 April 1773
x ANNA b. 17 April 1760
xi MOSES b. 15 June 1762

References: Stafford CT PR #630(Silvanus Delano). Tolland CT VR 1:12(b. Elizabeth), 153(1st m.; b. ch.), 154(d. Silvanus, Eliz.; 2nd m.).

900 ELIZABETH DELANO[5] (Jonathan[4], Mercy[3] Warren, Nathaniel[2], Richard[1]) b. Dartmouth 15 May 1722.

She m. Tolland CT 3 July 1744 JOSEPH CHAMBERLAIN, b. Billerica 22 Feb. 1721; son of Joseph and Mary (Johnson) Chamberlain.

On 6 Feb. 1745/6 Joseph Chamberlain of Tolland sold 80 acres in Tolland to Joseph Chamberlain Jr. On 20 Jan. 1747/8 Joseph Chamberlain of Tolland sold 70 acres in Tolland to Barnabas Delano of Tolland.

On 16 Jan. 1747/8 Christopher West of Coventry sold 70 acres in Coventry to Joseph Chamberlain of Tolland. On 20 July 1754 Joseph Chamberlain of Coventry sold 40 acres in Coventry to Jehiel Rose.

No probate record has been found for Joseph Chamberlain or any later records.

Children (CHAMBERLAIN) b. Tolland CT:

i SUSANNA[6] b. 16 July 1745
ii JOEL b. 4 Oct. 1747
iii ABNER b. 14 Nov. 1751

References: Tolland CT VR 1:158(m.; b. Joel, Susanna). Coventry CT VR D:24(b. Abner). DELANO GEN p. 388. VR BILLERICA 1:37(b. Joseph). Tolland CT LR 4:78, 186(Joseph Chamberlain). Coventry CT LR 3:526(Christopher West); 4:298 (Joseph Chamberlain).

901 SUSANNA DELANO[5] (Jonathan[4], Mercy[3] Warren, Nathaniel[2], Richard[1]) b. Tolland CT 23 June 1724; d. Coventry CT 16 Aug. 1804 ae 84.

She m. Tolland CT 5 Nov. 1746 NOAH GRANT, b. Tolland CT 12 July 1718; d. French and Indian War 20 Sept. 1756; son of Noah and Martha (Huntington) Grant.

On 13 May 1751 Noah Grant of Tolland sold 129 acres in Tolland to Capt. Ebenezer Grant of Windsor.

On 17 March 1756 Noah Grant was appointed Captain of the 7th Company, 2nd Regiment.

No probate found for Noah Grant.

Children (GRANT):

i NOAH[6] b. Tolland CT 23 June 1748 [sic]
ii ELIZABETH (twin) b. 2 July 1748 [sic]; d. 5 days after
iii son [prob. SOLOMON] (twin) b. 2 July 1748 [sic]; d. "as soon as born."
iv SUSANNAH b. ca. 1751; d. Coventry CT 16 Aug. 1821 ae 70; unm.
v PETER b. Coventry; d. at sea; unm.

References: THE GRANT FAMILY, Arthur H. Grant, Poughkeepsie, 1898 pp. 15-6, 33. Tolland CT VR 1:9(m.; b. son Noah, b. twins), 18(b. father Noah). DELANO GEN p. 388. Tolland CT LR 4:396(Noah Grant). PUBLIC RECORDS OF THE COLONY OF CONNECTICUT (1877), 10:472(Captain). COLL. CONN. HIST. SOC. (1903) 9:122(Noah reported dead). DELANO GEN (1999) pp. 104-5.

NOTE: Great grandparents of President U.S. Grant.

902 THOMAS DELANO[5] (Jonathan[4], Mercy[3] Warren, Nathaniel[2], Richard[1]) b. Coventry CT 24 Dec. 1726; d. Sharon CT 8 Sept. 1803 ae 77.

He m. ca. 1747 LOIS -----, b. ca. 1729; d. Sharon CT 27 Oct. 1798 ae 69.

On 15 May 1759 Samuel Doty of Sharon sold 110 acres in Sharon [CT] to Thomas Delano, late of Tolland, now of Sharon.

On 10 Feb. 1760 Lois Delano brought recomendations from the Tolland CT Church to join the church in Amenia NY.

Thomas Delano served in the Revolutionary War from CT.

On 23 Jan. 1786 Thomas Delano of Sharon sold 10 acres in Sharon to Stephen Delano.

No probate found for Thomas Delano in Sharon CT or Dutchess Co. NY.

Children (DELANO) last 4 bp. Amenia NY:

i BENJAMIN[6] b. ca. 1750
ii HANNAH b. ca. 1749
iii STEPHEN b. 1 April 1753
iv REUBEN b. 1755
v JETHRO b. 1758
vi THOMAS bp. 20 July 1760

vii ELISHA bp. 11 Feb. 1764
viii FREDERICK bp. 19 May 1765
ix LOIS bp. 4 Oct. 1767

References: DELANO GEN p. 390(ch.). SHARON CT CEMS p. 69(d. Thomas, Lois). NYGBR 35:108(bp. Thomas), 110(bp. Elisha), 111(bp. Frederick), 203(bp. Lois). CT MEN IN THE REV p. 611. DELANO GEN (1999) pp. 105-6. Sharon CT LR 4:261(Samuel Doty); 9:116(Thomas Delano).

903 TIMOTHY DELANO[5] (Jonathan[4], Mercy[3] Warren, Nathaniel[2], Richard[1]) b. Tolland CT 4 Nov. 1729; d. there 12 April 1777 in 48th yr.

He m. Tolland CT 1 Aug. 1754 LYDIA LATHROP; b. Tolland CT 21 Jan. 1736; living 1801; dau. of John and Ann (Thatcher) Lothrop, a descendant of Pilgrim John Howland. She m. (2) bef. 16 June 1778 John Chamberlain.

Timothy Delano served in the Rev. War as a Private.

On 24 May 1777 David Lathrop and Lydia Delano posted bond as administrators of the estate of Timothy Delano of Tolland. The 29 Sept. 1777 distribution went to eldest son Calvin Delano, he to pay other children: males at 21 and females at 18 with a third to widow Lydia. On 15 May 1779 she signed as Lydia Chamberlain. (Dr. Jno. Chamberlain had a bill for doctoring Nathan Delano, youngest heir.) In 1778 guardians were appointed for Lydia (ae 14), Nathan (ae 3), Amy (ae 16), Jethro (ae 5), Luther (ae 18) and Roger (ae 11).

In 1801 John Chamberlain Esq. and wife Lydia, late of Dutchess Co. NY but now of Tioga Co. NY, conveyed land in Amenia NY.

Children (DELANO):

i TRIPHENA[6] b. 18 Aug. 1755
ii CALVIN b. 10 Nov. 1756
iii ROXANNA b. 26 July 1758
iv LUTHER b. 13 April 1760; d. in the army in 1780; unm.
v AMY b. ca. 1762
vi LYDIA b. ca. 1763
vii NATHAN b. 16 Nov. 1764
viii SARAH b. ca. 1765; d. 27 Sept. 1775 ae 10 yrs.
ix ROGER b. 9 Aug. 1767
x TIMOTHY b. 28 April 1769; d. 5 Oct. 1775 in 7th yr.
xi JETHRO b. ca. 1773
xii NATHAN b. 1775

References: Stafford CT PR #631(Timothy Delano). Tolland CT VR 1:55(m.; b. 1st 4 ch.), 90(b. Lydia). DELANO

GEN p. 410. NEHGR 72:68(d. Timothy, Luther, Sarah, son Timothy). CT MEN IN THE REV p. 23. DELANO GEN (1999) pp. 107-8.

904 JETHRO DELANO[5] (Jonathan[4], Mercy[3] Warren, Nathaniel[2], Richard[1]) b. Tolland CT 29 Oct. 1732.

He m. prob. Tolland CT ELIZABETH LATHROP.

On 4 April 1754 Nathan Delano of Coventry sold 25 acres in Tolland [CT] to Jethro Delano of Tolland.

On 5 June 1754 Jethro Delano of Tolland sold 40 acres in Tolland to Roger Pitkin.

Jethro Delano moved to Dutchess Co. NY.

No probate or land records were found for Jethro Delano in Dutchess Co. NY.

Children (DELANO) b. Armenia NY (?):

i AMY[6] b. 10 July 1764
ii ROGER b. 1766
iii NATHAN b. 1768
iv JETHRO b. 1770

References: DELANO GEN p. 413. Tolland CT LR 5:21(Nathan Delano); 5:35(Jethro Delano).

905 MARY DELANO[5] (Jabez[4], Mercy[3] Warren, Nathaniel[2], Richard[1]) b. Dartmouth 12 April 1712; d. Tolland CT 14 May 1743.

She m. Dartmouth 7 Oct. 1731 ZEBULON WEST, bp. 16 March 1707 or 16 Nov. 1707; d. Tolland CT 4 Dec. 1770 ae 64; son of Francis and Mary (Minor) West. He m. (2) Tolland CT 22 Feb. 1744 Sarah (Avery) Sluman by whom he had Sarah, Desire, Jeremiah, Nathaniel, Prudence and Sarah.

Zebulon West was the first representative from Tolland CT in the legislature and was elected for 53 sessions and held many other offices.

Children (WEST) b. Tolland CT:

i MARY[6] b. 17 Dec. 1732
ii child b.&d. 5 Nov. 1734
iii STEPHEN b. 2 Nov. 1735
iv ANN b. 19 March 1738; d. 5 Jan. 1755
v THANKFUL b. 14 July 1740; d. 5 Dec. 1754
vi ELIJAH b. 6 April 1743; d. 26 July 1743

References: VR DARTMOUTH 2:533(m.). Tolland CT VR 1:82(d. Mary; m.; b. ch.; d. Elijah), 83(2nd m.; d. Ann, Thankful); 2:79(d. Zebulon). NEHGR 60:146-7(West Gen.). DELANO GEN (1999) pp. 108-9.

906 JONATHAN DELANO^5 (Jabez^4, Mercy^3 Warren, Nathaniel^2, Richard^1) b. Dartmouth 13 Feb. 1713/4; d. prob. New Bedford bef. 2 May 1797.

He m. Dartmouth 14 Nov. 1734 ABIGAIL HAMMOND, b. ca. 1714; d. 1775; dau. of Samuel and Priscilla (Samson) Hammond; a descendant of Pilgrim Henry Samson.

On 2 May 1797 Lemuel Wiliams was appointed administrator of the estate of Jonathan Delano, late of New Bedford, mariner.

Children (DELANO) b. Dartmouth:

i JABEZ^6 b. 7 May 1735
ii JONATHAN b. 16 Sept. 1736; d. bet. 22 July 1767 and 25 April 1768. The will of Jonathan Delano Jr. of Dartmouth, mariner, dated 22 July 1767, proved 25 April 1768, names wife Lydia; father and mother Jonathan and Abigail Delano; bros. Amasa and Stephen.
iii AMASA b. 18 Feb. 1737/8
iv PHILLIP b. 23 Aug. 1739
v PRISCILLA b. 14 Oct. 1740
vi MARY b. 4 June 1744
vii STEPHEN b. 12 May 1748

References: VR DARTMOUTH 1:76-9(b. ch.); 2:155(m.). DELANO GEN p. 421. Bristol Co. PR 20:278; 21:165(Jonathan Delano Jr.); 149:175(Jonathan Delano). MF 20:1:89-90.

907 SUSANNA DELANO^5 (Jabez^4, Mercy^3 Warren, Nathaniel^2, Richard^1) b. Dartmouth 16 Nov. 1717; d. there 30 Dec. 1749.

She m. Dartmouth 31 March 1737 ABRAHAM SHERMAN, b. Dartmouth 30 Nov. 1713; d. there 18 June 1773 ae 60; son of Philip and Hannah (Smith) Sherman. He m. (2) Dartmouth 13 April 1758 Mary (Chase) Howland by whom he had Mary, Deborah, David, Hannah and Abijah.

On 7 July 1773 the inventory of the estate of Abraham Sherman of Dartmouth was taken. On 20 Aug. 1773 the dower was set off to Mary Sherman, widow. The 24 April 1775 division names daughters Eunice Church, Abigail Church and Susanna Potter; sons Philip and Abraham Sherman; children Mary Sherman, Deborah Sherman, Abigail Sherman and David Sherman.

Children (SHERMAN) b. Dartmouth:

i EUNICE^6 b. 2 Jan. 1738
ii PHILIP b. 5 Aug. 1739
iii RHODA b. 11 July 1741; d. 26 Jan. 1742
iv ABIGAIL b. 6 Jan. 1743

v ABRAHAM b. 11 Feb. 1745
vi SUSANNA b. 14 March 1747

References: VR DARTMOUTH 1:219(b. Abraham), 219-31(b. ch.); 2:421(both m.); 3:63(d. Abraham), 64(d. Rhoda, Susanna). SHERMAN DESC pp. 443-4. Bristol Co. PR 22:523; 23:348-50, 487-8; 27:115-9; 31:58 (Abraham Sherman).

908 ABIGAIL DELANO[5] (Jabez[4], Mercy[3] Warren, Nathaniel[2], Richard[1]) b. Dartmouth 1 May 1719.

She m. Dartmouth 19 Oct. 1740 ISAAC SHERMAN, b. Dartmouth 22 Jan. 1712; d. prob. shortly after the marriage; son of Isaac and Sarah (-----) Sherman.

The will of Isaac Shearman of Dartmouth, yeoman, dated 10 March 1745 mentions son Isaac "on condition he return to Dartmouth personally any time within the space of five years after my decease."

No children.

No Bristol Co. PR for Isaac or Abigail Sherman.

References: VR DARTMOUTH 1:224(b. Isaac). SHERMAN DESC p. 437(m.). Bristol Co. PR 19:10-2(Isaac Sherman).

909 JABEZ DELANO[5] (Jabez[4], Mercy[3] Warren, Nathaniel[2], Richard[1]) b. Dartmouth 28 April 1723; d. Rochester Jan. 1768.

He m. (1) Falmouth 26 March 1747 DEBORAH BARLOW, b. Rochester 30 March 1731; d. bef. 24 Aug. 1760 (2nd m.); dau. of Nathan and Hannah (Bowerman) Barlow.

He m. (2) Rochester 24 Aug. 1760 RUTH GOODSPEED, b. Rochester 16 Nov. 1736; d. aft. 5 June 1769; dau. of John and Bethia (-----) Goodspeed.

On 2 May 1768 Philip Turner of Rochester was appointed administrator of the estate of Jabez Delano, late of Rochester, husbandman dec.

Children (DELANO) b. Rochester; 6 by first wife, 5 by second:

i HARPER[6] b. 29 Dec. 1747
ii STEPHEN b. 17 Jan. 1749
iii BEULAH b. 27 Jan. 1751
iv HANNAH b. 26 June 1754; d. Sept. 1755 ae abt. 15m
v NATHAN b. 9 July 1756
vi JABEZ b. 15 June 1758
vii DEBORAH b. 15 May 1761
viii ANNA b. 5 Nov. 1762
ix BETHIAH b. 21 Sept. 1764
x HANNAH b. 18 May 1766
xi MARA b. 30 Jan. 1768

References: VR FALMOUTH p. 154(1st m.). VR ROCHESTER 1:20(b. Deborah), 103-7(b. ch. except Anna), 119(b. Anna), 136(b. Ruth); 2:107(2nd m.), 373(d. Hannah). Plymouth Co. PR 20:46, 82, 214, 242(Jabez Delano).

910 MERCY DELANO[5] (Jabez[4], Mercy[3] Warren, Nathaniel[2], Richard[1]) b. Dartmouth 27 Aug. 1725; d. White Creek NY 12 Feb. 1799.

She m. Dartmouth 16 Feb. 1743 DANIEL BRIGGS, b. Dartmouth 9 Nov. 1723; d. White Creek NY 14 July 1801; son of Thomas and Mary (Allen) Briggs.

Daniel Briggs was 3-0-5 in the 1790 census of Beekman Town, Dutchess Co. NY.

No Dutchess Co. or Washington Co. NY LR or PR for Daniel Briggs.

Children (BRIGGS):

i ABRAHAM[6] b. 27 June 1744
ii JABEZ b. 1746
iii STEPHEN b. 1748
iv THANKFUL b. 1751
v ELIAKIM b. 1753
vi JERATHMAYL b. 1754
vii SUSANNA b. 1760
viii MARY b. 1764
ix LAVINA b. 1766

References: VR DARTMOUTH 1:45(b. Daniel); 2:78(m.). JOHN BRIGGS OF NEWPORT AND PORTSMOUTH RI AND HIS DESCENDANTS by Lilla B. Sampson p. 45 (ch.).

911 EUNICE DELANO[5] (Jabez[4], Mercy[3] Warren, Nathaniel[2], Richard[1]) b. Dartmouth 31 May 1727; d. aft. 6 Nov. 1758.

She m. Dartmouth 27 Aug. 1747 NATHANIEL PADDOCK, b. Yarmouth 27 Feb. 1723/4; d. Rochester 6 Nov. 1758; son of Judah and Alice (Alden) Paddock, a descendant of Pilgrim John Alden.

On 6 Nov. 1758 Eunice Paddock was appointed administratrix of the estate of Nathaniel Paddock of Rochester, husbandman.

Children (PADDOCK) b. Rochester:

i ALICE[6] b. 23 Nov. 1748
ii STEPHEN b. 25 June 1750
iii GRACE b. 22 March 1752
iv DANIEL b. 19 Aug. 1754
v HANNAH b. 4 Dec. 1756

References: VR DARTMOUTH 2:341(m.). VR ROCHESTER 1:227(b. ch.). YARMOUTH VR 1:35(b. Nathaniel). Plymouth Co. PR 15:57(Nathaniel Paddock).

912 SARAH DELANO[5] (Jabez[4], Mercy[3] Warren, Nathaniel[2], Richard[1]) b. Dartmouth 30 June 1734; d. Cambridge NY 1802.

She m. Dartmouth 30 Aug. 1753 FORTUNATUS SHERMAN, b. Dartmouth 24 Sept. 1728; d. Cambridge NY 19 Feb. 1803; son of Jabez and Jedidiah (Hawes) Sherman.

They moved to Washington Co. NY about 1778.

On 7 Oct. 1778 Fortunatus Sherman of Dartmouth, carpenter, sold land in Dartmouth to John Howland of Dartmouth; wife Sarah also signed.

The will of Fortunatus Sherman of Cambridge, dated 17 Feb. 1803, proved 11 April 1803, divides his estate into twelve equal shares among son Lemuel; grandson Fortunatus; granddaughter Sarah; son Amasa and his dau. Hannah half share each; Stephen and Delano sons of Amasa half share each; daughter Rhoda Wells 2 shares; granddaughter Sarah Wells; daughter Eunice Bishop; her daughter Sarah Bishop; and grandson Fortunatus Berry and granddaughter Rhoda Norton half share each.

Children (SHERMAN) b. Dartmouth.

i LEMUEL[6] b. 19 Aug. 1756
ii STEPHEN b. 28 April 1760
iii HANNAH b. 8 July 1763; d. 8 April 1766 ae 2y 9m
iv AMASA b. 11 Sept. 1765
v SARAH b. 8 Sept. 1770
vi RHODA b. 8 July 1772
vii EUNICE b. 2 Sept. 1775

References: VR DARTMOUTH 1:223(b. Fortunatus), 219-31(b. ch.); 2:426(m.); 3:63(d. Hannah). SHERMAN DESC pp. 492-3(deaths). Bristol Co. LR 59:69(Fortunatus Sherman). Washington Co. NY Wills 1:349(Fortunatus Sherman).

913 AMY HATCH[5] (Mercy Delano[4], Mercy[3] Warren, Nathaniel[2], Richard[1]) b. Tolland CT 10 Oct. 1713; d. there 8 Aug. 1756.

She m. Tolland CT 8 July 1730 AMASA WEST, bp. Stonington CT 27 March 1704; living 17 July 1776 (ack. deed); son of Francis and Mercy (Minor) West. He m. (2) Tolland CT 20 Sept. 1757 Bethsheba (Pope) Gibbs by whom he had Levi.

On 26 March 1753 Amasa West of Tolland gave son Francis West of Tolland 65 acres in Tolland.

On 13 July 1776, ack. 17 July 1776, Amasa West of Tolland sold land in Tolland to Phinehas Brainard.

No CT PR for Amasa West.

Children (WEST) b. Tolland CT:

i FRANCIS[6] b. 1 Nov. 1731
ii OLIVER b. 2 Oct. 1733
iii PHEBE b. 2 Sept. 1735
iv LUCY b. 9 Aug. 1738
v REBECCA b. 26 Nov. 1740; d. 10 Dec. 1749
vi AMEY b. 8 Dec. 1741
vii MERCY b. 16 Sept. 1744
viii MEHITABLE b. 7 Feb. 1746; d. 24 March 1755
ix AMASA b. 1 May 1749; d. 24 March 1755
x SUSAN b. 8 March 1754; d. 25 March 1755

References: Tolland CT VR 1:78(d. Amy; m.; b. & d. ch.); 2:5 (2nd m.). NEHGR 60:146(West Gen.). Tolland CT LR 4:494; 7:300(Amasa West).

914 JOSEPH HATCH[5] (Mercy Delano[4], Mercy[3] Warren, Nathaniel[2], Richard[1]) b. Tolland CT 12 Sept. 1715; d. there 23 Feb. 1773 ae 58y.

He m. Tolland CT 10 March 1741 MARY CLARK, b. Lebanon CT 11 July 1720; d. Tolland CT 13 April 1810 ae 89y; prob. dau. of Joseph and Rebecca (Huntington) Clark.

The will of Joseph Hatch of Tolland CT dated 24 Aug. 1772, codicil 16 Sept. 1772, names wife Mary; dau. Mary West; son Jonathan Hatch; dau. Mercy Grigs; son William Hatch; son Joseph Hatch; daus. Ellice Hatch; Bethiah Hatch; Anna Hatch and Rebecca Hatch (last 4 under 15 yrs.); sons Daniel Hatch and Isaac Hatch (under 21). In 1793 the administration was appealed by Isaac Hatch of Sharon CT.

Children (HATCH) b. Tolland CT:

i MARY[6] b. 15 Jan. 1741/2
ii JONATHAN b. 24 Sept. 1743
iii MERCY b. 28 Feb. 1745/6
iv WILLIAM b. 28 Dec. 1747
v JOSEPH b. 13 April 1750
vi ALLISE b. 12 May 1753
vii BETHIA b. 13 Jan. 1755
viii DAN b. 29 Dec. 1757
ix ANNA b. 18 Sept. 1759
x TIMOTHY b. 1 Feb. 1761; d. 25 Oct. 1761
xi ISAAC (twin) b. 24 May 1763
xii REBECCA (twin) b. 24 May 1763

References: Stafford CT PR #988(Joseph Hatch). Tolland CT VR 1:27(m.; d. Joseph; b.&d. ch.). Lebanon CT VR p. 115(b. Mary). DELANO GEN (1999) pp. 136-7.

915 MERCY HATCH[5] (Mercy Delano[4], Mercy[3] Warren, Nathaniel[2], Richard[1]) b. Tolland CT 23 Aug. 1717; d. Falmouth 25 Sept. 1771 ae 54.

She m. Falmouth 5 Nov. 1741 SAMUEL SHIVERICK, b. Falmouth 10 Feb. 1715/6; d. there 7 Oct. 1771 ae 55y; son of Thomas and Kezia (Hatch) Shiverick.

The will of Samuel Shiverick of Falmouth, gent., dated 26 Aug. 1771, proved 15 Oct. 1771, names wife Mercy; nephew Samuel Shiverick; Susanna Chadwick "wifes niece whom we have brought up."

No known children.

References: VR FALMOUTH pp. 115(b. Samuel), 207(m.), 257 (deaths). Barnstable Co. PR 12:468(Samuel Shiverick).

916 JONATHAN HATCH[5] (Mercy Delano[4], Mercy[3] Warren, Nathaniel[2], Richard[1]) b. Tolland CT 29 Sept. 1718; d. there 5 Feb. 1742/3.

He m. Tolland CT 1 Sept. 1740 THANKFUL HINCKLEY, b. Barnstable 2 Dec. 1725; d. Weathersfield VT in 1802; dau. of Ichabod and Mary (Bassett) Hinckley.

The will of Jonathan Hatch dated 27 Jan. 1743/4 names wife Thankful; daughters Rebecca and Thankful.

Children (HATCH) b. Tolland CT:

i REBECCA[6] b. 14 Feb. 1740/1; d. 28 Nov. 1749
ii THANKFUL b. 24 Oct. 1742

References: Tolland CT VR 1:138(d. Jonathan; m.; b.&d. ch.). HATCH GEN p. 39. Hartford CT PR #2632(Jonathan Hatch).

917 LOIS HATCH[5] (Mercy Delano[4], Mercy[3] Warren, Nathaniel[2], Richard[1]) b. Tolland CT; d. Lee 28 July 1812.

She m. Falmouth 18 Jan. 1753 JOSEPH HANDY, b. ca. 1715; d. bet. 1800 and 1810; son of Isaac and Eleanor (Stewart) Handy. He m. (1) int. Rochester 25 Nov. 1749 Elizabeth Norris.

On 31 Dec. 1780 Lois Handy was admitted to the First Church of Lee.

On 10 March 1794 Joseph Handy of Lee, yeoman, sold land in Lee to David Fort.

No probate found for Joseph Handy.

Children (HANDY) b. Falmouth:

i SILAS[6] b. 26 Oct. 1753; d. 20 Nov. 1754

ii MARTHA b. 23 Sept. 1756; d. Lee 26 May 1773 in 17th yr.
iii JOSEPH b. 20 May 1759
iv SUSANNA CHADWICK bp. Falmouth 18 July 1762
v NATHANIEL b. 15 Sept. 1764
vi SETH b. 31 Oct. 1767
vii ALICE bp. 4 Aug. 1771

References: VR FALMOUTH pp. 61-2(b. ch.), 172(m.). VR LEE p. 204(deaths). VR ROCHESTER 2:161(int. his 1st m.). NEHGR 125:254-6(Handy fam.). DELANO GEN (1999) pp. 116-7. Berkshire Co. LR (Middle District) 34:137(Joseph Handy). RECORDS OF THE TOWN OF LEE, Lee 1900, p. 247(adm. to church).

918 ALICE HATCH[5] (Mercy Delano[4], Mercy[3] Warren, Nathaniel[2], Richard[1]) b. Tolland CT; d. Willington CT 25 Feb. 1769.

She m. Tolland CT 30 April 1742 JONATHAN CASE, b. Windham CT 16 May 1718; d. Willington CT 15 July 1796; son of Barnard and Abigail (Rudd) Case. He m. (2) Pomfret CT 22 Nov. 1769 Mehitabel (Goodell) Dana. On 7 April 1741 Barnard Case of Tolland deeded 50 acres of land to his son Jonathan Case.

On 20 Oct. 1746 Jonathan Case conveyed land to his father Joseph Hatch of Tolland. On 25 Dec. 1746 Joseph Hatch conveyed land to his son Jonathan Case.

No CT PR for Jonathan Case.

Children (CASE) first 8 b. Tolland CT; last 2 b. Willington CT:

i REBECCA[6] b. 30 March 1743
ii MERCY b. 3 Aug. 1745
iii ABIGAIL b. 21 March 1748; d. 1749
iv BARNARD b. 1 May 1750
v JONATHAN b. 29 March 1752; d. 5 June 1753
vi ABIGAIL b. 6 March 1754
vii ALICE b. 5 March 1756
viii LOIS b. 20 Aug. 1758
ix ZIPPORAH b. 25 June 1761
x MOLLENY b. 20 June 1766

References: TAG 48:18-21(good account). Tolland CT VR 1:143 (m.; b. 1st 8 ch). Willington CT VR B:17(d. Alice, Jonathan; b. last 2 ch.; 2nd m.). Windham CT VR 1:32 (b. Jonathan). HATCH GEN p. 107(1746 deed).

919 MERIBAH DELANO[5] (Nathan[4], Mercy[3] Warren, Nathaniel[2], Richard[1]) b. Middleboro 18 Sept. 1709; living 9 June 1756.

She m. int. Rochester 4 Aug. 1731 CONSTANT DEXTER, b. Rochester 27 Nov. 1706; d. there bet. 9 June 1756 and 7 March 1757; son of Benjamin and Sarah (Arnold) Dexter.

The will of Constant Dexter of Rochester dated 9 June 1756, proved 7 March 1757, names wife Meribah; children Betty, Meribah, Drusilla, Sarah, Nathan, Isaac, Thomas, Stephen and Gideon.

No Plymouth Co. PR for Meribah Dexter.

Children (DEXTER) b. Rochester:

i BETTY[6] 19 March 1733/4
ii MERIBAH b. 16 Jan. 1735/6
iii DRUSILLA b. 12 March 1737
iv SARAH b. 28 Jan. 1739
v NATHAN b. 8 Feb. 1741
vi ISAAC b. 13 June 1744
vii THOMAS b. 7 March 1745
viii STEPHEN b. 30 Jan. 1747
ix GIDEON b. 29 June 1750

References: VR ROCHESTER 1:109(b. Constant), 108-17(b. ch.); 2:109(int.). Plymouth Co. PR 14:340(Constant Dexter).

920 SUSANNA NYE[5] (Susanna Delano[4], Mercy[3] Warren, Nathaniel[2], Richard[1]) b. Tolland CT 16 Jan. 1718/9; d. Ellington CT 22 Oct. 1799 ae 81 yrs.

She prob. m. (1) ca. 1735 SOLOMON LATHROP, b. Barnstable 10 Sept. 1710; d. Tolland CT 28 Feb. 1738; son of Hope and Elizabeth (Lathrop) Lathrop.

She prob. m. (2) ca. 1740 BENJAMIN PINNEY, b. Windsor CT 1715; d. Ellington CT 25 Nov. 1777 ae 62 yrs.; son of Samuel and Sarah (Phelps) Pinney. By his first wife he had Elizabeth, Louisa and Benjamin.

The will of Benjamin Pinney of East Windsor dated 30 Sept. 1774, proved 11 Dec. 1777, names eldest son Eleazer executor; sons Lemuel and Ebenezer; wife Susannah; daughters Betty, Louisa, Abi, Jedidah, Thankful, Ruth and Chloe.

Children (LATHROP) b. Tolland CT:

i MERCY[6] b. 1 Oct. 1736
ii SUSANNA b. 2 April 1738

Children (PINNEY) named in will:

iii JEDIDAH
iv ELEAZER b. Feb. 1753
v LEMUEL
vi ABI
vii THANKFUL
viii RUTH

ix CHLOE
x EBENEZER b. 1761 or 1762

References: WINDSOR CT BY STILES 2:611. TAG 49:81-4(Claude Barlow presenting arguments). Tolland CT VR 1:119(b. Lathrop ch.; d. Solomon). Ellington CT Cemetery (g.s. Susanna, Benjamin). DELANO GEN (1999) pp. 119-20. Stafford CT Probate Dist. #1712; 1:370(Benjamin Pinney).

921 BRIDGET DELANO[5] (Nathaniel[4], Mercy[3] Warren, Nathaniel[2], Richard[1]) b. Dartmouth 6 Feb. 1722/3; d. there 23 June 1802 in 80th yr.

She m. Dartmouth 31 July 1746 JONATHAN HATHAWAY, b. Dartmouth 17 Oct. 1715; d. there 23 May 1783 in 68th yr.; son of Jonathan and Susanna (Pope) Hathaway; a descendant of Pilgrim Francis Cooke.

The will of Jonathan Hathaway of Dartmouth, cordwainer, dated 19 March 1783, proved 7 Oct. 1783, names wife Bridget; sons Robert, Paul, Arthur and Nathaniel; daus. Susanna and Elizabeth.

Children (HATHAWAY) b. Dartmouth:

i ROBERT[6] b. 5 Nov. 1747
ii SUSANNAH b. 16 Sept. 1749
iii PAUL b. 9 Nov. 1751
iv ISSACHER b. 20 Jan. 1754; d. Roxbury 29 June 1775; unm.
v ARTHUR b. 11 June 1756
vi ELIZABETH b. 11 July 1759
vii JONATHAN b. 27 Feb. 1762; d. aboard prison ship in NY Harbor 4 Feb. 1783; unm.
viii NATHANIEL b. 7 April 1765

References: VR DARTMOUTH 1:112(b. Jonathan), 110-14(b. ch.); 2:232(m.); 3:35(d. Bridget), 36(d. Jonathan). HATHAWAY GEN (1970) p. 767. Bristol Co. PR 27:555(Jonathan Delano). MF 12:317.

922 SARAH DELANO[5] (Nathaniel[4], Mercy[3] Warren, Nathaniel[2], Richard[1]) b. Dartmouth 18 March 1724/5; d. there 24 Oct. 1815 ae 93y 6m 25d.

She m. Dartmouth 28 Dec. 1747 ISAIAH ELDRIDGE, b. Dartmouth 11 Oct. 1724; d. New Bedford 28 Feb. 1812 ae 88; son of Elnathan and Hannah (Kelley) Eldridge.

The will of Isaiah Eldridge dated 13 Jan. 1804, presented 5 May 1812, names wife Sarah; sons Phineas and Killey; daughters Ruby Allen, Mary Terry, Bethiah Russell and Sarah Woodward.

Child (ELDRIDGE) b. Dartmouth:

i RUBY[6] b. 23 Oct. 1750; d. Fairhaven 13 Dec. 1835
ii MARY b. 24 March 1753
iii PHINEAS b. 29 Nov. 1755
iv BETHIAH b. 20 May 1759
v SARAH b. 31 July 1761
vi KILLEY b. 16 Sept. 1764
vii RHODA b. 26 Aug. 1766; d. 29 Oct. 1766
viii ISAIAH b. 19 Dec. 1771 (not in will)

References: VR DARTMOUTH 1:85(b. Phineas); 2:177(m.). VR NEW BEDFORD 3:63(d. Isaiah). Bristol Co. PR 47:219-20(Isaiah Eldridge). NEHGR 94:300(Bible rec. - b. ch.).

923 NATHANIEL DELANO[5] (Nathaniel[4], Mercy[3] Warren, Nathaniel[2], Richard[1]) b. Dartmouth 23 Dec. 1728; d. New Bedford 12 Sept. 1797.

He m. (1) Dartmouth 12 Dec. 1751 MARY TABER, b. Dartmouth 11 Sept. 1731; d. ca. 1770; dau. of Jonathan and Lois (West) Taber, a descendant of Pilgrim Francis Cooke. The will of Jonathan Taber, tanner of Dartmouth, dated 15 Sept. 1770 names dau. Mary Delano.

He m. (2) Sandwich 12 3rd mo. 1772 DINAH ALLEN, b. Dartmouth 2 June 1742; d. New Bedford 8 July 1818 ae 76; dau. of George and Rachel (Smith) Allen.

On 29 April 1771 Nathaniel Delano, yeoman, posted bond as guardian of Durphy, Mercy, Nathaniel Jr., Elizabeth, Stephen and Jonathan Delano [children by his first wife].

The inventory of the estate of Nathaniel Delano was taken 10 March 1798, acknowledged 1 Oct. 1799 by Dinah Delano administratrix of the estate.

Children (DELANO) b. Dartmouth; 7 by 1st wife; 6 by 2nd wife:

i LOIS[6] b. 2 Feb. 1753; d. 28 April 1754
ii MARCY b. 3 March 1755
iii JONATHAN b. 23 Oct. 1756
iv NATHANIEL b. 17 Dec. 1758
v ELIZABETH b. 16 March 1761
vi DURPHEY b. 14 Aug. 1765
vii STEPHEN b. 3 Oct. 1766
viii GEORGE b. 9 Jan. 1773
ix WILLIAM b. 6 May 1775
x MARY b. 19 Dec. 1777
xi RACHEL (twin) b. 14 Nov. 1780
xii TIMOTHY (twin) b. 14 Nov. 1780
xiii ROBERT b. 22 Aug. 1783
xiv PELEG b. 16th 11 mo. 1785

References: VR DARTMOUTH 1:20(b. Dinah), 77-9(b. 1st 13 ch.), 270(b. Mary); 2:156(1st m.); 3:28(d. Lois). VR NEW BEDFORD 3:56(d. Nathaniel, Dinah). Bristol Co. PR alphabetical file(Nathaniel Delano). MF 12:147-8. SANDWICH VR 2:1285(b. last 7 ch.); 2:1349(2nd m.).

924 PELEG DELANO[5] (Nathaniel[4], Mercy[3] Warren, Nathaniel[2], Richard[1]) b. Dartmouth 11 Feb. 1730/1; living Sidney ME in 1810.

He m. Dartmouth 30 Jan. 1755 SARAH SAMSON b. Dartmouth bef. 5 May 1733; living there 1 June 1779; dau. of Joseph and Sarah (Samson) Samson, a descendant of Pilgrims John Alden, Henry Samson and Myles Standish. On 5 May 1747 James Cushman of Dartmouth was appointed guardian of Sarah Samson over 14.

On 1 June 1779 Peleg Delano of Dartmouth sold his homestead; wife Sarah also signed the deed.

On 3 July 1779 Remington Hobly sold 100 acres in Vassalborough [ME] to Peleg Delano of Dartmouth. On 19 March 1796 Peleg Delano of Sidney [ME], yeoman, sold the same land to Peleg Delano of Sidney, yeoman.

In the 1810 census of Sidney ME Peleg Delano was living with two men over 45 and 2 women over 45.

Children (DELANO) recorded Sandwich Quaker records:

i BENJAMIN[6] b. 9th day 7th mo. 1759
ii PELEG (twin) b. 27 day 10 mo. 1761
iii SARAH (twin) b. 27 day 10 mo. 1761
iv BRIDGET b. 10 day 4 mo. 1764
v JOSEPH b. 11 day 6 mo. 1766
vi ALMY b. 20 day 9 mo. 1773

References: VR DARTMOUTH 2:156(m.). Bristol Co. LR 69:135 (Peleg Delano). SANDWICH VR 2:1285(b. ch.). Lincoln Co. ME LR 14:178(R. Hobley); 38:75(to son Peleg). DELANO GEN (1999) pp. 122-3. MD 23:177(gdn. Sarah).

925 RICHARD DELANO[5] (Nathaniel[4], Mercy[3] Warren, Nathaniel[2], Richard[1]) b. Dartmouth 29 Oct. 1733; d. New Bedford 21 June 1797.

He m. Sandwich 28 Nov. 1765 MERCY TABER, b. Dartmouth 31 July 1733; d. New Bedford 19 Nov. 1822; dau. of Jonathan and Lois (West) Taber, a descendant of Pilgrim Francis Cooke.

The will of Richard Delano of Dartmouth, yeoman, dated 13th 1st mo. called Jan. 1777, inv. 11 Sept. 1797, names wife Mercy; namesake Richard Taber son of Joseph and Elizabeth Taber; sons Richard, Seth and Amaziah; brother-in-law Jonathan Taber and wife Mercy.

No Bristol Co. PR for Mercy Delano.

Children (DELANO) b. Dartmouth:

i RICHARD[6] b. 28 Jan. 1767
ii SETH b. 25 Dec. 1769
iii AMAZIAH b. 15 Feb. 1771

References: VR DARTMOUTH 1:270(b. Mercy). VR NEW BEDFORD 3:56(deaths). Bristol Co. PR alphabet. file(Richard Delano & Nathaniel Delano). SANDWICH VR 2:1285(b. ch.), 1346(m.).

926 MARY DELANO[5] (Nathaniel[4], Mercy[3] Warren, Nathaniel[2], Richard[1]) b. Dartmouth 16 March 1736; living 19 Sept. 1801.

She m. Dartmouth 15 Jan. 1764 JUDAH SAMSON, b. Duxbury 10 Aug. 1735; d. New Bedford 27 Nov. 1797; son of Miles and Sarah (Studley) Samson, a descendant of Pilgrim Myles Standish.

The inventory of the estate of Judah Samson was taken 11 Dec. 1797.

The 19 Sept. 1801 division of the estate of Judah Sampson, late of New Bedford, names widow Mary Sampson; son Nathaniel Samson; oldest dau. Elizabeth Drew; youngest dau. Mary Taber.

Children (SAMSON) named in division:

i ELIZABETH[6]
ii NATHANIEL
iii MARY b. 9 July 1772

References: VR DARTMOUTH 2:413(m.). VR NEW BEDFORD 3:146(d. Judah). Bristol Co. PR 35:335; 38:207; 39:112 (Judah Samson). MF 14:63. VR DUXBURY pp. 82(b. dau. Mary Gifford), 146(b. Judah).

927 ELIZABETH DELANO[5] (Nathaniel[4], Mercy[3] Warren, Nathaniel[2], Richard[1]) b. Dartmouth 18 Sept. 1738; d. Fairhaven 8 Oct. 1823.

She m. int. Dartmouth 24 Feb. 1759 JOSEPH TABER, b. Dartmouth 28 Feb. 1731/2; d. bef. 12 May 1796; son of Benjamin and Susanna (Lewis) Taber, a descendant of Pilgrims Francis Cooke and Edward Doty.

The will of Joseph Taber, yeoman of New Bedford, dated 6 Oct. 1795, proved 5 May 1796, names wife Elizabeth; youngest son Nathaniel; eldest son "Archelins"; sons Elnathan, Lewis, Sanford and Peleg.

Children (TABER) b. Dartmouth:

i ARCHELAUS[6] b. 3 Oct. 1759

ii ELNATHAN b. 15 April 1762
iii RICHARD b. 29 Aug. 1764 (not in will)*
iv LEWIS b. 10 May 1767
v SANFORD b. 24 Sept. 1769
vi PELEG b. 14 Dec. 1771
vii NATHANIEL b. 1776 (named in will)

References: TABER DESC pp. 21-2. VR DARTMOUTH 1:269(b. Joseph), 267-71(b. ch.); 2:487(int.). MF 12:519-20. Bristol Co. PR 34:92(Joseph Taber).

*RICHARD was still living when the will was written (DELANO GEN (1999) p. 125).

928 SUSANNA DELANO[5] (Nathaniel[4], Mercy[3] Warren, Nathaniel[2], Richard[1]) b. Dartmouth 21 Nov. 1741.

She m. Rochester Nov. 1777 REUBEN TRIPP, son of Jesse and Experience (Delano) Tripp, a descendant of Pilgrim Francis Cooke.

Reuben Tripp of Rochester served in the Revolutionary War.

No Plymouth, Bristol, Middlesex or Suffolk Co. PR or LR for Reuben or Susanna Tripp.

Possible Children (TRIPP):*

i NEBUDCHANEZER[6]
ii MARY
iii SUSANNA
iv REUBEN b. 1785
v poss. JOSEPH

References: VR ROCHESTER 2:307(m.). DELANO GEN (1999) p. 125.

*The only source for the 5 children is the "Desc. of Joseph, son of John Tripp" manuscript at the New Bedford Library by George L. Randall, pp. 17-8. Proof needed.

929 EXPERIENCE DELANO[5] (Jethro[4], Mercy[3] Warren, Nathaniel[2], Richard[1]) b. Dartmouth 1 Feb. 1727/8.

She m. Dartmouth 29 Sept. 1748 JESSE TRIPP, b. ca. 1722; d. bef. 6 Nov. 1806; son of Joseph and Elizabeth (Wilcox) Tripp, a descendant of Pilgrim Francis Cooke.

The will of Jesse Tripp of Rochester, yeoman, dated 5 Aug. 1787, proved 6 Nov. 1806, names sons Jesse, Jonathan, Reuben, Calvin and John; daus. Mercy Ellis, Elizabeth Tripp and Hannah Tripp.

Children (TRIPP) named in will:

i MERCY[6]
ii JONATHAN b. 1753
iii JOHN b. 25 March 1761
iv JESSE b. 1763
v REUBEN
vi CALVIN
vii ELIZABETH
viii HANNAH

References: TG 4:92. VR DARTMOUTH 2:508(m.). Plymouth Co. PR 40:526(Jesse Tripp). DELANO GEN (1999) pp. 125-6.

930 BETHIAH DELANO[5] (Jethro[4], Mercy[3] Warren, Nathaniel[2], Richard[1]) b. Dartmouth 17 March 1730; d. Middleboro 16 Dec. 1803 in 74th yr.

She m. int. Dartmouth 12 March 1768 SETH EATON, b. Middleboro 6 April 1739; d. there 20 Feb. 1823 in his 84th yr.; son of Barnabas and Mehitabel (Alden) Eaton, a descendant of Pilgrims John Alden, Francis Eaton and Samuel Fuller. He m. (1) int. Dartmouth 3 March 1764 Sarah Delano.

On 10 Oct. 1774 Joseph Alden sold land in Middleboro to Seth Eaton of Dartmouth, laborer.

Seth Eaton was a private in the Revolutionary War.

No Plymouth Co. PR for Seth Eaton.

Child (EATON):

i SETH[6] b. ca. 1773 (based on age at death)

References: MF 9:58. VR DARTMOUTH 2:174(both int.). MIDDLEBORO DEATHS p. 60. MIDDLEBORO VR 1:65(b. Seth). Plymouth Co. LR 58:208(Joseph Alden). DAR PATRIOT INDEX p. 213.

931 NATHAN DELANO[5] (Jethro[4], Mercy[3] Warren, Nathaniel[2], Richard[1]) b. Dartmouth 28 April 1732; d. New Bedford bef. 1 Jan. 1805 (inv.).

He m. (1) Dartmouth 23 July 1752 SARAH TRIPP, b. ca. 1730; d. bet. 15 June 1775 (last child) and 6 Jan. 1788 (2nd m. int.); dau. of Joseph and Elizabeth (Wilcox) Tripp, a descendant of Pilgrim Francis Cooke.

He m. (2) int. New Bedford 6 Jan. 1788 ABIGAIL EVANS, b. Freetown 12 Sept. 1758; living 6 May 1806; dau. of Thomas and Hannah (Hathaway) Evans.

Nathan Delano was 1-4-4 in 1790 census of New Bedford.

On 1 Jan. 1805 an inventory was ordered on the estate of Nathan Delano, late of New Bedford. On 5 Feb. 1805 Abigail Delano, widow of Nathan, posted bond as executrix. On 6 May 1806 she rendered 2nd account.

Children (DELANO) 13 by 1st wife, 8 by 2nd, b. New Bedford:

- i REBEKAH[6] (twin) b. Dartmouth 18 Oct. 1752 (VR DARTMOUTH says 1754)
- ii THOMAS (twin) b. Dartmouth 18 Oct. 1752 (VR DARTMOUTH says 1754)
- iii JOSEPH b. 4 July 1754
- iv THANKFUL b. 8 Feb. 1756
- v ELIASHIB (twin) b. 15 Jan. 1758
- vi JETHRO (twin) b. 15 Jan. 1758
- vii ESTHER b. 18 April 1760
- viii ELIZABETH b. 13 April 1762
- ix JOHN b. 2 Oct. 1765
- x REUBEN b. 22 Aug. 1767; d.y.
- xi ROSANNA b. 23 Nov. 1769
- xii ABRAHAM b. 6 Dec. 1771; d.y.
- xiii PAUL b. 15 June 1775
- xiv DEBORAH b. 1 June 1788
- xv ABRAHAM (twin) b. 9 Aug. 1790
- xvi REUBEN (twin) b. 9 Aug. 1790
- xvii SARAH b. 23 May 1792
- xviii BETSY b. 1795; d. unm.
- xix MARY b. 1798
- xx ABBY b. Oct. 1799
- xxi FANNY b. 1800

References: VR DARTMOUTH 1:78(b. Rebekah), 79(b. Thomas); 2:156(m.). VR NEW BEDFORD 1:143-5(b. 1st 17 ch.); 2:165(int.). TG 4:92. Bristol Co. PR alphabet. file(Nathan Delano). DELANO GEN p. 461(last 4 ch.). MF 12:323-4. FREETOWN VR(b. Abigail).

932 REUBEN DELANO[5] (Jethro[4], Mercy[3] Warren, Nathaniel[2], Richard[1]) b. Dartmouth 15 May 1734; d. bef. 6 June 1809 (inv.).

He m. int. Dartmouth 23 March 1762 ELIZABETH SOUTHWORTH, d. bef. 9 Oct. 1812 (inv.).

Reuben Delano was 3-1-5 in 1790 census of New Bedford.

The inventory of the estate of Reuben Delano was taken 6 June 1809. On 4 May 1810 necessaries were set off to the widow.

Children (DELANO) b. Dartmouth:

- i SARAH[6] b. 15 Oct. 1765
- ii JEFFREY b. 15 May 1768
- iii EBENEZER b. 6 Dec. 1770
- iv HANNAH b. 1 March 1773

v NATHAN b. 5 June 1775
vi BETHYAH b. 28 July 1777

References: VR DARTMOUTH 1:76-8(b. ch.); 2:156(int.). Bristol Co. PR 45:21, 273(Reuben Delano); 150:350(Elizabeth Delano).

933 CALVIN DELANO[5] (Jethro[4], Mercy[3] Warren, Nathaniel[2], Richard[1]) b. Dartmouth 20 Oct. 1736; d. Fairhaven 2 Dec. 1813 ae 76.

He m. (1) Middleboro 31 Aug. 1764 MARY ALDEN, b. Middleboro 11 Nov. 1741; d. Fairhaven 8 Sept. 1773; dau. of John and Lydia (Lazell) Alden, a descendant of Pilgrims John Alden, Francis Cooke and Stephen Hopkins.

He m. (2) Dartmouth 11 Dec. 1777 BETHIAH HOWLAND, b. Plymouth 22 April 1743; d. Fairhaven 24 Feb. 1827; dau. of Consider and Ruth (Bryant) Howland, a descendant of Pilgrim John Howland.

Calvin Delano was 1-1-4 in 1790 census of New Bedford.

The will of Calvin Delano of Fairhaven, gentleman, dated 29 Dec. 1813, presented 4 Jan. 1814, names wife Bethiah; son Calvin; daus. Lydia Stoddard and Elizabeth Howland Stetson wife of William Stetson; children of late dau. Deborah Delano.

No Bristol Co. PR for Bethiah Delano.

Children (DELANO) 3 by each wife, 1st 3 b. Middleboro, last 3 b. Dartmouth:

i LYDIA[6] b. 8 Oct. 1766
ii ALDEN b. 23 July 1767; d. 23 Aug. 1783
iii DEBORAH b. 23 Aug. 1770
iv MARY b. 24 Feb. 1779; d. 21 June 1806; unm.
v CALVIN b. 24 June 1780; d. St. Petersburg, Russia 12 Nov. 1814
vi ELIZABETH HOWLAND bp. Dartmouth 27 Jan. 1782

References: MD 13:175(b. Bethiah). VR DARTMOUTH 1:77(bp. Elizabeth Howland); 2:155(2nd m.); 3:28(d. Mary). MIDDLEBORO VR 1:84(b. Mary), 149(1st m.). Bristol Co. PR alphabetical file (Calvin Delano). PLYMOUTH VR p. 80(b. Bethiah). DELANO GEN p. 478(b. ch.; d. Bethiah; son Calvin). New Bedford Mercury News Obits(d. Calvin).

934 DEBORAH DELANO[5] (Jethro[4], Mercy[3] Warren, Nathaniel[2], Richard[1]) b. Dartmouth 11 May 1739; d. there 17 May 1770 ae 30y 11m 23d.

She m. int. Dartmouth 3 July 1762 DANIEL EGGERY, b. Hingham 21 Sept. 1734; d. Hardwick 23 Oct. 1801 ae 67y 1m 2d; son of Deming and Rachel (Thorn) Eggery. He m. (2) Rochester 21 Nov. 1771 Mary Perry by whom he had Deborah, William,

Thomas, Job, Nathan and Samuel. He m. (3) Taunton 27 Nov. 1796 Martha Cobb.

On 12 Aug. 1763 Daniel Egery, late of Scituate now residing in Dartmouth, bought land from Thomas Hathaway.

On 1 Feb. 1771 Daniel Egery of Dartmouth, shipwright, sold part of a tract in Highham that was granted to [his mother] Rachel Egery, to Urian Oaks.

On 5 Dec. 1777, ack. 19 Feb. 1784, Daniel Egery of Dartmouth sold land to Lemuel Williams.

Daniel Egery served as a Captain in the Rev. War.

On 24 Nov. 1777 Joseph Nye Jr. of Hardwick sold 50 acres in Hardwick to Daniel Eagrey of Dartmouth, gent.

The will of Daniel Egery of Hardwick, gentleman, dated 22 Oct. 1801, proved 27 Oct. 1801, names wife Martha; sons Daniel, William, Thomas, Samuel and Nathan; daughters Sarah wife of Samuel Stewart, Bathsheba wife of Silas Burbank, Mary Egery and Deborah wife of Stephen Putnam.

Children (EGGERY) b. Dartmouth:

i SARAH[6] b. 11 Aug. 1764
ii BARSHABE b. 15 April 1766
iii DANIEL b. 26 Dec. 1767

References: VR DARTMOUTH 1:85(b. ch.); 2:176(m.; his 2nd m.); 3:30(d. Deborah). VR HARDWICK p. 293(d. Daniel). VR ROCHESTER 2:123(2nd m.). Bristol Co. LR 46:423(Thomas Hathaway); 62:499(Daniel Egery). NEHGR 115:193. MSSR 5:251, 555. HINGHAM HIST 2:211(b. Daniel). VR TAUNTON 2:171(3rd m.). Suffolk Co. LR 123:68(Daniel Egery). Worcester Co. LR 38:530 (Joseph Nye Jr.). Worcester Co. PR 30:389 (Daniel Egery).

935 SARAH DELANO[5] (Jethro[4], Mercy[3] Warren, Nathaniel[2], Richard[1]) b. Dartmouth 14 Oct. 1741.

She m. int. Dartmouth 3 March 1764 SETH EATON. There is no evidence the marriage took place. He married Dartmouth 12 March 1768 Bethia Delano, Sarah's sister.

References: VR DARTMOUTH 2:174(int.).

936 JOSHUA DELANO[5] (Jethro[4], Mercy[3] Warren, Nathaniel[2], Richard[1]) b. Dartmouth 29 Jan. 1746/7; d. Fairhaven 20 May 1819.

He m. Dartmouth 26 Dec. 1776 PATIENCE SNOW, b. ca. 1751; d. Fairhaven 15 Oct. 1829.

On 18 Sept. 1819 Patience Delano declined to administer the estate of Joshua Delano and asked that her eldest son Joshua be appointed administrator. On 5 Oct. 1819 Joshua Delano was appointed administrator.

Children (DELANO):

i BETSEY[6] b. 5 Oct. 1776
ii ISAAC b. 18 Jan. 1778
iii ESTHER b. 19 May 1779
iv SETH b. 3 July 1781; d. Sligo, Ireland 3 April 1807; unm.
v JOSHUA b. 21 Jan. 1783
vi JETHRO b. 26 Sept. 1784
vii CHARLES b. 6 Sept. 1786
viii HENRY b. 19 Sept. 1788
ix ALDEN b. 26 Sept. 1790; d. NY 31 Jan. 1812; unm.
x SYLVIA b. 4 May 1792; d. 31 Oct. 1807
xi EBENEZER b. 28 Oct. 1794
xii EUNICE b. 27 Oct. 1796

References: VR DARTMOUTH 2:156(m.). Bristol Co. PR 56:215 (Joshua Delano). DELANO GEN p. 479(b. ch., etc.).

937 JETHRO DELANO[5] (Jethro[4], Mercy[3] Warren, Nathaniel[2], Richard[1]) b. Dartmouth 17 Sept. 1749; d. bef. 6 May 1783 (div. of father's estate).

He m. Falmouth ca. 1775 ABIGAIL ELDRIDGE, d. Fairhaven Feb. 1830; dau. of John and Mary (Coleman) Eldridge. She m. (2) New Bedford 18 Dec. 1788 Obed Freeman.

Jethro Delano served as a Pvt. in the Rev. War.

On 6 Oct. 1784 Calvin Delano was appointed administrator of the estate of Jethro Delano, late of Dartmouth.

On 5 March 1793 Jethro Hathaway and Peter Fuller sold real estate of Jethro Delano, late of New Bedford, dec. with widow's dower set out to Abigail Freeman late Delano.

Children (DELANO) b. Fairhaven:

i BETSY[6] b. 9 Oct. 1777
ii MARY b. 2 Oct. 1779

References: VR NEW BEDFORD 2:208(her 2nd m.). Bristol Co. PR alphabetical file; 148:209(Jethro Delano). DELANO GEN p. 484(b. ch.; d. Abigail). MSSR 4:646. VR FALMOUTH p. 154(int. her 2nd m.).

938 THOMAS DELANO[5] (Thomas[4], Mercy[3] Warren, Nathaniel[2], Richard[1]) b. Dartmouth 12 Aug. 1729; d. Nantucket Island 23 Oct. 1799 ae 67.

He m. Nantucket 28 Feb. 1750 ELIZABETH SWAIN, b. Nantucket 20 10th mo. 1730; d. there 29 May 1811 ae 82; dau. of Stephen and Elinor (Ellis) Swain.

On 23 Nov. 1799 Elizabeth Delano, widow, was named administratrix of the estate of Thomas Delano of Nantucket.

On 14 April 1801 Elizabeth Delano and Elizabeth Delano and John Cartwright as attorneys for Henry Delano, Thomas Delano and wife Susannah, Abishi Delano and wife Elizabeth, Foster Swift and wife Deborah, Humphrey Howland and wife Elizabeth and Beriah Fitch and wife Salley sold to Simeon Hussey land formerly owned by Thomas Delano, dec.

On 27 July 1802 Elizabeth Delano, widow of New Bedford, for herself and her children sold to Samuel Swain land derived from her father Stephen Swain and her husband Thomas Delano.

No probate for Elizabeth Delano.

Children (DELANO) b. Nantucket:

i EPHRAIM[6] b. 16 May 1752; d.y.
ii HENRY b. ca. 1754
iii THOMAS b. 13 May 1758
iv ELIZABETH b. ca. 1760 (based on age at death)
v DEBORAH b. 1762
vi ABISHAI b. 12 July 1763
vii WILLIAM d. Havana, Cuba 21 June 1800; unm.
viii SALLY

References: VR NANTUCKET 1:405(b. ch. mostly without dates); 2:536(b. Elizabeth); 3:382(m.); 5:228(d. Thomas, Elizabeth). DELANO GEN p. 484(b. ch.). Nantucket Co. LR 16:377; 17:69(Elizabeth Delano). VR NEW BEDFORD 3:56(d. William), 90(d. dau. Elizabeth).

939 ABISHA DELANO[5] (Thomas[4], Mercy[3] Warren, Nathaniel[2], Richard[1]) b. Dartmouth 9 July 1731; d. New Bedford 19 June 1818 ae 87.

He m. (1) Dartmouth 19 Feb. 1756 HANNAH JENNE, b. Dartmouth 30 June 1731; d. New Bedford 29 Oct. 1794; dau. of Cornelius and Elizabeth (-----) Jenne, a descendant of Pilgrim Richard Warren.

He m. (2) New Bedford 1 Dec. 1795 MARY (TOBEY) PARKER, b. Dartmouth 9 Sept. 1747; d. there 5 Nov. 1836 ae 92; dau. of Zacheus and Sarah (Pope) Tobey. She m. (1) Dartmouth 17 April 1766 Avery Parker by whom she had Jonathan, Zacheus, Elisha and Avery.

The will of Abishai Delano of New Bedford, yeoman, dated 9 Feb. 1818, sworn 6 Oct. 1818, names wife Mary; dau. Betsy Adams; sons Cornelius, Philip and Gideon; grandson Willard Warner.

Children (DELANO) b. Dartmouth:

i BETTY[6] b. 7 Oct. 1756
ii JABEZ b. 29 Sept. 1758; d. 15 June 1759 ae 9m
iii PHILIP b. 12 April 1760
iv CORNELIUS bp. 10 July 1768
v JANE bp. 10 July 1768; d. 9 Nov. 1795; unm.
vi JOSEPH bp. 10 July 1768; d. 14 Nov. 1791; unm.
vii SARAH bp. 4 June 1769; d. 16 Nov. 1793; unm.
viii GIDEON bp. 18 Aug. 1771
ix ABISHAI b. 10 Oct. 1774; d. 10 Sept. 1777

References: VR DARTMOUTH 1:76-8(b. & bp. ch.), 277(b. Mary); 2:155(both m.), 343(Mary's 1st m.); 3:28(d. Mary, Jabez). VR NEW BEDFORD 3:55(d. Abisha). Bristol Co. PR alphabetical file(Abishai Delano). DAR PATRIOT INDEX p. 185(b. Philip). DELANO GEN (1999) pp. 133-4(deaths). NEHGR 113:170 (Parker).

940 EPHRAIM DELANO[5] (Thomas[4], Mercy[3] Warren, Nathaniel[2], Richard[1]) b. Dartmouth 14 Aug. 1733; d. Fairhaven 15 July 1815.

He m. Dartmouth 27 Nov. 1760 ELIZABETH CUSHMAN, b. Dartmouth 29 July 1739; d. there 24 Nov. 1809; dau. of James and Sarah (Hatch) Cushman, a descendant of Pilgrims Isaac Allerton and Degory Priest.

Ephraim Delano served as a Pvt. in the Rev. War.

The will of Ephraim Delano of Fairhaven, yeoman, dated 17 June 1815, sworn 3 Oct. 1815, names son Ephraim; brother Abisha Delano; daus. Hannah, Elizabeth, Deborah, Sarah and Temperance; sons Jabez, Aldeton and Warren.

Children (DELANO):

i THOMAS[6] b. 16 Oct. 1761; d. on a prison ship Feb. 1782
ii JABEZ b. 27 April 1763
iii HANNAH b. 12 April 1766
iv ALLERTON b. 2 Dec. 1767
v son b. 1769; d.y.
vi EPHRAIM (twin) b. 1 March 1771
vii ELIZABETH (twin) b. 1 March 1771
viii DEBORAH b. 26 July 1773; d. 9 March 1851; unm.
ix SARAH b. 4 May 1776; d. 25 Sept. 1820; unm.
x WARREN b. 28 Oct. 1779
xi TEMPERANCE b. 27 May 1782; d. 22 April 1872; unm.

References: VR DARTMOUTH 1:72(b. Elizabeth); 2:155 (int.). Bristol Co. PR alphabetical file (Ephraim Delano).

DELANO GEN pp. 500-4(d. Thomas, Deborah, Sarah, Temperance). MF 8:105-6; 17:159. FAIRHAVEN VR p. 18(b. m. d. Elizabeth, Ephraim). CUSHMAN GEN p. 142. MSSR 4:644.

NOTE: None of the children are in VR DARTMOUTH.

941 GIDEON DELANO[5] (Thomas[4], Mercy[3] Warren, Nathaniel[2], Richard[1]) b. Dartmouth 25 Sept. 1736; d. New Bedford 17 May 1813 in 77th yr.

He m. (1) Dartmouth 31 March 1768 PATIENCE (-----) TABER.

He m. (2) New Bedford 26 April 1789 ABIGAIL ALLEN.

No Bristol Co. PR for Gideon Delano.

No known children.

References: VR DARTMOUTH 2:155(1st m.). VR NEW BEDFORD 2:165(2nd m.); 3:56(d. Gideon).

942 DEBORAH DELANO[5] (Thomas[4], Mercy[3] Warren, Nathaniel[2], Richard[1]) b. Dartmouth 14 June 1739; d. Pawling, Dutchess Co., NY 21 March 1804.

She m. int. Dartmouth 17 June 1758 BENJAMIN SHERMAN, b. Dartmouth 11 Feb. 1734/5; d. Pawling, Dutchess Co., NY 1805; son of Jabez and Jedidah (Hawes) Sherman, a descendant of Pilgrim John Howland.

Benjamin Sherman moved to Quaker Hill NY in the Spring of 1764.

No Dutchess Co. NY PR or LR for Benjamin Sherman.

Children (SHERMAN) first 4 b. Dartmouth; rest b. Quaker Hill NY:

i JETHRO[6] b. 1 Dec. 1759
ii ABIEL b. 11 March 1761
iii DARIUS b. 1763
iv SYLVIA b. 1764
v URIAL b. 1765
vi EZRA b. 1767
vii SHADRACK b. 1769
viii MISHALL b. 1774
ix WILLIAM b. 1775
x BENJAMIN b. 1779
xi DEBORAH b. 1780

References: VR DARTMOUTH 1:220(b. Benjamin); 2:423(int.). SHERMAN DESC p. 459. DELANO GEN (1999) pp. 135-6(b. ch.). POUGHKEEPSIE JOURNAL of 3 April 1804(d. Deborah). HISTORY OF DUTCHESS CO. NY, James H. Smith, Interlaken NY, reprint 1980, p. 551.

943 JANE DELANO[5] (Thomas[4], Mercy[3] Warren, Nathaniel[2], Richard[1]) b. Dartmouth 3 Dec. 1743; d. Conway 4 Nov. 1837.

She m. Dartmouth 5 Jan. 1765 PRINCE TOBEY, b. Dartmouth 7 June 1741; d. Conway 7 July 1810 ae 69; son of Zacheus and Sarah (Pope) Tobey.

Prince Tobey served as a Pvt. in the Rev. War.

The will of Prince Tobey of Conway dated 1 May 1809, proved 11 Sept. 1810, names son Benjamin executor and names wife Jane; sons Elijah, Elisha and Prince; daughters Deborah, Elizabeth, Sarah, Christiania and Pamelia; grandchildren Pollina, Richard, Jane and Ardelia Bond.

Children (TOBEY) first 8 b. Dartmouth, rest b. Conway:

- i SILAS[6] b. 10 Oct 1765; d. 26 Aug. 1769
- ii ELIJAH b. 31 Jan. 1767
- iii DEBORAH b. 22 May 1768; d. 31 Aug. 1761 ae 1 yr.
- iv DEBORAH b. 9 March 1770
- v ELIZABETH b. 22 May 1772
- vi son b. 28 May 1774; d. June 1774 ae 35d
- vii JANE b. 26 Aug 1775
- viii EZRA b. 8 April 1777 (not in will)
- ix ELISHA b. 22 Feb. 1779
- x JOSEPH (twin) b. 23 Jan. 1781; d. 22 Sept. 1800
- xi BENJAMIN (twin) b. 23 Jan 1781
- xii SARAH b. 27 May 1783
- xiii PRINCE b. 22 Jan. 1785
- xiv CHRISTIANA b. 4 May 1787; d. unm. 9 Sept. 1809 ae 22
- xv PAMELIA b. 23 March 1789

References: VR CONWAY p. 267(d. Prince, Christiana). VR DARTMOUTH 1:277(b. Prince); 2:501(int.). TOBEY (TOBIE, TOBY) GENEALOGY, Rufus B. Tobey and Charles H. Pope, Boston, 1905, pp. 77-8(b. ch.). Hampshire Co. PR 27:2(Prince Tobey). DAR PATRIOT INDEX p. 881. DELANO GEN (1999) pp. 136-7.

944 WILLIAM SEVER[5] (Sarah[4] Warren, James[3], Nathaniel[2], Richard[1]) b. Kingston 12 Oct. 1729; d. there 15 June 1809 ae 80 yrs.

He m. (1) Plymouth 2 Dec. 1755 SARAH WARREN, b. Plymouth 23 May 1730; d. Kingston 15 March 1797; dau. of James and Penelope (Winslow) Warren, a descendant of Pilgrims Richard Warren and Edward Winslow (see #953).

He m. (2) Plymouth 19 June 1798 MERCY (FOSTER) RUSSELL, b. Plymouth 2 Dec. 1737; d. Kingston 9 Feb. 1810 ae 72; dau. of Nathaniel and Mercy (Thatcher) Foster. She m. (1) Plymouth 1 Aug. 1757 John Russell.

William Sever graduated from Harvard in 1745.

The will of William Sever of Kingston dated 30 April 1802, proved 14 Aug. 1809, names wife Mercy; grandson William James Sever, son of William Sever late of Worcester; granddau. Penelope Winslow Sever, dau. of William and Anne Warren Sever; dau. Mary Sever widow of son William Sever; granddau. Sarah Russell, dau. of Thomas Russell late of Boston and Sarah Russell late wife of Thomas; sons James and John Sever of Kingston.

Children (SEVER) b. Kingston by Sarah:

i SARAH[6] b. 3 Oct. 1757
ii WILLIAM b. 23 June 1759
iii JAMES b. 3 Nov. 1761
iv ANNE WARREN b. 25 Sept. 1763; d. Kingston 17 Jan. 1788 ae 24; unm.
v JOHN b. 7 May 1766

References: VR KINGSTON pp. 131-2(b. ch.), 277(m.), 379(d. Ann), 380(d. William, Sarah, Mercy). HARVARD GRADS 12:487-8. Plymouth Co. PR 43:18, 483; 44:428-30(William Sever). MF 5:21-2. PLYMOUTH VR pp. 82(b. Sarah), 116(b. Mercy), 348(1st m.), 373(2nd m.), 349(Mercy's 1st m.), 373(2nd m.). MD 7:171(d. Anne, Sarah), 172(d. William).

945 JOHN SEVER[5] (Sarah[4] Warren, James[3], Nathaniel[2], Richard[1]) b. Kingston 22 Feb. 1730/1; d. there 24 Dec. 1760 ae 30 yrs.

He m. Boston 13 Dec. 1753 JUDITH COOPER, b. ca. 1731; d. Kingston 16 Feb. 1764 ae 33. She m. (2) Kingston 10 Sept. 1761 William Rand by whom she had Lucy and William.

On 20 Feb. 1761 Mrs. Judith Sever of Kingston was appointed administratrix of the estate of John Sever of Kingston, physician.

Child (SEVER) b. Kingston:

i JUDITH[6] b. 24 Dec. 1754; d. 7 April 1759 ae 4y 3m

References: VR KINGSTON pp. 132(b. dau. Judith), 265(her 2nd m.), 371(d. dau. Judith), 379(d. John). Plymouth Co. PR 17:11(John Sever). BOSTON VR 30:325(m.).

946 SARAH FORD[5] (Alice[4] Warren, James[3], Nathaniel[2], Richard[1]) b. Marshfield 23 Sept. 1721; d. there 17 April 1777 in 55th yr.

She m. Kingston 22 Feb. 1738 CORNELIUS WHITE, b. Marshfield 9 March 1708; d. there 9 Jan. 1796 in 88th yr.;

son of Cornelius and Hannah (Randall) White, a descendant of Pilgrim William White.

On 1 Dec. 1774 Nathaniel Ford, Elisha Kent and wife Lusanna and Cornelius White and wife Sarah, all of Marshfield, heirs of Alice Ford, late wife of Peleg Ford, sold their part of a cedar swamp in Plympton which formerly belonged to James Warren of Plymouth dec.

No Plymouth Co. PR for Cornelius or Sarah White.

Children (WHITE) b. Marshfield:

i CHARLES[6] b. 11 Oct. 1740
ii ALICE b. 4 Sept. 1742
iii SARAH b. 16 June 1744
iv RUTH b. 11 April 1746
v LUCY b. 8 June 1748
vi CORNELIUS b. 4 June 1750; d. 16 Oct. 1751
vii CORNELIUS b. 15 Feb. 1752; d. 10 July 1753
viii OLIVE b. 5 April 1754
ix CORNELIUS b. 22 June 1756
x WARREN b. 18 Oct. 1758
xi PELEG b. 12 Aug. 1760

References: MF 13:106. MARSHFIELD VR 1:31(b. Corn.), 73(b. all ch.; d. both Corn.), 353(m.), 371(d. Corn.), 372(d. Sarah). Plymouth Co. LR 58:160(Nathaniel Ford, etc.). VR KINGSTON p. 302(m.).

947 LUSANAH FORD[5] (Alice[4] Warren, James[3], Nathaniel[2], Richard[1]) b. Marshfield 1 Oct. 1723; living 25 May 1786 (deed).

She m. Marshfield 11 June 1741 ELISHA KENT, b. Marshfield 22 July 1712; living 25 May 1786 (deed); son of John and Sarah (-----) Kent.

On 25 May 1786 Elisha Kent of Marshfield, yeoman, sold son William Kent of Marshfield, mariner, a wood lot which came from the estate of his father John Kent. Lusannah released her dower.

No Plymouth Co. PR for Elisha or Lusanah Kent.

Children (KENT) b. Marshfield:

i WILLIAM[6] b. 31 Oct. 1742
ii SMITH b. 2 Oct. 1744
iii ELISHA b. 13 Sept. 1746
iv PELEG b. 4 Oct. 1748
v LUCE b. 5 Oct. 1750
vi PHEBE b. 15 July 1752; "lived 1 yr, 10d."
vii CHARLES b. 7 Jan. 1754
viii SARAH b. 19 Feb. 1756

ix NATHANIEL b. 25 Dec. 1757; d. March 1759
x NATHANIEL b. 25 Dec. 1760
xi WARREN b. 20 Dec. 1764
xii ELSE b. 22 April 1766
xiii son b. & d. 17 March 1769

References: MARSHFIELD VR pp. 31(b. Elisha), 76(b. Smith thru Charles; b. Nath. thru son), 77(b. Sarah, Nath., Wm.; d. Nath.), 172(m.). Plymouth Co. LR 66:257(Elisha Kent).

948 ABIGAIL FORD[5] (Alice[4] Warren, James[3], Nathaniel[2], Richard[1]) b. Marshfield 14 Sept. 1725; d. Woolwich ME 5 June 1766.

She m. Marshfield 24 Oct. 1746 ISRAEL SMITH, b. Hanover 24 Nov. 1723; bp. Scituate 3 Nov. 1734; d. Woolwich ME 23 Jan. 1798; son of Joseph and Rachel (Randall) Smith. He m. (2) Woolwich ME Sarah Thomson by whom he had Rachel, Joanna, Sarah, Lucinda, Mary and Isaac. He m. (3) Woolwich ME 15 Feb. 1776 Jane Webb.

On 26 March 1760 Samuel Denney of Georgetown sold 250 acres in Woolwich to Israel Smith of Georgetown.

On 5 June 1760 Israel Smith of Woolwich in the county of York sold to Thomas Oldham his tenement in Scituate.

On 27 Nov. 1776 Israel Smith of Woolwich, yeoman, sold 50 acres in Woolwich to Charles Smith.

On 4 June 1798 widow Jane Smith was appointed administratrix of the estate of Israel smith.

Children (SMITH) b. Scituate:

i JOSEPH[6] b. 21 April 1747
ii ABIGAIL b. 7 April 1750
iii PELEG b. 6 May 1752
iv LUCY b. 9 April 1754
v CHARLES b. 29 Oct. 1755
vi ALICE b. 14 June 1757
vii ISRAEL b. Woolwich ME 3 Jan. 1764

References: VR SCITUATE 1:324(bp. Israel; b. ch.). MARSHFIELD VR p. 173(m.). Plymouth Co. LR 48:100(Israel Smith). HANOVER VR p. 10(b. Israel). Woolwich ME VR 1752-1895, p. 13(b. Israel; d. Abigail; b. ch. by Sarah; d. Israel). Woolwich Church records pp. 8(d. Israel), 29(3rd m.). Georgetown ME VR 1:176(2nd m.). Lincoln Co. ME PR 8:95, 273; 9:6 (Israel Smith). Lincoln Co. ME LR 1:229(Samuel Denny); 12:102 (Israel Smith).

949 NATHANIEL FORD[5] (Alice[4] Warren, James[3], Nathaniel[2], Richard[1]) b. Marshfield 11 July 1731; living 26 June 1789 (deed).

He m. Marshfield 12 Feb. 1756 EUNICE ROGERS, living 26 June 1789 (deed).

On 26 June 1789 Nathaniel Ford of Marshfield, yeoman, sold to Isaac Porter the whole of his homestead and other lots in Marshfield. Eunice Ford relinquished her right to dower.

No Plymouth Co. PR for Nathan or Eunice Ford.

Children (FORD) b. Marshfield:

i PELEG[6] b. 19 April 1757
ii NATHANIEL b. 20 March 1759
iii CHARLES b. 5 Aug. 1761
iv JAMES b. 20 Oct. 1763
v EUNICE b. 3 April 17--
vi ELSE b. Sept. 1768
vii LYDIA b. 2 Nov. 1770
viii FEBE b. 7 --- 1773

References: MARSHFIELD VR pp. 147(m.), 155(b. Peleg thru Lydia), 156(b. Febe). Plymouth Co. LR 69:111 (Nathaniel Ford).

950 HANNAH STACY[5] (Patience[4] Warren, James[3], Nathaniel[2], Richard[1]) b. Plymouth 21 Jan. 1722/3; d. Cambridge 22 Sept. 1788 ae 66 yrs.

She m. Kingston 27 Sept. 1744 JAMES READ, b. Cambridge 9 Oct. 1721; d. there 31 July 1770 in 48th yr.; son of James and Sarah (Batson) Read.

On 29 Aug. 1770 Hannah Read was appointed administratrix of the estate of James Reed of Cambridge, Gentleman. On 21 Jan. 1789 James Read and Joseph Stacy Read gave receipts as "only heirs at law."

Children (REED) b. Cambridge:

i MARY[6] bp. 13 Oct. 1745; d. 12 Aug. 1748 ae 3y
ii SARAH bp. 1 Nov. 1747
iii JAMES bp. 25 Feb. 1749/50; d. 29 July 1750
iv JAMES bp. 6 July 1751
v JOSEPH bp. 14 Sept. 1753; d.y.
vi JOSEPH STACY bp. 10 Nov. 1754
vii HANNAH bp. 25 Sept. 1757

References: VR CAMBRIDGE. VR KINGSTON p. 266(m.). Middlesex Co. PR 48:426; 51:497(James Read). CAMBRIDGE HIST p. 636(bp. ch.; deaths).

951 SARAH STACY[5] (Patience[4] Warren, James[3], Nathaniel[2], Richard[1]) b. Plymouth 15 Jan. 1726/7; living 11 March 1763 (deed).

She m. Pembroke Nov. 1743 EVANS SKINNER, b. Berkeley NC; living 14 Aug. 1789; son of Richard and Sarah (Creecy) Skinner of Perquimans Co. NC.

On 10 April 1746 Evans Skinner of Kingston, mariner, gave his wife Sarah Skinner, power of attorney to do what was needed to settle the estate of her father Rev. Joseph Stacey of Kingston.

On 13 Oct. 1752 Ezra Skinner of Kingston, mariner, and wife Sarah, sold to Joseph Stetson of Scituate two pieces of land in Kingston.

On 11 March 1763 Evans Skinner of the county of Chowan in the Province of North Carolina, and wife Sarah, sold lands in Plymouth which belonged to her grandfather James Warren.

Evan Skinner was a Pvt. in the Rev. War.

The will of Evan Skinner of Chowan Co. NC dated 14 Aug. 1789 names sons William John, Samuel and Richard and daughter Mary Topping.

Children (SKINNER) 1st 3 b. Kingston:

i HANNAH[6] b. 13 July 1745 (not in will)
ii PATIENCE b. 3 May 1747; d. 4 May 1747
iii JOSEPH STACEY b. 16 April 1748 (not in will)
iv WILLIAM JOHN
v SAMUEL
vi RICHARD
vii MARY

References: VR KINGSTON pp. 134(b. Hannah, Joseph), 135(b. Patience), 381(d. Patience). VR PEMBROKE p. 347 (m.). Plymouth Co. PR 10:232(Joseph Stacey). Plymouth Co. LR 42:6; 48:94(Evans Skinner). THE SKINNER KINSMAN, Doris S. Wahl and Cynthia W. Rummel, p. 15.

952 JAMES[5] WARREN (James[4-3], Nathaniel[2], Richard[1]) b. Plymouth 28 Sept. 1726; d. there 28 Nov. 1808.

He m. Barnstable 14 Nov. 1754 MERCY OTIS, b. Barnstable 14 Sept. 1728; d. Plymouth 19 Oct. 1814 ae 86 yrs.; dau. of James and Mary (Allyn) Otis, a descendant of Pilgrim Edward Doty. The will of James Otis of Barnstable dated 21 April 1774 names dau. Mercy Warren and five grandsons, sons of James Warren Esqr., namely James Warren Jr., Winslow Warren, Charles Warren, Henry Warren and George Warren.

James Warren graduated from Harvard in 1745. He was president of the Provincial Congress of Massachusetts. He was a General during the Rev. War. His wife Mercy was a noted author and sister of James Otis, the patriot.

The will of James Warren of Plymouth Esqr. dated 8 June 1792, proved 28 Dec. 1808, names wife Mercy; sons James Warren, Henry Warren and George Warren.

Children (WARREN) b. Plymouth:

i JAMES[6] b. 18 Oct. 1757; d. Plymouth 5 Aug. 1821 ae 64 apparently unm.
ii WINSLOW b. 24 March 1759; killed by Indians at the forks of the Miami River in Ohio 4 Nov. 1791. No PR.
iii CHARLES b. 14 April 1762; d. St. Lucar, Spain 30 Nov. 1784; apparently unm. No PR.
iv HENRY b. 21 March 1764
v GEORGE b. 20 Sept. 1766

References: MD 13:201(d. James); 19:151(b. ch.); 31:10(m.); 32:154(b. Mercy). MF 5:20-1. PLYMOUTH CH RECS 2:661(d. Mercy), 669(d. son James). WARREN GEN p. 28(d. Winslow, Charles). PLYMOUTH VR p. 199(b. ch.; d. James; d. ch.). Plymouth Co. PR #21876; 42:419(James Warren). Barnstable Co. PR 20:224(James Otis). HARVARD GRADS 11:584-606.

953 SARAH[5] WARREN (James[4-3], Nathaniel[2], Richard[1]) b. Plymouth 23 May 1730; d. Kingston 15 March 1797 ae 67.

She m. Kingston 2 Dec. 1755 WILLIAM SEVER, b. Kingston 12 Oct. 1729; d. there 15 June 1809 ae 80; son of Nicholas and Sarah (Warren) Sever, a descendant of Pilgrims Edward Doty and Richard Warren. He m. (2) Plymouth 19 June 1798 Mercy (Foster) Russell. (See #944)

William Sever graduated from Harvard in 1744.

The will of William Sever of Kingston, Esquire, dated 30 April 1802, proven 14 Aug. 1809, mentions his marriage contract with Mercy Russell now his wife; names grandson William James Sever, son of William Sever late of Worcester deceased; granddau. Penelope Winslow Sever, dau. of son William; granddau. Anne Warren Sever, dau. of son William; dau. Mary Sever, the widow of son William Sever; granddau. Sarah Russell, the dau. of Thomas Russell, late of Boston deceased and of Sarah Russell, late wife of sd Thomas Russell, my dau.; sons James Sever and John Sever of Kingston.

Children (SEVER) b. Kingston:

i SARAH[6] b. 3 Oct. 1757
ii WILLIAM b. 23 June 1759
iii JAMES b. 3 Nov. 1761
iv ANN WARREN b. 25 Sept. 1763; d. Kingston 19 Jan. 1788 ae 25; unm.
v JOHN b. 7 May 1766

References: VR KINGSTON pp. 131-2(b. ch.), 132(b. William), 277(m.), 379(d. Anne), 380(deaths). MF 5:21-2. MD 7:171-2(d's.); 25:11(1st m. int.). Plymouth Co. PR #17842;

43:18(William Sever). PLYMOUTH VR pp. 348(m.), 373(his 2nd m.). HARVARD GRADS 12:487-8. Plymouth Co. PR #17842; 43:18; 44:428-30(William Sever).

954 ROBERT BRADFORD[5] (John[4], Mercy[3] Warren, Joseph[2], Richard[1]) b. Plymouth 18 Oct. 1706; d. Kingston 9 or 12 Aug. 1782 in 76th yr. or ae 77.

He m. Kingston 4 Nov. 1726 SARAH STETSON, b. Plymouth 26 Aug. 1708; d. Kingston 23 Feb. 1792 ae 84; dau. of Elisha and Abigail (Brewster) Stetson, a descendant of Pilgrim William Brewster. Order for settlement of the estate of Elisha Stetson late of Kingston dec. dated 20 July 1756 names daus. Sarah, wife of Robert Bradford; and Zerash, wife of Benjamin Bradford.

On 25 July 1782 Robert Bradford of Kingston, gentleman, sold to his son John Bradford of Kingston, yeoman, 3 acres.

The will of Robert Bradford of Kingston dated 8 Aug. 1782, proved 2 Sept. 1782, mentions "wife"; and names dau. Orpah (no surname); sons Stetson, Robert and Peleg; dau. Zilpah and heirs of dau. Rebecca (no surnames); friend William Drew to be executor. On 13 April 1784 dower was set off to Sarah Bradford, widow of Captain Robert Bradford, late of Kingston deceased.

In April 1789 the following heirs participated in the division of Robert's estate: Zilpha Loring, John Bradford, Stetson Bradford, Rebecca Holmes, Orpha Bradford, all of Kingston.

Children (BRADFORD) b. Kingston:

i PELEG[6] b. 9 March 1727
ii ZILPAH b. 6 April 1728 (not in will)
iii REBECCA b. 31 Dec. 1730
iv JOHN b. 18 Oct. 1732 (not in will)
v ELTHEA b. 13 Dec. 1734; d. 11 June 1737
vi ORPHA b. 28 Dec. 1736; d. Kingston 3 May 1830 ae 93
vii STETSON b. 17 Feb. 1738/9
viii ROBERT b. 19 Jan. 1740/1; d. Sept. 1747
ix SARAH b. 20 Feb. 1742/3; d. Sept. 1747
x CONSIDER b. 3 Dec. 1744/5; d. Sept. 1747
xi SARAH b. 4 Feb. 1747/8 (not in will)
xii ROBERT b. 11 July 1750

References: MD 7:23(d. Robert); 7:178(b. Sarah). VR KINGSTON pp. 26-31(b. ch.), 182(m.), 319(d. Consider, Elthea), 321(d. Orpha, Robert, son Robert), 322(d. Sarah, dau. Sarah). WATERMAN GEN 1:626. BRADFORD DESC p. 46. Plymouth Co. PR 15:97 (Elisha Stetson); 28:460-1; 29:135(Robert Bradford).

PLYMOUTH VR p. 44(b. Sarah). Plymouth Co. LR 69:60 (div.); 90:20(Robert Bradford).

955 REBECCA BRADFORD^5 (John^4, Mercy^3 Warren, Joseph^2, Richard^1) b. Plymouth 14 Dec. 1710; d. bet. 6 Aug. 1770 (swore to inv.) and 7 Jan. 1771.

She m. int. Kingston 18 Oct. 1729 JOHN BREWSTER, b. prob. Duxbury ca. 1697; d. Kingston 24 June 1766; son of Wrestling and Mary (-----) Brewster, a descendant of Pilgrim William Brewster.

The will of John Brewster of Kingston, innholder, dated 24 June 1766, proved 1 Jan. 1770, names wife Rebecca executrix; dau. Rebecca Samson dec. and her children Elisha and Rebecca Samson; dau. Abigail Brewster, wife of Lemuel Brewster; and dau. Sarah Brewster. The administration mentions John Brewster d. 24 June 1766.

On 7 Jan. 1771 Robert Bradford was appointed administrator of the estate of John Brewster of Kingston, left incomplete by the death of widow Rebecca.

Children (BREWSTER) b. Kingston:

i JOHN^6 b. 7 Oct. 1730; d. 23 July 1748 ae 17y 9m 16d
ii REBECCA b. 25 March 1733
iii ABIGAIL b. 17 Dec. 1736
iv SARAH b. 15 Sept. 1745; d. 25 Sept. 1747 ae 2y 14d
v SARAH bp. 28 Oct. 1750

References: MD 7:24(d. Sarah, son John). VR KINGSTON pp. 31-3(b. ch.), 186(m.), 324(d. Sarah), 325(d. John). WATERMAN GEN 1:626. BRADFORD DESC pp. 14, 46. Plymouth Co. PR 20:296, 409; 27:494(John Brewster). GEN ADVERTISER 2:29.

956 MARY MITCHELL^5 (Alice Bradford^4, Mercy^3 Warren, Joseph^2, Richard^1) b. Bridgewater 19 July 1709; d. Hingham 4 Sept. 1745 in 37th yr.

She m. Hingham 30 Jan. 1728/9 JOSHUA HERSEY JR., b. Hingham 22 Dec. 1704; d. there 1 Nov. 1784 ae 80; son of Joshua and Sarah (Hawke) Hersey. He m. (2) Hingham 15 June 1750 Mary (Fearing) Lincoln by whom he had Mary and Rachel. He m. (3) Boston 27 May 1762 Sarah (Foster) Hanners.

The will of Joshua Hersey of Hingham, gentleman, dated 26 Sept. 1776, probated 24 Nov. 1784, gives wife Sarah Hersey "the household stuff she brought me at marriage"; names sons Abel and Joshua; dau. Mercy Lincoln; son Bradford Hersey; dau. Mary Thaxter; and dau. Rachel Hersey deceased who was heir to Daniel Lincoln deceased. [Dau. by 2nd m.].

Children (HERSEY) b. Hingham:

- i ABEL[6] b. 23 Jan. 1729/30
- ii JOSHUA b. 11 Feb. 1731/2
- iii MERCY b. 29 March 1733; d. 15 Aug. 1733
- iv EDWARD b. 15 Dec. 1734; d. 3 Feb. 1735/6
- v EDWARD b. 7 April 1736; d. 20 Aug. 1736
- vi MERCY b. 21 Sept. 1737
- vii EDWARD b. 24 Feb. 1738/9; d. 23 April 1740
- viii BRADFORD b. 3 April 1741
- ix BENJAMIN b. 20 Oct. 1744; d. 31 Oct. 1751

References: HINGHAM HIST 2:302. BRADFORD DESC p. 46. Suffolk Co. PR 83:1021(Joshua Hersey). BOSTON VR 30:51(3rd m.).

957 ALICE MITCHELL[5] (Alice Bradford[4], Mercy[3] Warren, Joseph[2], Richard[1]) b. Bridgewater 23 Dec. 1714; d. Hingham 20 Dec. 1779 in 66th yr.

She m. Hingham 12 Feb. 1735/6 NOAH HERSEY, b. Hingham 24 Feb. 1709/10; d. there 29 June 1755 ae 45; son of Joshua and Sarah (Hawke) Hersey.

The will of Noah Hersey of Hingham, yeoman, dated 26 June 1755, probated 21 July 1744, names wife Alice; eldest son Peleg; dau. Sarah; sons Noah, Jacob and Levi, all of the children under 21.

Children (HERSEY) b. Hingham:

- i PELEG[6] b. 22 Nov. 1737
- ii SARAH b. 28 Aug. 1741
- iii JACOB b. 23 April 1744; d. 12 Jan. 1747/8
- iv NOAH b. 6 Oct. 1746
- v JACOB b. 6 Aug. 1748; d. Hingham 7 Aug. 1773
- vi LEVI b. 23 July 1751

References: HINGHAM HIST 2:302-3. BRADFORD DESC p. 47. Suffolk Co. PR 50:356(Noah Hersey).

958 EDWARD MITCHELL[5] (Alice Bradford[4], Mercy[3] Warren, Joseph[2], Richard[1]) b. Bridgewater 7 Feb. 1715/6; d. E. Bridgewater 25 Dec. 1801 ae 85y 10m.

He m. Hingham 14 Dec. 1738 ELIZABETH CUSHING, b. Hingham 21 May 1714; d. E. Bridgewater 9 May 1799 ae 85; dau. of Elisha and Leah (Loring) Cushing.

The will of Edward Mitchell of Bridgewater, yeoman, dated 10 Feb. 1787, proved 15 Jan. 1802, names wife Elizabeth; daus. Bettee Keith, wife of Eleazer; Molly Keith, wife of James Jr.; Celia Harris, wife of Arthur; and Sarah Mitchell; granddaughter Alice Keith, dau. of John; and sons Edward,

Cushing, Elisha, John, William, Bradford and Bela. A codicil dated 3 March 1790 gives Elisha's share, he since deceased, to his son Asa Mitchell.

Children (MITCHELL) b. Bridgewater:

i EDWARD[6] b. 1 Sept. 1739
ii CUSHING b. 8 Dec. 1740
iii ELIZABETH b. 26 April 1742
iv ALICE b. 5 April 1744 (not in will)
v ELISHA b. 28 March 1746
vi JOHN b. 8 March 1747/8
vii WILLIAM b. 13 March 1749/50
viii BRADFORD b. 17 May 1752
ix MARY b. 1754
x CELIA b. 20 Aug. 1757
xi SARAH b. 26 April 1759
xii BELA b. 30 Oct. 1761

References: VR BRIDGEWATER 1:225-31(b. ch.). VR E. BRIDGEWATER p. 372(d. Edward, Eliz.). BRADFORD DESC p. 47. Plymouth Co. PR 38:3(Edward Mitchell). HINGHAM HIST 2:154(b. Elizabeth; m.).

959 SARAH HERSEY[5] (Alice Bradford[4], Mercy[3] Warren, Joseph[2], Richard[1]) b. Hingham 4 July 1719; d. there 24 Oct. 1798.

She m. Hingham 17 May 1739 THOMAS LORING, b. Hingham 30 Aug. 1713; d. there 23 Aug. 1795; son of John and Jane (Baker) Loring.

The will of Thomas Loring of Hingham, hatter, dated 21 Feb. 1795, presented 8 Sept. 1795, names wife Sarah; daus. Jane Thaxter, Rachel Loring and Christiana Loring; sons Asa, Thomas and Jotham. A codicil dated 29 July 1795 directs that at Asa's death his share be divided among Jotham, Thomas, Rachel and Christiana.

Children (LORING) b. Hingham:

i JOTHAM[6] b. 30 April 1740
ii ASA b. 17 March 1741/2; d. Hingham 24 June 1800; unm.
iii THOMAS b. 29 July 1744; d. 31 Dec. 1745
iv SARAH b. 20 July 1747; d. 31 Dec. 1764
v JANE b. 10 Dec. 1749; d. 5 April 1752
vi JANE b. 5 Nov. 1752
vii THOMAS b. 10 March 1755
viii RACHEL b. 17 July 1758; d. Hingham 6 Nov. 1813; unm.
ix CHRISTIANA b. 16 June 1760; Hingham 12 May 1827; unm.

References: LORING GEN p. 32(b.m.d. Thomas; b. 9 ch.), 53. BRADFORD DESC p. 47. Suffolk Co. PR 94:122(Thomas Loring). HINGHAM HIST 3:30, 32(b. Sarah; m.).

960 JONATHAN FREEMAN[5] (Mercy Bradford[4], Mercy[3] Warren, Joseph[2], Richard[1]) b. Harwich 26 March 1709/10; d. bef. 13 July 1748.

He m. Plymouth 19 Dec. 1728 SARAH RIDER, b. Plymouth 25 Dec. 1712; perhaps the "Sarah Curtis widow" who d. Plymouth 19 Jan. 1800; dau. of John and Mary (-----) Rider. She prob. m. (2) Plymouth 31 Jan. 1750/1 Edward Curtis. She apparently had no children by either marriage.

The will of Jonathan Freeman of Halifax, yeoman, dated 12 Jan. 1743, proved 13 July 1748, leaves all to his wife Sarah.

References: MD 12:223(b. Sarah); 13:72(m.). PLYMOUTH VR pp. 55(b. Sarah), 95(m.), 148(her 2nd m.). Plymouth Co. PR #8114(Jonathan Freeman).

961 MERCY FREEMAN[5] (Mercy Bradford[4], Mercy[3] Warren, Joseph[2], Richard[1]) b. Harwich 24 April 1711; d. bef. 5 Jan. 1763.

She m. Plympton 12 June 1728 THOMAS WATERMAN, b. Plympton in Oct. 1707; d. there 22 Aug. 1789 in 82nd yr.; son of Robert and Mary (Cushman) Waterman, a descendant of Pilgrim Isaac Allerton. He m. (2) Plympton 5 Jan. 1763 Joanna (Paddock) Harlow. He m. (3) Kingston 1 Aug. 1765 Lydia (Faunce) Washburn.

The will of Thomas Waterman of Halifax dated 16 July 1784, proved 5 Oct. 1789, names sons Thomas and Freeman; the children of dau. Rebecca Heferds dec.; dau. Mercy Josling; and grandson Robert Waterman.

Children (WATERMAN) b. Plympton:

i JONATHAN[6] b. 17 Dec. 1730 (not in will)
ii ABIGAIL b. 16 May 1733 (not in will)
iii REBECCA b. 19 April 1736
iv MARY (or MERCY) b. 10 June 1739
v THOMAS b. 23 July 1742
vi PRISCILLA b. 22 April 1745; d.y.
vii FREEMAN b. 16 July 1748

References: WATERMAN GEN 1:38, 82, 84. BRADFORD DESC p. 48. Plymouth Co. PR 31:78(Thomas Waterman). VR PLYMPTON pp. 220(b. ch.), 421(m.; his 2nd m.), 529(d. Thomas). MF 17:121. VR KINGSTON p. 300(his 3rd m.).

962 BRADFORD FREEMAN^{5} (Mercy Bradford^{4}, Mercy^{3} Warren, Joseph^{2}, Richard^{1}) b. Harwich 15 Aug. 1713; d. after 9 Nov. 1758.

He m. Kingston 4 Sept. 1734 SARAH CHURCH, b. Plymouth 26 Feb. 1717/8; living 17 Oct. 1758; dau. of Charles and Mary (Pope) Church, a descendant of Pilgrim Richard Warren. (see #629)

No Plymouth Co. PR found for Bradford or Sarah Freeman, nor guardianships for the children, and the only LR was dated 17 Oct. 1758 when Bradford Freeman of Plympton sold land in Plympton with wife Sarah giving up her dower. He ack. his signature 9 Nov. 1758.

Children (FREEMAN) b. Plympton:

i CHARLES^{6} b. 15 Oct. 1735; d. 28 Sept. 1736
ii HANNAH b. 19 July 1737
iii MOLLEY b. 20 Oct. 1739; d. 22 Oct. 1756
iv MERCY b. 10 Oct. 1742
v JONATHAN b. 24 Oct. 1745
vi CHARLES b. 26 March 1751
vii MARY b. 18 April 1757

References: MD 5:56(b. Sarah). VR PLYMPTON pp. 102-3(b. ch.). BRADFORD DESC p. 48. Plymouth Co. LR 46:138(Bradford Freeman). PLYMOUTH VR p. 40(b. Sarah). VR KINGSTON p. 224(m.).

963 ICHABOD FREEMAN^{5} (Mercy Bradford^{4}, Mercy^{3} Warren, Joseph^{2}, Richard^{1}) b. Harwich 2 Aug. 1714; d. Columbia CT 12 Jan. 1782 ae 66.

He m. ANNE -----, b. ca. 1728; d. Columbia CT 10 Feb. 1792 ae 64.

On 17 Nov. 1750 Ichabod Freeman of Lebanon CT, laborer, sold one acre in Halifax to John Waterman Jr.

On 9 March 1785 widow Anne Freeman; dau. Phebe Loomis "only surviving child"; and her husband Nathan Loomis divided the estate of Ichabod Freeman.

Child (FREEMAN):

i PHEBE^{6} b. ca. 1755 (based on age at d.).

References: Old Cemetery, Columbia CT p. 14(d. Ichabod, Anne, Phebe). Plymouth Co. LR 41:185(Ichabod Freeman). Windham CT PR #1471(Ichabod Freeman).

964 FEAR CUSHMAN^{5} (Mercy Bradford^{4}, Mercy^{3} Warren, Joseph^{2}, Richard^{1}) b. Plympton 10 July 1718; d. Kent CT 29 May 1760.

She m. Plympton 11 Dec. 1734 NEHEMIAH STURTEVANT, b. Plympton 18 Nov. 1710; d. Kent CT 18 April 1774; son of Nehemiah and Ruth (Sampson) Sturtevant.

On 21 March 1747 Nehemiah Sturtevant of Plimton and wife Fear sold land she had received from the estate of her father Isaac Cushman deceased.

On 8 Dec. 1748 Nehemiah Sturtevant of Lebanon CT and wife Fear bought land in Kent CT.

There are no CT wills for Nehemiah or Fear Sturtevant.

Children (STURTEVANT) b. Plympton (exc. Lucy); rec. Kent CT:

i PELEG[6] b. 25 Jan. 1735/6
ii PERES b. 15 Nov. 1737
iii REMEMBER b. 6 Oct. 1740
iv RUTH b. 12 Sept. 1743
v FEAR b. 6 Dec. 1745
vi ABIAH b. 27 Nov. 1748
vii LUCY (or LUCIA) b. Kent CT 6 Oct. 1752

References: VR PLYMPTON pp. 202-6(b. ch.), 206(b. Nehemiah), 405(m.). BRADFORD DESC pp. 48, 49. Kent CT LR 1:6(b. Peleg, Remember, Ruth, Fear, Abiah, Lucy), 62(d. Fear, Nehemiah), 367(Nehemiah Sturtevant deed). Plymouth Co. LR 40:190(Nehemiah Sturtevant). MF 17:112.

965 PRISCILLA CUSHMAN[5] (Mercy Bradford[4], Mercy[3] Warren, Joseph[2], Richard[1]) b. Plympton 12 Dec. 1719; d. Kent CT 30 July 1763 in 44th yr.

She m. Plympton 6 Sept. 1739 ISRAEL HOLMES, b. ca. 1713; d. Burlington VT 29 Aug. (prob. 1807) ae 95; son of John Holmes. He m. (2) Kent CT 7 May 1766 Anna Noble.

On 7 June 1743 Israel Holmes of Plimton, cordwainer, and wife Priscilla sold land from the estate of their father Isaac Cushman of Plimton dec.; he acknowledged the deed 7 July 1743.

The will of Israel Holmes of Warren, Litchfield Co. CT dated 25 Aug. 1803, established 22 Dec. 1807 (inv. certified in Warren 10 Dec. 1807 stating he d. in Burlington VT) names daus. Sarah Buel, Priscilla Buel, Betty Bliss, Abigail Bentley; sons Gurshom and Peleg.

Children (HOLMES) first 2 b. Plympton, third b. Lebanon CT, fourth unknown, rest b. Kent CT:

i SARAH[6] b. 1 May 1742
ii PRISCILLA bp. 24 June 1744
iii BETTEY b. 31 July 1746
iv ABIGAIL (named in will)

v GERSHOM b. 27 Sept. 1752
vi PELEG b. 15 May 1755

References: VR PLYMPTON pp. 120(b. Sarah, bp. Priscilla), 334 (m.). BRADFORD DESC p. 49. Plymouth Co. LR 36:36 (Israel Holmes). Litchfield CT PR(Israel Holmes). Kent CT VR 2:19(b. Gershom, Peleg; d. Priscilla, Israel; 2nd m.). Lebanon CT VR 1:148(b. Betty). MF 17:112-3.

966 ABIGAIL CUSHMAN[5] (Mercy Bradford[4], Mercy[3] Warren, Joseph[2], Richard[1]) b. Plympton 31 Dec. 1722; d. there 8 Feb. 1784 in 62nd yr.

She m. Plympton 31 Dec. 1741 GIDEON SAMPSON, b. Plympton 15 Oct. 1719; d. Plympton 30 Oct. 1794 ae 75y 6d; son of George and Hannah (Soule) Sampson, a descendant of Pilgrims George Soule and Myles Standish. He m. (2) Duxbury 22 Dec. 1784 Rebecca Soule.

The will of Gideon Sampson of Plympton dated 28 Oct. 1794, proved 9 Dec. 1794, names wife Rebecca; kinswomen Rebecca Killey, Hannah Perkins, Elizabeth Cushman, Abigail Cushman, dau. of Joseph Cushman of Duxborough; relative Joseph Cushman.

Apparently no children.

References: VR DUXBURY pp. 298(2nd m.). VR PLYMPTON pp. 176(b. Gideon), 382(m.), 513(d. Abigail, Gideon). MD 11:117(d. Abigail), 118(d. Gideon). Plymouth Co. PR 35:193 (Gideon Sampson).

967 JOHN BRADFORD[5] (Samuel[4], Mercy[3] Warren, Joseph[2], William[1]) b. Plympton 8 April 1717; d. there 28 Sept. 1770 ae 53y 5m 9d.

He m. Plymouth 10 Nov. 1743 ELIZABETH HOLMES, b. Plymouth 13 Oct. 1723; d. Plympton 30 Dec. 1806 in 85th yr.; dau. of Eleazer and Hannah (Sylvester) Holmes, a descendant of Pilgrim Richard Warren.

On 22 Nov. 1770 widow Elizabeth Bradford and John Bradford, yeoman, both of Plimton, were appointed administrators on the estate of Capt. John Bradford late of Plympton deceased. Division of the estate into 12 shares on 31 May 1776 gave 2 shares to eldest son Capt. John Bradford, and single shares to sons Perez, Oliver and William, and daus. Elizabeth Magoun, Mary Churchel, Priscilla Rider, Hannah Waterman, Lydia Bradford, Mercy Bradford and Sarah Bradford.

On 2 Jan. 1807 Perez Bradford of Plympton gave his bond as administrator on the estate of Elizabeth Bradford, widow, deceased.

On 20 April 1807 the estate of Elizabeth Bradford was divided among: John Bradford, heirs of Elizabeth Magoun, Lydia Bryant, heirs of William Bradford, Mary Churchill, Priscilla

Rider, Marcy Sears, Oliver Bradford, Perez Bradford, Hannah Waterman and Sarah Bosworth.

Children (BRADFORD) b. Plympton:

- i ELIZABETH[6] b. 9 Aug. 1744
- ii MOLLY (or MARY) b. 15 May 1746
- iii JOHN b. 18 July 1748
- iv PRISCILLA b. 4 Sept. 1750
- v PEREZ b. 10 Nov. 1752
- vi HANNAH b. 16 Jan. 1755
- vii LYDIA b. 16 Feb. 1757
- viii OLIVER b. 10 Jan. 1759
- ix MARCY b. 20 Dec. 1761
- x WILLIAM b. 8 June 1766
- xi SARAH b. 8 Oct. 1769

References: MD 8:153-4(deaths); 12:12(b. Elizabeth); 14:160 (m.); 17:131. VR PLYMPTON pp. 31-9(b. ch.), 446(d. Elizabeth), 447(d. John). BRADFORD DESC p. 49. Plymouth Co. PR 20:409; 24:116(John Bradford); 39:97; 42:141 (Elizabeth Bradford). PLYMOUTH VR pp. 49(b. Elizabeth), 103 (m.).

968 GIDEON BRADFORD[5] (Samuel[4], Mercy[3] Warren, Joseph[2], William[1]) b. Plympton 27 Oct. 1718; d. there 18 Oct. 1793 in 75th yr.

He m. Plymouth 8 Oct. 1741 JANE PADDOCK, b. Yarmouth 30 Aug. 1717; d. Plympton 18 April 1795 in 78th yr.; dau. of Ichabod and Joanna (Faunce) Paddock.

The will of Gideon Bradford of Plympton Esq. dated 11 May 1784, proved 11 Nov. 1793, names wife Jane; sons Levi, Joseph, Samuel, Gideon and Calvin who were to have all his law books; and daus. Sarah Ellis, wife of Freeman, and Jane Bisbee, wife of Noah.

The will of Jane Bradford of Plympton, widow of Gideon Bradford Esq., dated 31 May 1794, sworn 4 Jan. 1796, names son Levi; dau. Jenny Bisbee, wife of Noah; and dau. Sarah Ellis, wife of Freeman.

Children (BRADFORD) b. Plympton:

- i LEVI[6] b. 16 Feb. 1742/3
- ii JOSEPH b. 19 Oct. 1745
- iii SARAH b. 19 May 1748
- iv SAMUEL b. 20 June 1750
- v GIDEON b. 30 May 1752
- vi CALVIN b. 25 July 1754
- vii JENNY (or JANE) b. 12 March 1756

References: MD 8:153-4(deaths); 14:159(m.). VR PLYMPTON pp. 30-8(b. ch.), 447(d. Gideon, Jane). YARMOUTH VR 1:40(b. Jane). BRADFORD DESC pp. 49-50. Plymouth Co. PR 33:467(Gideon Bradford); #2550(Jane Bradford). PLYMOUTH VR p. 102(m.).

969 MARY BRADFORD[5] (Samuel[4], Mercy[3] Warren, Joseph[2], William[1]) b. Plympton 16 Oct. 1722; d. Tiverton RI 3 Feb. 1792 in 70th yr.

She m. Tiverton 1 Dec. 1743 ABIEL COOKE, b. Tiverton ca. 1719; d. there 15 July 1808; son of John and Alice (Southworth) Cooke, a descendant of Pilgrim John Alden. This is not a Mayflower Cooke line. Abiel Cooke had four illegitimate children by Mary "Moll" Briggs.

Abiel Cooke was a Loyalist in the Revolutionary War.

Abiel Cooke of Tiverton died intestate and his dau. Sarah Cook was appointed administratrix of his estate. On 6 Feb. 1809 she was named guardian of her brothers Nathaniel and William and her sister Priscilla who were apparently unable to take care of their portions.

On 9 July 1812 the heirs of Abiel Cook signed a deed. They were David Cook and wife Alice of Plymouth; Gilbert Eddy and wife Nancy of Oxford; Samuel Knight of Oxford, Chenango Co.; Philip Knight [worn] of Schenectady; Samuel Swain and wife Mary of Nantucket; Sarah Cook of Tiverton, singlewoman; Sarah Cook as guardian of Nathaniel and William Cook; Abiel Cook; and Priscilla Cook.

Children (COOKE) b. Little Compton RI:

i MARY[6] b. 8 Aug. 1744
ii JOSEPH b. 21 Aug. 1746
iii WILLIAM b. ca. 1750; d. bef. 1818; unm.
iv ALICE b. 6 June 1752
v SAMUEL b. 4 Oct. 1754
vi NATHANIEL b. 28 Dec. 1756; d. Little Compton RI 4 Jan. 1817
vii SARAH b. 2 July 1759; d. summer 1840; unm. The will of Sarah Cook, singlewoman of Little Compton dated 29 April 1837, proved 3 Aug. 1840, names kinsmen Joseph Cook, John Stanton Cook and Isaac Sanford Cook, sons of kinsman Samuel Cook Sr.; Mary, wife of Pardon Almy and her dau. Mary Almy and Nabby Hill and "her second daughter" all of whom were daughters or granddaughters of kinsman Samuel Cook Sr.
viii PRISCILLA b. 10 Dec. 1761; d. aft. 6 Feb. 1809; unm.

References: RIVR Little Compton 4:6:108(b. ch. except William). BRADFORD DESC p. 50. COOK (THOMAS) GEN 1:158-161(d. Abiel, Nathaniel). Tiverton RI PR 12:2(Sarah Cook). RIVR Tiverton 4:7:16(m.). NEHGR 117:21(d. Mary). Little Compton RI LE 6:183-7(heirs).

NOTE: No proof found for a son THADDEUS listed in BRADFORD DESC.

970 SARAH BRADFORD[5] (Samuel[4], Mercy[3] Warren, Joseph[2], William[1]) b. Plympton 4 April 1725; living Pembroke 19 July 1756.

She m. Plympton 25 Nov. 1742 EPHRAIM PADDOCK, b. Yarmouth 15 April 1721; living Brookfield 15 Oct. 1763; d. Ware after 1790; son of Ichabod and Joanna (Faunce) Paddock.

The will of Elder Thomas Faunce of Plymouth drawn 21 March 1745, bequeathed lands in Middleboro to his daughter Joanna, wife of Ichabod Paddock [and mother of Ephraim].

On 19 July 1756 Ephraim Paddock of Pembroke, blacksmith, sold land in Pembroke with wife Sarah releasing her dower.

On 15 Oct. 1763 Ephraim Paddock of Brookfield, blacksmith, sold land in Middleboro which Elder Thomas Faunce late of Plymouth deceased gave to Jabez Barnes, provided he had issue. This deed was acknowledged 23 Aug. 1765 before Gideon Bradford, JP.

Ephraim Paddock was 1-0-1 in the 1790 census of Ware.

No probate found for Ephraim Paddock. No Worcester Co., Hampshire Co. or Springfield deeds.

Children (PADDOCK) 1st. 2 b. Pembroke:

i SARAH[6] b. 6 Jan. 1754
ii EPHRAIM bp. 20 June 1756
iii BRADFORD b. Warren 4 Nov. 1759

References: MD 18:118(int.). VR PEMBROKE p. 158(b. Sarah, bp. Ephraim). VR PLYMPTON p. 55(m). YARMOUTH VR 1:40 (b. Ephraim). BRADFORD DESC p. 50. Plymouth Co. PR 10:101(Thomas Faunce). Plymouth Co. LR 44:4; 50:82(Ephraim Paddock). VR WARREN p. 52(b. Bradford).

971 WILLIAM BRADFORD[5] (Samuel[4], Mercy[3] Warren, Joseph[2], William[1]) b. Plympton 4 Nov. 1728; d. Bristol RI 6 July 1808 ae 79.

He m. Plymouth 22 March 1750/1 MARY LE BARON, b. Plymouth 20 March 1731/2; d. Bristol RI 2 Oct. 1775; dau. of Lazarus and Lydia (Bartlett) LeBaron, a descendant of Pilgrim Richard Warren (see #306). The will of Lazarus LeBaron of Plymouth, physician, dated 24 Sept. 1772 names dau. Mary Bradford wife of Dr. Bradford of Bristol.

On 11 Nov. 1796 William Bradford of Bristol, physician, sold ten acres of his farm in Bristol to John Bradford of Bristol, gentleman.

William Bradford was a physician, lawyer, the last deputy governor of Rhode Island under the Crown and the first governor under the Continental Congress. He was U. S. Senator 1793-7.

The will of William Bradford of Bristol, physician and attorney, dated 9 Oct. 1807, proved 1 Aug. 1808, names sons William, John, Henry and LeBaron Bradford; Sarah, widow of LeBaron and their son LeBaron Bradford; daughters Mary Goodwin, widow; Hannah wife of Gustavus Baylis; Lydia wife of Charles Collins Jr.; grandson Henry Goodwin and niece Hannah LeBaron.

Children (BRADFORD) first b. Warren RI, next 7 b. Bristol RI:

i WILLIAM[6] b. 15 Sept. 1752
ii LE BARON b. 31 May 1754
iii JOHN b. 9 Oct. 1758; d. 30 Oct. 1765
iv MARY b. 2 Sept. 1760
v HANNAH b. 22 Nov. 1762; d. 1763
vi son b. 15 July 1764; d. 5 Aug. 1764
vii HANNAH b. 14 June 1767
viii JOHN b. 17 July 1768
ix ANN (or NANCY) b. 6 Aug. 1770 (not in will)
x EZEKIEL HERSEY b. 8 March 1772 (bp. as HENRY)
xi LYDIA b. 11 April 1774

References: MD 13:112(b. Mary); 16:167(int.), 171(m.). RIVR Bristol 6:1:65(b. 1st 4 ch.; 2nd Hannah, John), 119(d. William, Mary, children). PN&Q 3:105 (Bible rec.). BRADFORD DESC pp. 50-1. Plymouth PR 21:324(Lazarus LeBaron). Bristol RI PR 3:142(William Bradford). PLYMOUTH VR p. 148(m.). Bristol RI LE 7:95(William Bradford).

972 ABIGAIL BRADFORD[5] (Samuel[4], Mercy[3] Warren, Joseph[2], William[1]) b. Plympton 12 June 1732; d. there 31 Jan. 1776 in 44th yr.

She m. int. Plymouth 7 Sept. 1754 CALEB STETSON, bp. Plymouth Nov. 1734; son of Caleb and Deborah (Morton) Stetson.

On 24 Oct. 1783 Caleb Stetson, housewright, and Isaac Lobdell and wife Polly, heirs of Abigail Stetson late of Plympton, dec., and others, quitclaimed to Gideon Bradford items given Gideon in the will of Samuel Bradford deceased.

No Plymouth Co. PR for Caleb or Abigail Stetson.

Children (STETSON) first 2 b. Plymouth:

i CALEB[6] b. 12 Aug. 1755
ii BRADFORD b. 20 May 1757; d. 5 Sept. 1758 ae 1yr 3mo 13d
iii MARY (or MOLLY) b. 7 Sept. 1759

References: MD 11:163(d. Abigail); 18:216(b. 1st 2 ch.); 25:51 (int.). VR PLYMPTON p. 522(d. Abigail). BRADFORD DESC p. 52(b. Mary). Plymouth Co. LR 65:75(Caleb Stetson et al.) PLYMOUTH CH RECS 1:435(bp. Caleb). PLYMOUTH VR pp. 187(b. 1st 2 ch.), 244(int.). (PLYMOUTH) BURIAL HILL p. 34(d. Bradford).

973 PHEBE BRADFORD[5] (Samuel[4], Mercy[3] Warren, Joseph[2], William[1]) b. Plympton 30 March 1735; living Williamsburg 24 Oct. 1780.

She m. Plympton 10 Sept. 1753 SHUBAL NORTON, b. Chilmark 21 Aug. 1733; d. there 15 Feb. 1760 in 27th yr.; son of Jacob and Bethia (Mayhew) Norton.

On 27 Oct. 1780 Freeman Norton of Williamsburg, mariner, as attorney to his mother Phebe Norton also of Williamsburg, with Caleb Stetson and Isaac Lobdel and his wife Molly, all of Plympton, being heirs of Abigail Stetson late of Plympton dec., quitclaimed to Gideon Bradford items given Gideon in the will of Samuel Bradford late of Plympton dec.

Children (NORTON) b. Chilmark:

i FREEMAN[6] b. 21 Aug. 1754
ii SARAH b. 27 May 1756
iii BETHIA b. 20 Nov. 1758

References: VR CHILMARK pp. 26(b. Bethia, Freeman), 37(b. Sarah, Shubal), 92(d. Shubal). VR PLYMPTON p. 353(m. - no date). BRADFORD DESC p. 52. Plymouth Co. LR 65:75(Freeman Norton et al.).

974 SAMUEL BRADFORD[5] (Samuel[4], Mercy[3] Warren, Joseph[2], William[1]) b. Plympton 13 April 1740; d. Williamsburg 1 Aug. 1813.

He m. Chilmark 25 Nov. 1762 LYDIA PEASE, b. Chilmark in 1740; d. Williamsburg 21 Nov. 1825; dau. of John and Abigail (Burgess) Pease.

The will of Samuel Bradford of Williamsburg dated 3 Feb. 1801, with administrator's bond dated "last day of Feb. 1814", mentions "loving wife"; names son Shubel, dau. Sarah, sons Samuel, Edward Gray, and Pardon, with daughter Lydia to have use of a room in the house. On 22 Dec. 1813 Shubael Bradford and Edward Gray Bradford, both of Conway, Franklin Co., Ephraim Hill and wife Sarah, and Lydia Bradford, all of

Williamsburg, sold to Pardon Bradford of Williamsburg, real estate of their father Samuel Bradford late of Williamsburg dec.

Children (BRADFORD) b. Williamsburg:

i SARAH[6] b. 22 Sept. 1763; d. 30 Oct. 1763
ii SHUBAEL b. 5 Oct. 1764
iii JOHN b. 6 May 1766; d. Williamsburg 26 March 1782
iv SARAH b. 15 March 1768
v SAMUEL b. 5 Sept. 1770
vi EDWARD b. 22 Aug. 1772
vii son b. 13 March 1774; d. 3 May 1774
viii PARDON b. 27 June 1775
ix LYDIA b. 25 Sept. 1778; d. Williamsburg 16 March 1859; unm.
x ABIGAIL b. 28 Jan. 1782; d. Williamsburg 10 June 1790

References: VR CHILMARK p. 43(m.). BRADFORD DESC p. 52. Hampshire Co. PR Box 19:4(Samuel Bradford). Hampshire Co. LR 37:184(Shubael Bradford et al.). Williamsburg VR 1:26, repeated in 2:18(b. & d. ch.; d. Samuel, Lydia).

975 SETH CHIPMAN[5] (Priscilla Bradford[4], Mercy[3] Warren, Joseph[2], William[1]) b. Kingston 1 Nov. 1724; d. prob. at sea bef. 23 May 1766.

He m. Kingston 3 Dec. 1746 SARAH RIPLEY, b. Plympton 22 Jan. 1728; living Kingston 15 March 1770; dau. of William and Hannah (Bosworth) Ripley, a descendant of Pilgrim John Howland.

On 23 May 1766 Cornelius Samson of Kingston, gent., was appointed administrator on the estate of Seth Chipman late of Kingston, mariner.

On 15 March 1770 Sarah Chipman of Kingston, widow of Seth Chipman of Kingston, mariner, and her father William Ripley of Plimton, housewright, petitioned to sell land, she being left with two female children aged about 5 and 3 years.

On 14 Sept. 1771 William Ripley Jr. of Plimton was appointed guardian to Sarah and Mercy Chipman daus. of Seth Chipman Jr. late of Kingston, mariner, dec., minors under 14.

Children (CHIPMAN) b. Kingston:

i SARAH[6] b. 5 May 1764
ii MERCY b. 22 June 1766

References: VR KINGSTON pp. 40(b. ch.), 191(m.). VR PLYMPTON p. 170(b. Sarah). Plymouth Co. PR 17:162; 20:552 (Seth Chipman); 21:30(gdn.).

976 MERCY CHIPMAN[5] (Priscilla Bradford[4], Mercy[3] Warren, Joseph[2], William[1]) b. Kingston 19 Nov. 1725; d. there 13 Feb. 1782 in 57th yr.

She m. Kingston 7 Dec. 1763 BENJAMIN BRADFORD, b. Plymouth 17 Oct. 1705; d. Kingston 16 Oct. (or Nov.) 1783 ae 77; son of Israel and Sarah (Bartlett) Bradford, a descendant of Pilgrims John Alden, William Bradford, William Brewster and Richard Warren. He m. (1) int. Kingston 18 Dec. 1731 Zeresh Stetson by whom he had Thomas, Michael, Perez, Lydia, Benjamin, Marcy, Lemuel and Lydia.

On 7 April 1784 Levi Holmes was appointed administrator of the estate of Benjamin Bradford of Kingston, yeoman.

No children.

References: MD 13:167(b. Benjamin). VR KINGSTON pp. 179(m.; int. his 1st m.), 319(d. Benjamin), 322(d. Mercy). PLYMOUTH VR p. 72(b. Benjamin). Plymouth Co. PR 27:146(Benjamin Bradford).

977 BENJAMIN CHIPMAN[5] (Priscilla Bradford[4], Mercy[3] Warren, Joseph[2], William[1]) b. Kingston 23 May 1729; d. Poland ME May 1787.

He m. Kingston 9 May 1751 HANNAH WADSWORTH, b. Duxbury 6 Dec. 1732; d. Poland ME 26 Dec. 1822; dau. of Ichabod and Margaret (Marshall) Wadsworth.

On 30 Sept. 1774 Benjamin Chipman of Kingston, cooper, sold land in Kingston with buildings, with Hannah Chipman also signing.

On 16 May 1777 Barnabas Winslow of New Gloucester [ME] sold land in New Gloucester to Benjamin Chipman of New Gloucester, cooper.

On 22 April 1797 Hannah Chipman, widow of Benjamin Chipman, William Chipman, Daniel Chipman, John T. and Hannah Merrill and William and Margaret Allen, all of Poland [ME] conveyed land to Josiah Little of Newbury.

The Cumberland Co. ME probates for this period no longer exist.

Children (CHIPMAN) b. Kingston:

i BENJAMIN[6] b. 24 Jan. 1752
ii MARGARET b. 16 June 1756
iii SARAH b. 3 Dec. 1759
iv PRISCILLA b. 25 July 1761
v LYDIA b. 20 March 1763
vi WILLIAM b. 14 Aug. 1764

vii LEONA (twin) b. 18 Feb. 1766
viii DANIEL (twin) b. 18 Feb. 1766; d.y.
ix HANNAH b. 25 July 1769
x DANIEL b. 9 July 1771

References: VR DUXBURY p. 181(b. Hannah). VR KINGSTON pp. 39 (b. son Benjamin), 40(b. Margaret thru Leona), 191(m.). Plymouth Co. LR 58:117(Benjamin Chipman). Cumberland Co. ME LR 10:406(Barnabas Winslow); 30:528(Hannah Chipman, etc.). THE CHIPMAN FAMILY, Bert Lee Chipman, Winston-Salem NC, 1928, pp. 35-6.

978 JAMES BRADFORD[5] (William[4], Mercy[3] Warren, Joseph[2], William[1]) b. Plymouth 2 July 1717; d. prob. Plainfield CT 10 Dec. 1801 ae 84.

He m. (1) PRISCILLA SPAULDING, b. Plainfield CT 17 Jan. 1718/9; d. there 11 Feb. 1743 ae 24; dau. of Josiah and Sarah (Warren) Spaulding.

He m. (2) ca. 1743 ZERVIAH THOMAS, b. Marshfield 3 Oct. 1715; d. Plainfield CT 23 Nov. 1808 ae 93; dau. of John and Lydia (Waterman) Thomas, a descendant of Pilgrim Richard Warren (see #763). The will of John Thomas dated 12 May 1764 names dau. Zerviah wife of James Bradford of Plainfield.

On 12 May 1746 James Bradford of Plainfield CT sold to Samuel Foster land that belonged to his brother Zadock Bradford, dec.

The will of James Bradford of Plainfield CT "advanced in age" dated 17 May 1798, accepted 5 Jan. 1802, names wife Keziah [sic] also advanced in age; sons Anthony and Samuel; oldest dau. Persillah Dorrance, dau. Keziah Clift.

Children (BRADFORD) b. Plainfield CT by Zerviah:

i SAMUEL[6] b. ca. 1744
ii KEZIAH b. 15 Oct. 1747
iii ANTHONY b. 6 Sept. 1749
iv JAMES b. 20 Jan. 1751; d. 3 Dec. 1777; unm.
v PRISCILLA b. 20 Dec. 1752
vi JOSIAH b. 15 Oct. 1754 (not in will)
vii HANNAH b. 8 Nov. 1756; d. 25 June 1778; unm.
viii JOSEPH b. 30 Dec. 1758; d. 26 May 1759

References: MD 8:176(b. Zerviah). WATERMAN GEN 1:64-5; 627. BRADFORD DESC p. 53. CSL Hale Cem Recs: Plainfield. Plainfield CT PR #230(James Bradford). MARSHFIELD VR p. 42(b. Zerviah). THOMAS GEN p. 165. Plymouth Co. LR 38:71 (James Bradford). Plainfield CT VR 1:20(b. Priscilla).

NOTE: Neither m. nor ch. in IGI-CT or IGI-MA.

979 ELIPHALET BRADFORD[5] (William[4], Mercy[3] Warren, Joseph[2], William[1]) b. Plymouth 20 Jan. 1722/3; d. Duxbury 7 June 1795 in 72nd yr.

He m. (1) Duxbury 8 Aug. 1751 HANNAH PRINCE, b. Duxbury 22 Oct. 1730; d. there 11 July 1756 in 26th yr.; dau. of Thomas and Judith (Fox) Prince, a descendant of Pilgrim William Brewster.

He m. (2) Duxbury 9 Feb. 1758 HANNAH OLDHAM, b. 29 Oct. 1733; d. Duxbury 4 Nov. 1804 ae 71y 9d.

Eliphalet Bradford was 2-0-2 in the 1790 census of Duxbury.

No Plymouth Co. PR for Eliphalet Bradford.

Children (BRADFORD) b. Duxbury, 3 by 1st wife, rest by 2nd:

i HANNAH[6] b. 30 May 1752
ii LYDIA b. 28 Jan. 1754
iii EUNICE b. 8 May 1756
iv LUCY b. 9 Nov. 1758
v ABIGAIL b. 26 Dec. 1759
vi WILLIAM b. 17 Nov. 1761
vii ZADOCK b. 11 Aug. 1765
viii DEBORAH b. 16 Dec. 1767
ix MARY b. Sept. 1773; d. 16 May 1774

References: MD 9:160(d. wife Hannah); 11:237(b. Hannah Prince); 12:170(b. 1st 3 ch.); 16:168(int. 1st m.). VR DUXBURY pp. 27-32(b. ch.), 128(b. Hannah), 222(both m.), 352(d. Eliphalet, both wives), 392(d. Mary). BRADFORD DESC pp. 53, 54.

980 HANNAH BRADFORD[5] (William[4], Mercy[3] Warren, Joseph[2], William[1]) b. Plymouth 29 May 1724; d. Plainfield CT 2 March 1755 ae 29y 9m.

She m. Plainfield CT 20 Feb. 1745 WILLARD SPAULDING, b. Plainfield CT 1 March 1716/7; d. Killingly CT 19 Feb. 1766; son of Edward and Elizabeth (Hall) Spaulding.

On 15 March 1749/50 Willard Spaulding of Killingly CT, husbandman, and wife Hannah sold to John Brewster of Kingston land in Kingston that belonged "to our honoured father William Bradford."

The will of Willard Spaulding of Killingly CT "sick and weak" dated 21 March 1765, codicil 10 Dec. 1765, probated 4 March 1766, names only son Zadock, eldest daughter Mary, second dau. Hannah, youngest dau. Elizabeth. Brother Capt. James Bradford of Plainfield executor.

Children (SPAULDING) 1st b. Plainfield CT; rest b. Killingly CT:

i ZADOCK[6] b. 8 May 1746
ii MARY b. 4 Sept. 1748
iii HANNAH b. 29 June 1751
iv ELIZABETH b. 18 Nov. 1753

References: BRADFORD DESC p. 54. Plymouth Co. LR 41:58(Willard Spaulding). Killingly CT PR #2013(Willard Spaulding). Plainfield CT VR 1:17(b. Willard); 2:13(m.; b. Zadock), 29(d. Hannah). Killingly CT VR 1:47(b. Mary, Hannah), 53(b. Elizabeth), 174(d. Willard).

981 JOSEPH[5] WARREN (Joseph[4-3-2], Richard[1]) b. Plymouth 21 June 1724; d. there 3 Aug. 1770.

He m. Plymouth 15 Sept. 1763 MERCY (ATWOOD) TORREY, b. Plympton ca. 1730; d. Plymouth 12 Dec. 1770; dau. of Nathaniel and Mercy (Adams) Atwood. She m. (1) int. Plymouth 23 Feb. 1750/1 Josiah Torrey by whom she had Marcy and Joseph.

In 1769 [no date] Joseph Warren of Plymouth and wife Mercy sold to Joseph Barrows their share of a lot which had belonged to their father Nathaniel Atwood.

On 10 Jan. 1771 William Warren was appointed administrator of the estate of Joseph Warren. On 8 Feb. 1771 Sylvanus Bartlett was appointed guardian of Joseph Warren, son of Joseph.

Child (WARREN) b. Plymouth:

i JOSEPH[6] b. 18 Aug. 1765

References: MD 16:167(int. her 1st m.); 26:42(int.). WARREN GEN p. 28. Plymouth Co. PR 20:455, 477(Joseph Warren); 20:478(gdn.). MA MARR 2:19(m.). PLYMOUTH CH RECS 1:399(d. Joseph, Mercy). PLYMOUTH VR pp. 22(b. Torrey ch.), 145(int. her 1st m.), 218(b. son Joseph), 355(m.). Plymouth Co. LR 55:220(Joseph Warren).

982 ELIZABETH[5] WARREN (Joseph[4-3-2], Richard[1]) b. Plymouth 28 Sept. 1726; d. there 26 Oct. 1793 ae 67.

She m. Plymouth 6 Dec. 1744 SAMUEL NICHOLS NELSON, b. Plymouth 9 Aug. 1721; d. there 7 Aug. 1798 ae 77; son of Samuel and Bathsheba (Nichols) Nelson.

See #387 for an account of this family.

References: MD 12:222(b. Sam.); 16:171(m.). (PLYMOUTH) BURIAL HILL p. 70(d. Eliz.). PLYMOUTH CH RECS 1:428(d. Sam.). PLYMOUTH VR pp. 54(b. Samuel), 148(m.).

983 MARY^{5} WARREN (Joseph^{4-3-2}, Richard^{1}) b. Plymouth 25 Jan. 1729/30.

She m. (1) Plymouth 10 May 1750 WILLIAM MORTON, b. Plymouth 24 Oct. 1717; d. there 15 Nov. 1750; son of George and Rebecca (Churchill) Morton.

She m. (2) Plymouth 20 June 1754 ARTHUR SHEPARD.

The inventory of the estate of William Morton, late of Plymouth, dated 13 Feb. 1750 mentions part of real estate that once belonged to George Morton dec.

No Plymouth Co. PR or LR for Arthur or Mary Shepard.

Child (MORTON) b. Plymouth:

i WILLIAM^{6} b. 8 May 1751

References: MD 16:170(1st m.); 18:141(2nd m.). Plymouth Co. PR 12:245; 13:135(William Morton). PLYMOUTH VR pp. 52(b.&d. Wm.; b. son Wm.), 147(1st m.), 175(2nd m.).

984 PRISCILLA^{5} WARREN (Joseph^{4-3-2}, Richard^{1}) b. Plymouth 19 April 1733; d. there 2 Oct. 1757 ae 25y 5m 2d.

She m. Plymouth 4 Nov. 1751 LEMUEL DREW, b. Plymouth 18 Jan. 1724/5; d. there 29 July 1799; son of Lemuel and Hannah (Barnes) Drew, a descendant of Pilgrim Richard Warren (#316 iv).

No Plymouth Co. PR for Lemuel Drew.

References: MD 12:226(b. Lemuel); 16:87(d. Priscilla), 171 (m.). PLYMOUTH CH RECS 2:622(d. Lemuel). (PLYMOUTH) BURIAL HILL p. 33(d. Priscilla). PLYMOUTH VR pp. 58(b. Lemuel), 139(d. Priscilla), 148(m.).

985 WILLIAM^{5} WARREN (Joseph^{4-3-2}, Richard^{1}) b. Plymouth 18 June 1737; d. there 1 June 1793.

He m. (1) Plymouth 18 Oct. 1764 REBECCA EASDELL, d. Plymouth 26 Jan. 1770; dau. of James and Rebecca (Witherell) Easdell.

He m. (2) Plymouth 20 Jan. 1774 ELIZABETH (LOTHROP) KING, b. ca. 1741; d. Plymouth 26 Nov. 1799 ae 58 yrs.; dau. of Ansel and Mary (Thomas) Lothrop.

On 4 Feb. 1770 children Rebecca, Allethea and Molly were bp. in Plymouth.

On 14 Nov. 1793 Joseph Warren Nelson and Caleb Morton were appointed administrators of the estate of William Warren of Plymouth. The estate was declared insolvent 10 Dec. 1793. On 3 April 1794 a warrant was issued to set off to the widow Elizabeth Warren her right to dower.

Children (WARREN) b. Plymouth:

i REBECCA[6] b. 1 Sept. 1765
ii ALATHEA b. 1 April 1767
iii MARY (or MOLLY) bp. 4 Feb. 1770

References: WARREN GEN pp. 28-9. PLYMOUTH CH RECS 1:398(d. Rebecca), 420(d. Wm.), 458(bp. ch); 2:621(d. Eliz.). (PLYMOUTH) BURIAL HILL p. 84(d. Eliz.). MD 22:106(b. 1st 2 ch.). Plymouth Co. PR 27:459; 36:165-8(William Warren). PLYMOUTH VR pp. 221(b. 1st 2 ch.), 355(1st m.), 360(2nd m.).

986 JOHN LUCAS[5] (Joseph[4], Patience[3] Warren, Joseph[2], Richard[1]) b. Plympton 14 Dec. 1715; d. Carver 20 Feb. 1764 in 49th yr.

He m. Plympton 10 June 1739 LYDIA DOTEN, b. Plymouth 10 Feb. 1712/3; d. Carver 15 Nov. 1768 in 56th yr.; dau. of John and Mehitable (Nelson) Doty, a descendant of Pilgrim Edward Doty.

On 13 Feb. 1768 John Lucas of Plympton, house-wright, was appointed administrator of the estate of his father John Lucas, blacksmith. The 16 June 1768 division went to widow Lidia; eldest son Joseph; children Persis Cobb, John Lucas, David Lucas, Lidia Lucas, Hannah Lucas, Susanna Lucas and William Lucas.

On 9 March 1768 Samuel Lucas of Plimpton was appointed guardian to Lidia Lucas; Benjamin Lucas was appointed guardian to Hannah Lucas and Ebenezer Doten of Plimpton was appointed guardian to Susannah Lucas, all minor daughters to John Lucas, all over 14. John Cobb was appointed guardian to William Lucas minor son of John Lucas.

Children (LUCAS) b. Plympton:

i PERSIS[6] b. 15 Jan. 1741/2 [sic]
ii JOSEPH b. 3 Oct. 1742 [sic]
iii JOHN b. 5 July 1744
iv DAVID b. 5 May 1746
v LYDIA b. 27 March 1748
vi HANNAH b. 5 April 1750
vii SUSANNA b. 6 July 1752
viii WILLIAM b. 12 Oct. 1755

References: VR PLYMPTON pp. 134-5(b. ch.), 345(m.). MD 2:163 (b. Lydia). Plymouth Co. PR 20:19, 21, 22(gdn.); 167-8(John Lucas). PLYMOUTH VR p. 20(b. Lydia). VR CARVER p. 159(d. John, Lydia).

987 SAMUEL LUCAS[5] (Joseph[4], Patience[3] Warren, Joseph[2], Richard[1]) b. Plympton 19 Dec. 1719; d. Carver 3 Jan. 1792 ae 72y 3d.

He m. Plympton 9 Nov. 1749 ABIGAIL SHAW, b. Plympton ca. 1729; d. Carver 18 Oct. 1801 in 72nd yr.; dau. of John and Abigail (Perry) Shaw.

The will of Samuel Lucas of Plimpton, yeoman, dated 27 Oct. 1788, proved 1 March 1792, names wife Abigail; sons Samuel, Isaac Shaw, Abijah and Bezaleel Lucas; daughters Abigail Barrows wife of Malachi Barrows, Patience Robbins wife of Joseph Robbins, Elizabeth Lucas and Zilpha Lucas.

Children (LUCAS) b. Plympton:

i ISAAC[6] b. 23 Aug. 1750; d. 27 Aug. 1753 in 4th yr.
ii SAMUEL b. 15 June 1752
iii ABIGAIL b. 18 Aug. 1756; d. 16 Sept. 1756 ae 1 yr 1 mo
iv ISAAC SHAW b. 8 May 1757
v ABIJAH b. 5 Feb. 1759
vi JOSIAH d. 22 Aug. 1761 ae 14d
vii ABIGAIL b. 23 Aug. 1762
viii SOLOMON d. 22 Oct. 1764 ae 4d
ix PATIENCE b. 3 July 1766
x ELISABETH b. 1 Sept. 1768
xi BEZALEEL b. 22 April 1771
xii ZILPHA b. 22 April 1773; d. Carver 23 Oct. 1841 ae 68y 6m; unm.

References: VR CARVER pp. 158(d. Abigail, dau. Abigail), 159 (d. Isaac, Josiah), 160(d. Samuel, Solomon). VR PLYMPTON pp. 134-5(b. ch.), 346(m.), 987(d. Samuel, Abigail). Plymouth Co. PR 31:485-9; 33:32(Samuel Lucas).

988 PATIENCE LUCAS[5] (Joseph[4], Patience[3] Warren, Joseph[2], Richard[1]) b. Plympton 17 Jan. 1723/4.

She m. Plympton 22 Aug. 1751 JOSHUA PERRY, b. Sandwich 3 Feb. 1725/6; d. Middleboro 23 Jan. 1804; son of Elijah and Hannah (Damon) Perry.

In 1763 Joshua Perry of Middleboro was declared non compos mentis. Noah Perry, his guardian, rendered an account 6 Dec. 1773.

There was a Joshua Perry 2-1-3 in the 1790 census of Middleboro.

No Plymouth Co. PR for Joshua Perry.

References: VR PLYMPTON p. 355(m.). NEHGR 114:281-2. SANDWICH VR 1:125(b. Joshua). MIDDLEBORO VR 2:46(d. Joshua). Plymouth Co. PR 16:471, 509; 21:342(mental condition of Joshua Perry).

989 BARNABAS LUCAS[5] (Joseph[4], Patience[3] Warren, Joseph[2], Richard[1]) b. Plympton 30 Oct. 1729; d. bef. 3 Aug. 1778 (adm.).

He m. Pembroke 28 June 1753 JOANNA (or ANNA) PIERCE, b. Boston 6 April 1727; d. aft. 31 March 1799 (adm.); dau. of Isaac and Agnes (Kent) Pierce.

On 3 Aug. 1778 Joanna Lucas of Plympton, widow, was appointed administratrix of the estate of Barnabas Lucas, late of Plympton. On 2 June 1784 the estate was divided between Joanna Lucas, widow; sons Nehemiah, Elijah, Barnabas, Ephraim, Consider, Seth and Caleb Lucas; dau. Melatiah Wilton, wife of William Wilton; daus. Joanna, Molly, Elizabeth and Hannah Lucas.

On 28 May 1798 estate papers named Nehemiah of Carver, Elijah of Middleboro, Barnabas and Ephraim of Carver, Seth and Caleb minors, Consider of Woodstock, Joanna, Mary and Hannah of Carver, spinsters.

On 21 March 1798 Joanna Lucas of Carver, widow, was named adminstratrix of the estate of Elizabeth Lucas, spinster.

Children (LUCAS) named in division:

i MELATIAH[6]
ii NEHEMIAH
iii ELIJAH
iv BARNABAS
v EPHRAIM
vi CONSIDER
vii JOANNA
viii MOLLY (or MARY)
ix ELIZABETH
x HANNAH
xi SETH
xii CALEB

References: VR PEMBROKE p. 312(m.). Plymouth Co. PR 23:201; 25:115; 29:185, 418; 97:127(Barnabas Lucas); 34:155(Elizabeth Lucas). BOSTON VR 24:183(b. Joanna).

990 PHEBE LUCAS[5] (William[4], Patience[3] Warren, Joseph[2], Richard[1]) b. Plymouth 12 April 1725; d. bef. 12 May 1748 (2nd m.).

She m. Plymouth 25 April 1745 EBENEZER DUNHAM, b. Plympton 5 Feb. 1718/9; d. bef. 4 Aug. 1766; son of Israel and Joannah (Rickard) Dunham. He m. (2) Plympton 12 May 1748

Lydia (Perry) Fuller by whom he had Joanna, Ebenezer, Hannah, Jesse, Abigail, Nathaniel, Phebe and Silvanus.

On 4 Aug. 1766 Lidia Donham of Plymouth, widow, was appointed administratrix of the estate of Ebenezer Donham of Plimpton.

Child (DUNHAM) b. Plympton:

i LUCAS[6] b. 19 March 1745/6

References: VR PLYMPTON pp. 94(b. Ebenezer), 95(b. Lucas), 310(both m.). MD 17:5(m.). Plymouth Co. PR 17:166; 19:412-3(Ebenezer Dunham). PLYMOUTH VR p. 153(m.).

991 PRISCILLA LUCAS[5] (William[4], Patience[3] Warren, Joseph[2], Richard[1]) b. Plymouth 19 April 1727; living 8 April 1777.

She m. Plympton 7 Dec. 1762 ELEAZER ROBBINS, b. Plympton 9 June 1724; d. there 19 Oct. 1776 in 52nd yr.; son of Jeduthan and Rebecca (Crocker) Robbins, a descendant of Pilgrim John Howland. He m. (1) Plympton 7 May 1747 Rebecca Jackson by whom he had Rebecca, Elizabeth, Sarah, Eleazer, Jemima, Mary and Consider.

On 6 Jan. 1777 Eleazer Robbins of Plimpton, yeoman, was appointed administrator of the estate of Eleazer Robbins dec.

On 8 April 1777 a division was ordered with 1/3 to widow Priscilla Robbins and 2/3 divided between Eleazer Robbins, eldest son; sons Consider, Silvanus and Seth; dau. Rebecca Fuller, wife of John Fuller; dau. Sarah Sears, wife of Willard Sears; dau. Jemima Lucas, wife of Samuel Lucas; dau. Mary Lucas, wife of Abijah Lucas and dau. Mary Robbins and dau. Elizabeth Robbins. The division was completed 18 April 1793.

On 2 June 1777 Isaac Jackson was appointed guardian of Seth Robbins, aged 7 years. On the same day, Ebenezer Doten was named guardian of Elizabeth Robbins, aged 10 years. On the same date Isaac Jackson of Plymouth was named guardian of Sylvanus Robbins, a minor aged 13 years, son of Eleazer Robbins. On 6 April 1785 Seth Robbins, minor above the age of 14 years, son of Eleazer Robbins late of Plympton, yeoman, named John Fuller of Kingston his guardian.

Children (ROBBINS) b. Plympton*:

i JAMES[6] b. 19 Aug. 1763; d.y.
ii BENJAMIN b. 17 July 1765; d.y.
iii ELIZABETH b. 27 Feb. 1767
iv SETH b. 12 May 1769
v SYLVANUS

References: VR CARVER p. 166(d. Eleazer). VR PLYMPTON pp. 173(b. ch.), 378(both m. Eleazer). Plymouth Co. PR 23:119; 24:308-13; 33:325(Eleazer Robbins); 22:121-2(gdn. Seth); 22:122(gdn. Elizabeth); #17094(gdn. Sylvanus); 26:423 (Seth's 2nd gdn.).

*VR PLYMPTON calls mother "Elizabeth".

992 JOSEPH LUCAS[5] (William[4], Patience[3] Warren, Joseph[2], Richard[1]) b. Plymouth 12 June 1729; living 7 June 1810 (ack. deed).

He m. Kingston 8 March 1753 MARY RICKARD, b. Kingston 4 Aug. 173-; d. Carver 26 May 1778 in 44th yr.; dau. of Giles and Mary (Eddy) Rickard, a descendant of Pilgrim Francis Eaton.

Joseph Lucas served as a Pvt. during the Rev. War.

On 30 May 1777 Joseph Lucas of Plymouth, yeoman, sold land in Plympton to son Benjamin Lucas Jr. of Plymouth, laborer. On 21 Feb. 1780 he sold more land to son Benjamin Lucas which had come to him from his father William Lucas.

On 4 May 1779 Joseph Lucas of Plymouth sold one-eighth part of the sawmill to John Lucas of Plimpton.

On 13 Dec. 1800 Joseph Lucas of Plymouth, yeoman, sold all his homestead to Ansel Lucas of Plymouth, yeoman.

In May 1809, ack. 7 June 1810, Joseph Lucas of Plymouth, yeoman, sold Lazarus Lucas 9 acres at Swan Hole. On the same date Lazarus Lucas agreed to provide for his father Joseph Lucas until he died.

Children (LUCAS) b. Plymouth:

i BENJAMIN[6] b. 15 March 1755
ii PHEBE b. 24 Feb. 1757
iii LOVISA b. 8 July 1759
iv ELNATHAN b. 1 March 1762
v ANSELL b. 15 April 1764
vi MOLLE b. 18 April 1766
vii LAZARUS

References: VR CARVER p. 158(d. Mary). VR KINGSTON pp. 120(b. Mary), 251(m.). Plymouth Co. LR 58:269; 60:76; 61:41; 90:28; 145:174(Joseph Lucas). PLYMOUTH VR pp. 211(b. 1st 2 ch.), 212(b. ch. iii thru vi). MF 9:134-5. DAR PATRIOT INDEX p. 428.

NOTE: DOTY GEN and MF 11:1:144 gives them a youngest son Lazarus.

993 BENJAMIN LUCAS[5] (William[4], Patience[3] Warren, Joseph[2], Richard[1]) b. Plymouth 21 June 1731; living 15 March 1792 (deed).

He m. Plympton 3 April 1755 LYDIA CROCKER, b. Middleboro 28 Sept. 1731; dau. of Theophilas and Lydia (Eddy) Crocker.

On 15 March 1792 Theophelus Crocker of Shutesbury, yeoman, and Benjamin Lucas of Plymouth sold land in Carver which had been held in partnership with Abel Crocker and their father Theophilus Crocker dec. to Isaiah Tilson.

No Plymouth Co. PR for Benjamin Lucas.

Children (LUCAS) b. Plymouth:

i BELA[6] b. 3 Feb. 1757
ii ISAAC b. 6 Jan. 1759
iii ABIGAIL b. 8 March 1761
iv EZRA b. 19 May 1763
v LUCY b. 24 March 1765
vi LYDIA b. 24 July 1767
vii NAOMI b. 2 June 1770

References: VR PLYMPTON p. 345(m.). MD 16:14(b. Lydia); 19:6 (b. ch.). PLYMOUTH VR p. 189(b. ch.). Plymouth Co. LR 77:82(Theo. Crocker, etc.). MIDDLEBORO VR 1:79(b. Lydia).

994 MEHITABLE LUCAS[5] (William[4], Patience[3] Warren, Joseph[2], Richard[1]) b. Plymouth 24 Feb. 1737/8.

She prob. m. Plympton 27 March 1766 ELKANAH LUCAS, son of Elisha and Margaret (Shaw) Lucas.

On 17 Oct. 1780 Elkanah Lucas of Plympton, yeoman, sold land in Plympton to John Richard which had belonged to his father Elisha Lucas, late of Plympton, dec. Mehitable gave up her right to dower.

No Plymouth Co. PR for Elkanah Lucas.

References: VR PLYMPTON p. 345(m.; m. his parents). MD 28:86 (int.). PLYMOUTH VR p. 254(int.). Plymouth Co. LR 60:96(Elkanah Lucas).

995 SUSANNA HARLOW[5] (Patience Lucas[4], Patience[3] Warren, Joseph[2], Richard[1]) b. ca. 1724; d. Plympton 9 Jan. 1798 in 75th yr.

She m. Plympton 22 Nov. 1744 NOAH STURTEVANT, b. Plympton 7 Oct. 1717; d. there 1 Jan. 1792 ae 74y 2m 13d; son of Nehemiah and Ruth (Samson) Sturtevant.

On 28 March 1785 Noah Sturtevant of Plympton, yeoman, sold land in Plympton to Elijah Bisbee Jr. Susanna gave up her right to dower.

No Plymouth Co. PR for Noah or Susanna Sturtevant or later LR.

Children (STURTEVANT) b. Plympton:

i ANNA[6] b. 6 March 1745; d. Plympton 23 March 1823; unm.
ii ABIAH b. 2 Sept. 1747; d. 1 May 1756 ae 8y 7m 18d
iii NEHEMIAH b. 19 Sept. 1749
iv NATHANIEL b. 8 March 1752
v LYDIA b. 4 June 1756; d. 7 March or 4 May 1757 ae 9m 17d
vi NOAH b. 4 July 1758
vii SUSANNAH b. 29 Aug. 1760
viii LYDIA (in VR without birth date)
ix ICHABOD (in VR without birth date)

References: VR PLYMPTON pp. 202-7(b. ch.), 206(b. Noah), 405(m.), 522-4(deaths). Plymouth Co. LR 64:45(Noah Sturtevant). HARLOW GEN p. 222.

996 NATHANIEL HARLOW[5] (Patience Lucas[4], Patience[3] Warren, Joseph[2], Richard[1]) b. Plympton 15 March 1726; d. there 9 Aug. 1795 ae 69y 10m 13d.

He m. ca. 1754 SARAH BONNEY, b. Plympton 5 April 1731; d. Halifax 12 April 1819 ae 89y 11mo 27d; dau. of Isaac and Mary (Horrell) Bonney. She m. (2) Plympton 2 Oct. 1806 Ephraim Soule.

The will of Nathaniel Harlow of Plympton, yeoman, dated 5 Aug. 1795, proved 2 Nov. 1795, names wife Sarah; sons Nathaniel and Levi; daus. Patience Harlow and Sarah Shurtleff.

Children (HARLOW) b. Plympton:

i PATIENCE[6] b. 21 July 1755; d. Plympton 27 Jan. 1830 ae 74y 6m 6d; unm.
ii NATHANIEL b. 6 Oct. 1758
iii LEVI b. 6 April 1762
iv SARAH b. 17 July 1764

References: VR PLYMPTON pp. 25(b. Sarah), 113-4(b. ch.), 396 (her 2nd m.), 483(d. Nathaniel), 519(d. Sarah). Plymouth Co. PR 35:331(Nathaniel Harlow). MF 3:164.

997 SARAH BRADFORD[5] (Elizabeth Finney[4], Elizabeth[3] Warren, Joseph[2], Richard[1]) b. Plymouth 15 Dec. 1718; d. there 4 April 1794.

She m. Plymouth 23 Jan. 1738/9 ZEPHANIAH HOLMES, b. Plymouth 16 Jan. 1712/3; d. there 24 March 1774; son of Nathaniel and Joanna (Clark) Holmes.

On 27 Dec. 1739 Zephaniah Holmes of Plymouth, cordwainer, and wife Sarah sold to John Adams land in Kingston from the estate of her father William Bradford.

No Plymouth Co. PR for Zephaniah Holmes.

Children (HOLMES) b. Plymouth:

i BRADFORD[6] b. 9 Oct. 1739; d. 14 May 1740
ii ZEPHANIAH b. 30 July 1741
iii SARAH b. 23 Dec. 1743
iv LUCY b. 13 June 1747
v DEBORAH b. 8 April 1750

References: MD 2:80(b. Zephaniah); 14:158(m.); 15:162-3(b. ch.). PLYMOUTH CH RECS 1:403(d. Zephaniah), 422(d. Sarah). Plymouth Co. LR 33:74(Zephaniah Holmes). PLYMOUTH VR pp. 19(b. Zephaniah), 101(m.), 126(b.&d. Bradford), 127(b. last 4 ch.).

998 JERUSHA BRADFORD[5] (Elizabeth Finney[4], Elizabeth[3] Warren, Joseph[2], Richard[1]) b. Plymouth 20 Dec. 1722; d. Middleboro 23 April 1820 in 98th yr.

She m. (1) Plymouth 16 April 1741 EDWARD SPARROW; d. at sea bet. 20 June 1744 and 5 June 1745.

On 14 Nov. 1743 Edward Sparrow of Plymouth, mariner, and wife Jerusha sold to Thomas Adams land received from her father William Bradford.

On 5 June 1745 Jerusha Sparrow of Plymouth, widow of Edward late of Plymouth dec., gave her bond as administratrix of his estate. On 27 April 1747 Jerusha Carver, late Jerusha Sparrow, reported that the estate was insolvent.

She m. (2) Plymouth 22 Jan. 1746/7 JOSIAH CARVER, b. Plymouth 25 Sept. 1724; d. Middleboro 5 April 1799 aged 74y 7m 17d; son of Josiah and Dorothy (Coole) Carver.

The will of Josiah Carver of Middleboro dated 11 Feb. 1783, probated 2 May 1799, names wife Jerusha and appoints son-in-law [step-son] Edward Sparrow executor.

Child (SPARROW) b. Plymouth:

i EDWARD[6] b. 2 April 1745

References: MD 12:142(d. Jerusha); 13:169(b. Edward), 173 (Josiah); 16:254(1st m.); 17:5(2nd m.); 25:26-7(deed). MIDDLEBORO DEATHS p. 34 (Carver deaths). PLYMOUTH VR pp. 73(b. son Edward), 78(b. Josiah), 150(1st m.), 154(2nd m.). Plymouth Co. PR 9:46; 10:389(Edward Sparrow); 37:35 (Josiah Carver). Plymouth Co. LR 36:77(Edward Sparrow).

999 JOSIAH BRADFORD[5] (Elizabeth Finney[4], Elizabeth[3] Warren, Joseph[2], Richard[1]) b. Plymouth 29 March prob. 1724; d. there 26 April 1777.

He m. Plymouth 6 Nov. 1746 HANNAH RIDER, b. Plymouth 26 Nov. 1726; d. there 19 May 1790; dau. of Samuel and Mary (Sylvester) Rider, a descendant of Pilgrim Richard Warren (see #284iii)

On 10 Jan. 1757 a Josiah Bradford and family were warned from Middleboro.

On 30 Jan. 1797 Josiah Bradford, Samuel Bradford, Charles Bradford, Zepheniah Bradford, Ruth Bradford widow of William, Hannah Bradford, Lois Bradford, and Betsey Bradford, spinsters, all of Plymouth, and Thomas Perkins and wife Mercy of Halifax sold to Joshua Wright and Joseph Samson land that their grandmother Elizabeth Bradford deeded to their father Josiah Bradford.

No Plymouth Co. PR for Josiah Bradford.

Children (BRADFORD) b. Plymouth :

i WILLIAM[6] b. 30 Oct. 1749
ii HANNAH b. 9 July 1751
iii JOSIAH b. 7 Feb. 1754
iv SAMUEL
v CHARLES bp. 29 Aug. 1756
vi ZEPHANIAH
vii BETSEY
viii LOIS
ix MERCY

References: MD 3:121(b. 1st 3 ch.); 15:38(b. Hannah); 17:5 (m.); 134(int.). BRADFORD DESC p. 55. PLYMOUTH CO CT RECS 3:75. PLYMOUTH CH RECS 1:407(d. Josiah), 417(d. Hannah), 451(bp. Charles). PLYMOUTH VR pp. 30(b. 1st 5 ch.), 109(b. Hannah), 154 (m.). Plymouth Co. LR 82:40(Josiah Bradford, etc.).

1000 MERCY BRADFORD[5] (Elizabeth Finney[4], Elizabeth[3] Warren, Joseph[2], Richard[1]) b. Kingston 17 Jan. 1729; d. Plymouth 4 July 1762 in 34th yr.

She m. Plymouth 15 Dec. 1746 SAMUEL HARLOW, b. Plymouth 7 Sept. 1726; d. there 17 June 1767 in 41st yr.; son of William and Mercy (Rider) Harlow, a descendant of Pilgrim Richard Warren (see 262vii). He m. (2) Plymouth 24 Sept. 1763 Marcy Morton.

The will of Samuel Harlow of Plymouth, mariner, dated 26 Oct. 1765, codicil 30 Oct. 1765, proved 4 Aug. 1767, names wife Mary, executor, to have all the goods she brought to the marriage; children Samuel, Josiah, George, Mercy and Jerusha Harlow. On 7 July 1772 James Hovey Esq. and wife Mary, executor of the will of Capt. Samuel Harlow late of Plymouth dec., rendered an account on the estate. On 10 April 1787 John Davis of Plymouth was appointed administrator of Samuel's estate, his executrix dying before she could complete the administration.

Children (HARLOW) b. Plymouth:

i SAMUEL[6] b. 22 Oct. 1747
ii MERCY b. 20 Oct. 1749; d. 29 Sept. 1750
iii MERCY b. 10 April 1752
iv JERUSHA b. 13 Feb. 1754
v JOSIAH b. 2 Jan. 1756
vi JAMES b. 23 Nov. 1757; d. 10 Jan. 1788
vii GEORGE b. 18 Jan. 1759

References: MD 7:177-8(b. ch.; d. 2 ch.); 12:87(b. Samuel); 17:5(m.). (PLYMOUTH) BURIAL HILL pp. 28(d. dau. Mercy), 36(d. Mercy), 40(d. Samuel). PLYMOUTH VR pp. 43(b. & d. 1st 6 ch.), 44(b. George), 53(b. Samuel), 154(m.), 298(d. Mercy), 299(d. Samuel), 347(his 2nd m.). Plymouth Co. PR 19:511; 21:152; 27:511(Samuel Harlow).

1002 REBECCA FINNEY[5] (Robert[4], Elizabeth[3] Warren, Joseph[2], Richard[1]) bp. Plymouth 27 Sept. 1721.

She m. Plymouth 8 May 1739 DAVID MORTON, b. Plymouth 19 March 1716; son of John and Reliance (Phinney) Morton.

On 27 Feb. 1746/7 David Morton of Plymouth, seafaring man, sold two pieces of land in Plymouth to Mary Morton of Plymouth, wife of Joseph Morton. The land had been laid out to his father John Morton and given to his brother James Morton, dec. Wife Rebecca also signed.

No Plymouth Co. PR for David Morton.

References: MD 5:100(b. David); 16:254(m.). PLYMOUTH VR pp. 42(b. David), 150(m.). Plymouth Co. LR 38:170 (David Morton).

1003 ELIZABETH FINNEY[5] (Robert[4], Elizabeth[3] Warren, Joseph[2], Richard[1]) b. Plymouth 14 July 1724.

She m. Plymouth 13 May 1742 WILLIAM WOOD.

No Plymouth Co. PR or LR for William Wood.

Child (WOOD) b. Plymouth:

i ELIZABETH[6] b. 17 Aug. 1743; d. 3 March 1750/1

References: MD 15:161(b.&d. dau. Eliz.); 16:255(m.). PLYMOUTH VR pp. 125(b.&d. dau. Eliz.), 150(m.).

NOTE: Did she m. (2) Plymouth 31 Oct. 1748 JAMES DONHAM (MD 17:7)?

1004 JERUSHA FINNEY[5] (Robert[4], Elizabeth[3] Warren, Joseph[2], Richard[1]) b. Plymouth 19 April 1728.

She m. Plymouth 4 Jan. 1749/50 ISAAC HARLOW, b. Plymouth 3 Aug. 1725; son of Robert and Susanna (Cole) Harlow, a descendant of Pilgrims Isaac Allerton and Richard Warren.

On 13 May 1792 William Harlow and Isaac Harlow, both of Plymouth, mariners, sold their land in Plymouth to Benjamin Besse. [These are probably the sons.]

No Plymouth Co. PR for Isaac Harlow.

Children (HARLOW) b. Plymouth:

i REBECKAH[6] b. 21 Oct. 1750; d.y.
ii ISAAC b. 9 March 1753; d.y.
iii BETTE b. 18 Jan. 1755
iv WILLIAM b. 3 May 1757
v JERUSHA b. 8 Aug. 1759
vi REBECKAH b. 4 Jan. 1762
vii DEBORAH b. 3 Nov. 1764
viii LEMUEL b. 30 Nov. 1768

References: MD 2:79(b. ch.); 13:165(b. Isaac); 16:169(m.). PLYMOUTH VR pp. 18(b. ch.), 69(b. Isaac), 146(m.). Plymouth Co. LR 74:180(William & Isaac Harlow).

1005 ELIZABETH MARSHALL[5] (Priscilla Finney[4], Elizabeth[3] Warren, Joseph[2], Richard[1]) b. Plymouth 2 Jan. 1717/8.

She m. (1) Plymouth 27 May 1736 BENJAMIN CARTEE (or CARTER).

She m. (2) Pembroke 29 Dec. 1742 NATHANIEL CROADE (both were "of Plymouth").

No Plymouth Co. PR or LR for Benjamin Carter or Cartee.

Child (CARTEE) b. Plymouth:

i BENJAMIN[6] b. 22 Jan. 1739/40

Children (CROADE) b. Plymouth:

ii ELIZABETH b. 31 May 1743; d. 17 Sept. 1744
iii NATHANIEL b. 5 Sept. 1745

References: MD 13:111(b. Benj.); 14:156(m.). PLYMOUTH VR pp. 63(b. son Benj.), 95(1st m.), 99(m.), 131(b. Croade ch.) VR PEMBROKE p. 259(2nd m.).

1006 SAMUEL MARSHALL[5] (Priscilla Finney[4], Elizabeth[3] Warren, Joseph[2], Richard[1]) b. Plymouth 9 March 1719; d. there 28 Dec. 1800.

He m. Plymouth 10 Oct. 1748 SUSANNAH BARTLETT, b. Plymouth 1 March 1727/8; living 2 Aug. 1791 (ack. deed); dau. of Nathaniel and Abigail (Clark) Bartlett, a descendant of Pilgrims John Alden and Richard Warren (see #331 ii).

On [blank] Feb. 1791 Samuel Marshall of Plymouth, husbandman, sold to son Bartlett Marshall of Plymouth, mariner, his right to land in Plymouth which had belonged to his grandfather Mr. Josiah Finney which he had quitclaimed to his mother Priscilla Finney and her two sisters Elizabeth Bradford and Phebe Barnes, dec. and by his uncles Josiah Finney and John Finney. Susannah Marshall, wife of Samuel Marshall, gave up her right to dower. Ack. by both 2 Aug. 1791.

No Plymouth Co. PR for Samuel Marshall.

Children (MARSHALL) b. Plymouth:

i SAMUEL[6] bp. 22 July 1750
ii SUSANNA bp. 16 Sept. 1750
iii BARTLETT bp. 4 March 1752
iv PRISCILLA bp. 17 Aug. 1755
v BETTY bp. 17 Aug. 1760

References: MD 17:6(m.). PLYMOUTH CH RECS 1:446(bp. Sam., Susanna), 448(bp. Bartlett), 450(bp. Priscilla), 452(bp. Betty); 2:624(d. Samuel). PLYMOUTH VR pp. 79(b. Susanna), 131(b. Croade ch.), 155(m.). Plymouth Co. LR 81:72(Samuel Marshall).

1007 MARY MARSHALL[5] (Priscilla Finney[4], Elizabeth[3] Warren, Joseph[2], Richard[1]) b. Plymouth 28 June 1722; living 21 March 1792.

She m. (1) Plymouth 29 Oct. 1740 LEVI STEPHENS of Boston; b. Truro 27 Sept. 1709; d. bef. 28 July 1751(wife Mary was called widow when son Levi bapt.); son of Richard and Abigail (Treat) Stevens.

She m. (2) Plymouth 18 Oct. 1752 SYLVANUS MORTON, b. Plymouth 24 Feb. 1729/30; d. Liverpool, Queens Co. NS 26 Dec. 1778; son of Thomas and Abigail (Pratt) Morton.

On 21 Jan. 1757 Silvanus Morton of Plymouth, cordwainer, sold to Stephen Samson 100 acres which fell to him from the estate of his father Mr. Thomas Morton; wife Mary also signed. On 16 Aug. 1757 he sold to James Hovey his 1/9th share of his mother's dower interest in his father's land.

Sylvanus and Mary Morton moved to Liverpool NS ca. 1761.

On 21 March 1792 Benajah Collins as administrator of the estate of Silvanus Morton of Liverpool, dec. sold to Simeon Perkins, Esq. of Liverpool, a series of tracts formerly owned by Silvanus Morton, excepting the widow's dower.

On 1 Feb. 1792 Stephen Page sold to Silvanus Morton, James Morton and Dennis Freeman of Liverpool, yeomen, 100 acres in Liverpool; wife Priscilla also signed.

On 20 July 1792 Benajah Collins, as administrator of the estate of Silvanus Morton, filed his account.

No Plymouth Co. PR for Levi Stephens.

Children (STEPHENS) b. Plymouth:

i prob. PRISCILLA[6] b. ca. 1742*
ii prob. MARY b. ca. 1745*
iii HANNAH bp. 10 May 1747
iv LEVI bp. 28 July 1751

Children (MORTON) first 3 b. Plymouth, last b. Liverpool NS:

v ABIGAIL b. 10 June 1753
vi JAMES b. 3 Sept. 1755; d.y.
vii SILVANUS b. 5 July 1760
viii JAMES b. 3 Sept. 1762

References: MD 13:116(b. Sylvanus); 14:159(1st m.); 18:141(2nd m.), 213(b. 1st 2 Morton ch.). NEHGR 129:96(b. Morton ch.). PLYMOUTH CH RECS 1:443(bp. Hannah), 447(bp. Levi). PLYMOUTH VR pp. 69(b. Sylvanus), 102(1st m.), 175(2nd m.), 185(b. Abigail, James). Plymouth Co. LR 44:77; 44:168 (Silvanus Morton). Queen's Co. NS LR 4:72(Benajah Collins); 4:153(Stephen Page). TRURO VR p. 6(b. Levi). THE DIARY OF SIMEON PERKINS, Muriel M. F. Davidson ed., Brampton, Ontario, 1993, p. 8(d. Silvanus). Liverpool NS VR 1:6(b. Abigail, Silvanus, James). Queens Co. NS wills 1:62(Silvanus Morton).

*There are no Stevens/Stephens families in Liverpool NS before 1800. Therefore, it is likely that the Mary Stephens who m. Elijah Minard in Liverpool NS 28 July 1767 (VR 1:37) and the Priscilla Stephens who married Stephen Page in Liverpool 28 Nov. 1766 (VR 1:38) are unrecorded daughters of Levi and Mary (Marshall) Stephens. Note the 1792 deed.

1008 JOHN MARSHALL[5] (Priscilla Finney[4], Elizabeth[3] Warren, Joseph[2], Richard[1]) b. Plymouth Feb. 1725/6.

He m. Plymouth 5 Aug. 1755 JERUSHA (RIDER) WATKINS, bp. Plymouth 2 April 1727; d. there 14 Aug. 1769; dau. of John and Mary (-----) Rider. (See #291) She m. (1) Plymouth 29 July 1746 James Watkins.

No Plymouth Co. PR or LR for John Marshall.

References: MD 17:5(her 1st m.); 25:53(int.). PLYMOUTH CH RECS 1:234(bp. Jerusha), 398(d. Jerusha). TAG 36:195. PLYMOUTH VR pp. 154(her 1st m.), 345(m.).

1009 SARAH FINNEY[5] (John[4], Elizabeth[3] Warren, Joseph[2], Richard[1]) b. Plymouth 19 Nov. 1722; d. there 5 Oct. 1804 ae 86y.

She m. Plymouth 19 May 1742 EPHRAIM HOLMES, b. Plymouth 14 Feb. 1718/9; d. there 11 March 1769 ae 50y; son of Nathaniel and Joanna (Clark) Holmes.

No Plymouth Co. PR or LR for Ephraim or Sarah Holmes.

Children (HOLMES) b. Plymouth:

i ELIZABETH[6] b. 20 June 1743
ii EPHRAIM b. 16 Sept. 1745
iii JOANNA b. 19 Aug. 1748
iv NATHANIEL b. 14 April 1751
v son b. Aug. 1754; d. Aug. 1754
vi SARAH b. 3 May 1756
vii BATHSHEBA b. 19 Sept. 1758; d.y.
viii BATHSHEBA b. 28 Nov. 1763

References: MD 2:81(b. Ephraim); 15:163(b. ch.); 16:255(m.). PLYMOUTH VR pp. 19(b. Ephraim), 127(b. ch.; d. son), 150(m.). PLYMOUTH CH RECS 1:220(d. Ephraim), 234(d. Sarah). MF 12:449-50.

1010 PHEBE FINNEY[5] (John[4], Elizabeth[3] Warren, Joseph[2], Richard[1]) b. Plymouth 8 Feb. 1724/5.

She m. Plymouth 3 Aug. 1738 EDWARD DOTEN, b. Plymouth 7 Oct. 1716; son of Elisha and Hannah (Horton) Doten, a descendant of Pilgrim Edward Doty.

On 10 May 1757 Edward Doty of Plymouth, mariner, and wife Phebe sold their house and lot to Thomas Doty and Perez Tillson.

On 17 Jan. 1769 Edward Doten of Liverpool in Nova Scotia and wife and children Thomas, Lemuel, Phebe and Loes were warned from Plymouth.

No Plymouth Co. PR for Edward Doten.

Children (DOTEN) first 6 b. Plymouth; last 3 b. Nova Scotia:

i ELISHA[6] b. 21 Nov. 1743
ii EDWARD b. 13 Oct. 1745

iii THOMAS b. 6 March 1748
iv JOHN b. 9 Aug. 1750
v LEMUEL b. 7 Aug. 1753
vi JAMES b. 18 Nov. 1757
vii PHEBE b. Liverpool NS 6 Oct. 1761
viii LOIS b. ca. 1764 (based on age at d.) (named in warning)
ix HANNAH b. Nova Scotia 3 Sept. 1767

References: MD 16:254(m.). DOTY GEN pp. 158-9(b. Hannah). NEHGR 126:95(b. Phebe). PLYMOUTH VR pp. 42(b. Edward), 127(b. 1st 6 ch.), 150(m.), 165(int.), 478(d. Lois Robbins). PLYMOUTH CO CT RECS 3:276. Plymouth Co. LR 44:120 (Edward Doty). MF 11:1:57-8.

NOTE: The int. was dated 8 July 1738 (PLYMOUTH VR p. 165) so Phebe was only 13 years old if this is the right identification. In the int. she is called "Mrs."

1011 RUTH FINNEY[5] (John[4], Elizabeth[3] Warren, Joseph[2], Richard[1]) b. Plymouth 1 Oct. 1729; d. there 22 March 1752 in 24th yr.

She m. Plymouth 24 April 1750 JAMES DOTEN, b. Plymouth 27 Aug. 1728; d. there 25 July 1786 in 58th yr.; son of Elisha and Hannah (Horton) Doten, a descendant of Pilgrim Edward Doty. He m. (2) Plymouth 26 April 1753 Bathsheba Delano.

The will of James Doten of Plymouth dated 22 Sept. 1785, proved 7 Aug. 1786, names wife Bathsheba; James Doten the third, son to Stephen Doten; three sons of Stephen Doten's sons; brother Stephen Doten.

No known children.

References: MD 16:169(m.); 19:179-83(will). PLYMOUTH VR pp. 42(b. James), 146 (m.). PLYMOUTH CH REC 1:415(d. James). PLYMOUTH VR pp. 42(b. James), 146(m.), 147(his 2nd m.). (PLYMOUTH) BURIAL HILL p. 29(d. Ruth). Plymouth Co. PR #6589(James Doten).

1012 JOHN FINNEY[5] (John[4], Elizabeth[3] Warren, Joseph[2], Richard[1]) b. Plymouth 18 Oct. 1730; living 6 Dec. 1796 (deed).

He m. Plymouth 15 June 1757 REBECKAH HOLMES, prob. b. Plymouth 25 Oct. 1736; d. after 6 Dec. 1796 (deed); dau. of Jabez and Sarah (Clark) Holmes.

In a deed ack. 6 Dec. 1796 John Finney of Plymouth, yeoman, and wife Rebecca sold to Lemuel Lynch land in Plymouth which had come to Rebecca from her father Jabez Holmes.

No Plymouth Co. PR for John Finney.

Children (FINNEY) b. Plymouth:

i RUTH[6] b. 2 Feb. 1757
ii SARAH b. 19 Feb. 1758
iii ELIZABETH b. 22 Feb. 1761
iv JAMES b. 15 Aug. 1764
v JOHN b. 3 Sept. 1766

References: PLYMOUTH VR pp. 120(b. Rebecca), 220(b. ch.), 349(m.). MD 15:113(b. Rebecca); 22:106(b. ch.). Plymouth Co. LR 81:109(John Finney).

1013 JOSIAH FINNEY[5] (John[4], Elizabeth[3] Warren, Joseph[2], Richard[1]) b. Plymouth 17 Jan. 1739/40; living 13 March 1786.

He m. Plymouth 28 April 1763 ALICE BARNES, b. Plymouth 17 June 1744; living 13 March 1786; dau. of Lemuel and Lydia (Barnes) Barnes, a descendant of Pilgrim Richard Warren (see #322v).

On 29 Sept. 1796 Josiah Finney of Plymouth, mariner, sold land in Plymouth that had been assigned to his wife Else [Alice] in the division of the estate of "his father" Lemuel Barnes, dec. and grandfather William Barnes dec. to Thomas Jackson.

No Plymouth Co. PR for Josiah Finney.

Children (FINNEY):

i OLLEY[6] (or ALICE) b. 2 Feb. 1764
ii SUSANNAH
iii MARY
iv DANIEL

References: PLYMOUTH CH RECS 1:493(m.). MD 21:24(b. Olley); 26:42(int.). PLYMOUTH VR pp. 126(b. Alice), 206(b. Olley), 355(m.). Plymouth Co. LR 81:120-1(Josiah Finney). FINNEY-PHINNEY p. 16(list of ch.).

1014 ROBERT FINNEY[5] (John[4], Elizabeth[3] Warren, Joseph[2], Richard[1]) b. Plymouth 27 Sept. 1741; d. 15 Oct. 1781.

He m. Plymouth 12 Dec. 1765 LYDIA CLARK, b. Plymouth 23 June 1744; dau. of William and Experience (Doten) Clark; a descendant of Pilgrim Edward Doty.

Robert Finney was a Capt. in the Rev. War.

No Plymouth Co. PR for Robert Finney.

Children (FINNEY) b. Plymouth:

i LYDIA[6]
ii ROBERT b. 17 June 1768
iii CLARK

iv GEORGE
v JOSIAH
vi ELKANAH
vii EXPERIENCE

References: FINNEY-PHINNEY p. 16(list of ch.). MD 15:163(b. Lydia); 24:19(b. ch.). DOTY GEN p. 163. PLYMOUTH VR pp. 128(b. Lydia), 244(b. ch., but only date for Robert), 356(m.). MF 11:1:150-1. DAR PATRIOT INDEX p. 533(d. Robert).

1015 EZRA FINNEY[5] (John[4], Elizabeth[3] Warren, Joseph[2], Richard[1]) b. Plymouth 26 Nov. 1743; lost at sea 1787 ae 37 yrs.

He m. Plymouth 12 Jan. 1769 HANNAH LUCE, b. Plymouth 28 Aug. 1751; d. there 17 June 1814 ae 64 yrs.; dau. of Seth and Hannah (Morton) Luce. She m. (2) Plymouth 19 Dec. 1793 Neaman Holbrook.

No Plymouth Co. PR for Ezra Finney.

Children (FINNEY):

i HANNAH[6] b. Plymouth 8 Oct. 1769
ii LYDIA
iii ELIZABETH
iv EZRA b. 1776
v EPHRAIM
vi SETH b. 1780

References: FINNEY-PHINNEY pp. 16-7(list of children). MD 22:184(b. dau. Hannah). (PLYMOUTH) BURIAL HILL p. 58(d. Ezra, Hannah). PLYMOUTH CH REC 2:506(her 2nd m.), 661(d. Hannah). PLYMOUTH VR pp. 29(b. Hannah), 229(b. dau. Hannah), 352(m.), 370(her 2nd m.).

1016 SILVANUS FINNEY[5] (John[4], Elizabeth[3] Warren, Joseph[2], Richard[1]) b. Plymouth 10 Jan. 1745/6.

He m. Plymouth 1 Dec. 1768 MARY MORTON, b. Plymouth 5 April 1746; dau. of Josiah and Melatiah (Phinney) Morton.

No Plymouth Co. PR for Silvanus Finney.

Children (FINNEY):

i SOLOMON[6] b. 1773
ii SILVANUS
iii CALEB b. ca. 1774 (based on age at d.)

References: PLYMOUTH VR pp. 47(b. Mary), 352(m.), 626(d. Caleb). FINNEY-PHINNEY p. 17(list of children). MD 7:210(b. Mary).

1017 EPHRAIM FINNEY[5] (John[4], Elizabeth[3] Warren, Joseph[2], Richard[1]) b. Plymouth 1 Aug. 1748; d. Chesterfield 6 April 1814.

He m. Plymouth 16 June 1776 MARY BARTLETT, d. Chesterfield 26 March 1814; dau. of Samuel and Betsey (Moore) Bartlett, a descendant of Pilgrims John Alden, William Brewster and Richard Warren.

On 4 March 1777 Benjamin Bryant of Chesterfield sold Lot No. 63, 1st Division in Chesterfield to Ephraim Finney of Chesterfield, yeoman.

Ephraim Finney was 1-0-5 in the 1790 census of Chesterfield.

On 3 Nov. 1792 Ephraim Finney of Chesterfield, Hampshire Co. sold to Joseph Bartlett 4th of Plymouth 14 acres left to Ephraim's wife Mary by her father Samuel Bartlett Jr. of Plymouth, dec.

No Hampshire Co. PR for Ephraim Finney.

Children (FINNEY) b. Chesterfield:

i MARY[6] b. 28 April 1777
ii ELIZABETH b. 6 April 1779; prob. d.y.
iii HANNAH b. 13 Sept. 1781
iv SUSANNAH b. 31 Aug. 1786
v SARAH b. 16 Feb. 1789
vi EPHRAIM b. 14 July 1792

References: MD 27:177(int.). PLYMOUTH CH RECS 2:498(m.). PLYMOUTH VR p. 361(m.). Chesterfield VR 2:12(b. Susannah), 25(b. 1st 3 ch.); 3:36(deaths). HISTORY AND GENEALOGY OF THE FAMILIES OF CHESTERFIELD, MASS. 1762-1962, Northampton MA 1962, p. 160(births of ch.). Plymouth Co. LR 106:187(Ephraim Finney). Hampshire Co. LR 37:140(Benjamin Bryant).

1018 WILLIAM FINNEY[5] (John[4], Elizabeth[3] Warren, Joseph[2], Richard[1]) b. Plymouth 16 Nov. 1750.

He m. Plymouth 21 Oct. 1773 ELIZABETH SHERMAN, b. Marshfield 14 Nov. 1758; dau. of John and Elizabeth (Dingley) Sherman.

William Finney was a Corp. in the Rev. War.

No Plymouth Co. PR for William Finney.

Children (FINNEY):

i ELIZABETH[6]
ii SALLY
iii LEWIS b. ca. 1779 (based on age at d.)
iv RUTH b. ca. 1783
v WILLIAM b. 23 May 1784

References: MD 27:46(int.). MARSHFIELD VR p. 71(b. Elizabeth). FINNEY-PHINNEY p. 17(list of children). PLYMOUTH VR p. 360(m.). MF 11:1:152. DAR PATRIOT INDEX p. 533. (PLYMOUTH) BURIAL HILL p. 259(b. Lewis).

1019 MARGARET BARNES[5] (Phebe Finney[4], Elizabeth[3] Warren, Joseph[2], Richard[1]) b. Plymouth 14 June 1732; d. bef. 2 June 1808.

She m. Plymouth 12 April 1753 ZACHEUS BARTLETT, b. Plymouth 15 Jan. 1724/5; d. there 6 March 1800; son of Joseph and Elizabeth (Bartlett) Bartlett, a descendant of Pilgrims John Alden and Richard Warren.

Zacheus Bartlett was a Capt. in the Rev. War.

The division of the estate of Zacheus Bartlett, late of Plymouth, dated 12 April 1802, divided the estate between Joseph, Zacheus, George, Isaac and Melatiah Bartlett; Phebe Perry, Elizabeth Nye and Mary Mayhew. The widow's dower was divided 2 June 1808.

Children (BARTLETT) all b. prob. Plymouth:

i PHEBE[6] b. 16 March 1754
ii ELIZABETH b. 21 Oct. 1758
iii JOSEPH
iv ZACHEUS b. 20 Sept. 1765 (g.s.)
v GEORGE
vi ISAAC
vii MELATIAH
viii MARY

References: MD 18:141(m.); 19:8(b. 1st 2 ch.). Plymouth Co. PR 43:361(Zacheus Bartlett). (PLYMOUTH) BURIAL HILL p. 185(d. Zacheus). PLYMOUTH VR pp. 62(b.&d. Zacheus), 175(m.), 192(b. 1st 2 ch.). DAR PATRIOT INDEX p. 41.

1020 NATHANIEL BARNES[5] (Phebe Finney[4], Elizabeth[3] Warren, Joseph[2], Richard[1]) b. Plymouth 18 June 1740; d. there 28 May 1781.

He m. Plymouth 12 June 1766 JERUSHA BLACKMER, b. Plymouth 20 Jan. 1744/5; d. there 14 Sept. 1772; dau. of John and Sarah (Holmes) Blackmer.

On 9 July 1781 Zacheus Bartlett and Stephen Churchill of Plymouth were appointed to administer the estate of Nathaniel Barnes, late of Plymouth, housewright.

References: MD 15:40(b. Jerusha). PLYMOUTH CH RECS 1:401(d. Jerusha), 410(d. Nath.). Plymouth Co. PR 27:70; 28:236-7; 29:27(Nathaniel Barnes). PLYMOUTH VR pp. 111(b. Jerusha), 356(m.).

1021 ZACCHEUS BARNES[5] (Phebe Finney[4], Elizabeth[3] Warren, Joseph[2], Richard[1]) b. Plymouth 8 April 1743; living 26 June 1792 (deed).

He m. Plymouth 22 Sept. 1765 HANNAH CURTIS, b. Plymouth 24 April 1747; d. there 7 Feb. 1776; dau. of Jacob and Fear (Dunham) Curtis.

On 26 June 1792 Zaccheus Barnes of Plymouth, farmer, sold a lot of land in Plymouth that had been laid out to his grandfather Josiah Finney of Plymouth dec. to Nathaniel Goodwin.

No Plymouth Co. PR for Zaccheus Barnes or later LR.

Children (BARNES) b. Plymouth:

i PHEBE[6] b. 14 March 1766
ii HANNAH b. 10 Jan. 1768
iii LYDIA b. 12 March 1771
iv JONATHAN (in VR without date)
v JERUSHA (in VR without date)

References: MD 22:107(b. ch.). PLYMOUTH CH RECS 1:405(d. Hannah); 2:494(m.). Plymouth Co. LR 73:99(Zaccheus Barnes). PLYMOUTH VR p. 221(b. ch.; no dates given for last two). (PLYMOUTH) ANC LANDMARKS 2:13(names of ch.).

1023 JOSIAH FINNEY[5] (Joshua[4], Elizabeth[3] Warren, Joseph[2], Richard[1]) bp. Plymouth 11 April 1736.

Did he m. Plymouth 28 April 1763 ALICE BARNES? (see #1013). He is called Jr. in the marriage record, so that would imply it was #1013 as he is younger.

References: PLYMOUTH VR p. 355(m.).

1024 NATHANIEL FINNEY[5] (Joshua[4], Elizabeth[3] Warren, Joseph[2], Richard[1]) bp. Plymouth 11 April 1736.

Did he marry Falmouth 18 Dec. 1757 ABIGAIL HATCH? Or did he m. Sandwich 13 Jan. 1763 THANKFUL TUPPER?

References: VR FALMOUTH p. 160(m.). SANDWICH VR 1:208.

1026 WILLIAM RIDER[5] (Abigail[4] Warren, Benjamin[3], Joseph[2], Richard[1]) b. Plymouth 11 Oct. 1723; d. there 29 June 1772 in 49th yr.

On 6 May 1779 Benjamin Ryder the 3rd of Plymouth, cordwainer, was appointed to administer the estate of William Ryder, late of Plymouth, cordwainer. On 15 April 1782 the court ordered the estate to be divided between brothers Joseph Ryder and Benjamin Ryder and sister Abigail Holmes, wife of Lemuel Holmes.

No known children.

References: (PLYMOUTH) BURIAL HILL p. 43(d. Wm.). Plymouth Co. PR 21:296; 23:11; 30:328 (William Rider).

1027 ABIGAIL RIDER^{5} (Abigail^{4} Warren, Benjamin^{3}, Joseph^{2}, Richard^{1}) b. Plymouth 18 April 1726; living 15 April 1782 (div. of brother William's estate).

She m. Plymouth 28 April 1746 LEMUEL HOLMES, b. Plymouth 29 Oct. 1719; d. there 27 Dec. 1784; son of Eleazer and Hannah (Sylvester) Holmes, a descendant of Pilgrim Richard Warren (see #309 v).

No Plymouth Co. PR for Lemuel Holmes.

Children (HOLMES) b. Plymouth:

i MARTHA^{6} bp. 3 Sept. 1769
ii PRISCILLA bp. 3 Sept. 1769
iii JOSEPH bp. 3 Sept. 1769
iv LYDIA bp. 3 Sept. 1769

References: MD 12:12(b. Lemuel); 17:5(m.). NGSQ 74:216-7. PLYMOUTH CH RECS 1:413(d. Lemuel), 458(bp. ch.). PLYMOUTH VR pp. 49(b. Lemuel), 154(m.).

1028 JOSEPH RIDER^{5} (Abigail^{4} Warren, Benjamin^{3}, Joseph^{2}, Richard^{1}) b. Plymouth 15 June 1729; d. there 19 March 1794 ae 65 yrs.

He m. (1) Plymouth 13 July 1752 THANKFUL POLAND, b. Plymouth 9 Oct. 1725; d. there 23 Oct. 1789; dau. of John and Lidia (Tilson) Poland.

He m. (2) before 14 May 1791 (deed) MARTHA -----, living 27 April 1797.

On 14 May 1791 Joseph Rider and wife Martha sold 5 acres which he had received in the division of the estate of his brother William Rider to Seth Harlow.

On 11 Sept. 1794 Joseph Allerton and William Goodwin were appointed to administer the estate of Joseph Rider, late of Plymouth, gentleman. The inventory was taken in May 1795 and on 27 April 1797 the court set off to Martha Rider, widow of Joseph Rider, her dower.

Children (RIDER) b. Plymouth by 1st wife:

i SAMUEL^{6} b. 28 Nov. 1752; d. 19 Dec. 1752
ii SAMUEL b. 25 June 1754
iii dau. b. & d. 18 July 1757
iv HANNAH b. 17 Aug. 1760

References: MD 3:122(b. Thankful); 18:141(m.). PLYMOUTH CH RECS 1:417(d. Thankful). (PLYMOUTH) BURIAL HILL p. 70(d. Joseph). Plymouth Co. PR 34:32; 35:294; 36:164(Joseph Rider). PLYMOUTH VR pp. 31(b. Thankful), 146(1st m.), 190(b. 4 ch.; d. Samuel). Plymouth Co. LR 71:88(Joseph Rider).

1029 BENJAMIN RIDER[5] (Abigail[4] Warren, Benjamin[3], Joseph[2], Richard[1]) b. Plymouth 8 Sept. 1733; d. there 12 Oct. 1804 ae 71 yrs.

He m. Plymouth 27 Aug. 1775 PATIENCE HOWLAND, b. Plymouth 23 Sept. 1749; d. there 18 June 1791 in 42nd yr.; dau. of John and Patience (Spooner) Howland, a descendant of Pilgrim John Howland.

He was called Major Benjamin Ryder when the births of his children were recorded.

On 18 Dec. 1804 Rossiter Cotton and George Sampson were appointed to administer the estate of Benjamin Rider of Plymouth, gentleman.

Children (RIDER) b. Plymouth:

i PATIENCE[6] b. 16 Feb. 1777
ii ABIGAIL WARREN b. 2 June 1779

References: MD 12:224(b. Patience); 23:8(b. ch.); 27:177(m.). (PLYMOUTH) BURIAL HILL pp. 65(d. Patience), 103(d. Benj.). Plymouth Co. PR 34:388; 40:359. PLYMOUTH VR pp. 55(b. Patience), 231(b. ch.), 361(m.).

1030 HANNAH FAUNCE[5] (Hannah[4] Warren, Benjamin[3], Joseph[2], Richard[1]) b. Plymouth 2 Nov. 1725; d. aft. 23 May 1797.

She m. Plymouth 20 Sept. 1753 BENJAMIN MORTON, b. Plymouth 10 Oct. 1728; d. bef. 9 Jan. 1796 (adm.); son of Samuel and Lydia (Bartlett) Morton, a descendant of Pilgrims John Alden and Richard Warren (see #248iii).

On 19 April 1755 Benjamin Morton of Plymouth, bricklayer, and wife Hannah, sold part of the homestead "of our father Mr. Eleazer Faunce, dec."

On 30 Jan. 1756 Benjamin Morton, bricklayer of Plymouth, sold to Nathaniel Morton of Plymouth, joiner, land with dwelling "between my land and the land that was my father Samuel Morton's dec.". Wife Hannah gave up her dower.

On 9 Jan. 1796 Benjamin Morton of Plymouth was appointed administrator of the estate of Benjamin Morton of Rochester, mason. On 23 May 1797 the dower was set off to Hannah Morton, widow of Benjamin Morton, late of Rochester, mason.

Children (MORTON) b. Plymouth:

i LYDIA[6] b. 1 March 1754

ii HANNAH b. 15 Aug. 1755; d. 16 Oct. 1756
iii HANNAH b. 10 Jan. 1758
iv BARNABAS b. 4 Feb. 1759; d. 28 Aug. 1765
v BENJAMIN b. 28 Feb. 1763
vi BARTLETT b. 2 Oct. 1766

References: MD 12:11(b. 1st 4 ch.), 12(b. last 2 ch.). Plymouth Co. LR 44:30; 46:64(Benj. Morton). Plymouth Co. PR 34:60; 36:179(Benj. Morton). TAG 37:147. PLYMOUTH VR pp. 48(b. ch.), 78(b. Benjamin), 175(m.). (PLYMOUTH) BURIAL HILL pp. 32(d. dau. Hannah), 38(d. Barnabas).

1031 PATIENCE FAUNCE[5] (Hannah[4] Warren, Benjamin[3], Joseph[2], Richard[1]) b. Plymouth 22 Jan. 1729/30; d. there 1 Feb. 1767 ae 38 yrs.

She m. Plymouth 16 Nov. 1747 JOSIAH JOHNSON, b. Marshfield 17 Oct. 1723; son of Josiah and Abigail (Phillips) Johnson. He m. (2) Plympton 29 Oct. 1767 Bathsheba (Faunce) Barrows.

Children (JOHNSON) b. Plymouth:

i JOSIAH[6] b. 30 Sept. 1748
ii PATIENCE b. 10 March 1752
iii ELEAZER b. 3 Dec. 1755

References: MD 5:53(b. ch.); 17:5(m.). VR PLYMPTON p. 337(2nd m.). (PLYMOUTH) BURIAL HILL p. 39(d. Patience). MARSHFIELD VR p. 85(b. Josiah). PLYMOUTH VR pp. 37(b. ch.), 155(m.).

1032 MARY FAUNCE[5] (Hannah[4] Warren, Benjamin[3], Joseph[2], Richard[1]) b. Plymouth 2 June 1731; living 7 May 1795.

She m. Plymouth 16 Nov. 1756 PELEG FAUNCE, b. Plymouth 20 Nov. 1730; d. there 16 June 1795; son of Thomas and Lydia (Barnaby) Faunce, a descendant of Pilgrim Richard Warren (#376 vi).

All the children, except Benjamin, were baptized at Plymouth 18 Dec. 1774.

On 7 May 1795 Peleg Faunce of Plymouth, cordwainer, and wife Mary sold land in Plymouth that had been laid out to Thomas Faunce to Rossiter Cotton.

No Plymouth Co. PR for Peleg Faunce.

Children (FAUNCE) b. Plymouth:

i ELEAZER[6] b. 16 Dec. 1757
ii PELEG b. 2 Dec. 1759
iii JOSEPH b. 4 April 1763
iv BENJAMIN (or BARNABY) b. 18 Aug. 1765

v HANNAH
vi ABIGAIL b. 16 Sept. 1770

References: MD 19:92(b. 1st 4 ch.); 25:189(int.). PLYMOUTH VR pp. 46(b. Peleg), 196(b. 1st 4 ch.), 346(m.). PLYMOUTH CH RECS 1:423(d. Peleg), 461(bp. ch.). FAUNCE DESC pp. 40-1. Plymouth Co. LR 85:75(Peleg Faunce).

1033 ABIGAIL FAUNCE[5] (Hannah[4] Warren, Benjamin[3], Joseph[2], Richard[1]) b. Plymouth 22 Feb. 1734/5; d. there 27 Oct. 1780.

She m. Plymouth 16 July 1769 AMOS DUNHAM, b. Plymouth 21 Sept. 1716; d. there 14 Sept. 1782; son of Josiah and Ruth (Kempton) Dunham. He m. (1) Plymouth 1 April 1741 Abigail Hill. He m. (2) Plymouth 13 Feb. 1743/4 Ann McEvoy by whom he had Robert, Mary, Anne, Amos, Ruth, Mary, Josiah, Catherine and Abigail.

On 6 Oct. 1780 Amos Dunham and wife Abigail gave their dwelling house to their cousin Peleg Faunce Jr. of Plymouth.

No Plymouth Co. PR for Amos Dunham.

Apparently no children.

References: MD 16:85(d. Abigail). PLYMOUTH CH RECS 1:410(d. Abigail), 411(d. Amos). PLYMOUTH VR pp. 60(b. Amos), 102(his 1st m.), 103(his 2nd m.), 128-9(his ch. by Ann), 358(m.). Plymouth Co. LR 60:95(Amos Dunham).

1034 SARAH[5] WARREN (Nathaniel[4], Benjamin[3], Joseph[2], Richard[1]) b. Plymouth 8 Jan. 1742; d. there 3 March 1823 ae 81.

She m. Plymouth 3 March 1763 SETH HARLOW, b. Plymouth 10 Sept. 1736; d. there 30 June 1802 in 65th yr.; son of William and Mercy (Rider) Harlow, a descendant of Pilgrim Richard Warren (see #262x).

The will of Seth Harlow of Plymouth, housewright, dated 16 June 1802, proved 8 Sept. 1802, names wife Sarah; children Seth Harlow Jr., Benjamin Harlow; Elizabeth Churchill, widow of George; and Mercy Harlow. The division of 18 May 1824 names Seth Harlow, Elizabeth Leonard, Nathaniel Harlow, Sarah Kempton, Mercy Harlow and the heirs of Benjamin Harlow, Benjamin and Betsey; grandchildren Ebenezer Churchill, Elizabeth Churchill, Branch Churchill and Sarah Warren, children of dau. Elizabeth Churchill, widow of George.

Children (HARLOW) b. prob. Plymouth:

i BENJAMIN[6] b. 28 July 1764; d. 17 Oct. 1775 ae 11
ii SETH b. 14 July 1766
iii ELIZABETH b. ca. 1768 (based on age at d.)
iv SARAH b. ca. 1771 (based on age at d.)
v NATHANIEL b. ca. 1773 (based on age at d.)

vi MERCY b. ca. 1777; d. Plymouth 9 Nov. 1837 in 60th yr.; unm.
vii BENJAMIN b. ca. 1782 (based on age at d.)

References: PLYMOUTH VR pp. 209(b. 1st 2 ch.), 351(m.). Plymouth Co. PR 38:169; 48:139(Seth Harlow). (PLYMOUTH) BURIAL HILL pp. 46 (d. Benj.), 91(d. Seth), 191(d. Mercy). MD 21:95 (b. 1st 2 ch.). PLYMOUTH CH RECS 2:670(d. Sarah). HARLOW GEN pp. 93-5.

1035 HANNAH[5] WARREN (Nathaniel[4], Benjamin[3], Joseph[2], Richard[1]) b. Plymouth 14 March 1744; living 6 Oct. 1807.

She m. Plymouth 20 March 1766 PHILIP LEONARD, d. bef. 29 March 1803; son of Philip and Mary (Richmond) Leonard, a descendant of Pilgrim Thomas Rogers.

On 29 March 1803 Nathaniel Warren Leonard was appointed administrator of the estate of Philip Leonard of Plymouth, gent. On 6 Oct. 1807 the widow was granted 1/3 of the sales of the real estate. The remainder was divided equally by N. W. Leonard, Ephraim Leonard, Hannah Morton, Mary Ward and Phebe Leonard.

Children (LEONARD):

i NATHANIEL WARREN[6] b. Plymouth 7 Feb. 1768
ii EPHRAIM (in VR without date)
iii HANNAH (in VR without date)
iv MARY (in VR without date)
v PHEBE b. 6 May 1779

References: PLYMOUTH VR pp. 226(b. Nathaniel), 351(m.), 424(b. ch.). MD 22:181(b. Nath. W.). Plymouth Co. PR 34:367; 38:340, 457, 506; 42:201(Philip Leonard). MF 19:201.

1036 SUSANNAH[5] WARREN (Nathaniel[4], Benjamin[3], Joseph[2], Richard[1]) b. Plymouth 8 June 1746; d. there 3 Jan. 1834.

She m. Plymouth 9 April 1767 EZRA HARLOW, b. Plymouth 28 Aug. 1741; d. there 17 April 1826 ae 84; son of John and Mary (Rider) Harlow, a descendant of Pilgrim Richard Warren (see #290vi).

Ezra Harlow was 2-1-2 in the 1790 census of Plymouth.

On 25 Feb. 1839 the estate of Ezra and Susannah Harlow was divided between Susannah Leach, Martha Whiting, Ezra Harlow and the estate of John Harlow dec.

Children (HARLOW) named in division:

i MARTHA[6]
ii SUSANNA

iii EZRA b. ca. 1772
iv JOHN b. 15 Sept. 1777

References: PLYMOUTH VR pp. 110(b. Ezra), 351(m.). Plymouth Co. PR 18:180-3(Ezra Harlow). PLYMOUTH CH RECS 2:674(d. Ezra). MD 15:39(b. Ezra). HARLOW GEN pp. 267-8(d. Susanna; b. of ch.).

1037 RUTH[5] WARREN (Nathaniel[4], Benjamin[3], Joseph[2], Richard[1]) b. Plymouth 20 Aug. 1749; living 16 Oct. 1826.

She m. int. Plymouth 5 Aug. 1775 THOMAS MORTON of Greenwich, Eng. and Plymouth MA, b. 26 Dec. 1748; d. bef. 21 March 1825 (adm.); son of Josiah Morton.

On 21 March 1825 a letter of administration was granted to Thomas Morton of Plymouth, yeoman, on the estate of Thomas Morton of Plymouth dec. On 16 Oct. 1826 one-third was set off to Ruth Morton, widow as dower.

On 19 March 1827 the estate was divided among the heirs Thomas Morton, Josiah Morton, Sarah Bramhall, Jane Burgess, Betsey Langford, Susan Morton and George Bramhall Jr.

Children (MORTON):

i SARAH[6] b. 8 Feb. 1776
ii LUCY b. 7 Oct. 1777 (not in divison)
iii THOMAS b. 22 Oct. 1779
iv JOSIAH b. 11 Feb. 1782
v JANE b. May 1784
vi BETSEY b. 14 Oct. 1786
vii SUSANNAH b. 2 April 1789
viii HANNAH b. 14 Feb. 1792 (not in division)

References: MD 27:177(int.); 42:50-1(Bible record - b. Thomas; b. ch.). PLYMOUTH VR p. 264(int.). Plymouth Co. PR 52:348; 59:278; 63:83, 384-91(Thomas Morton).

1038 BENJAMIN[5] WARREN (Benjamin[4-3], Joseph[2], Richard[1]) b. Plymouth 13 March 1739/40; d. there 12 June 1825 ae 85 yrs.

He m. (1) int. Plymouth 1 Jan. 1763 JANE STURTEVANT, b. Kingston 7 April 1737; d.there 28 Feb. 1797 in 59th yr.; dau. of David and Sarah (Holmes) Sturtevant.

He m. (2) Plymouth 15 Oct. 1797 LOIS (HARLOW) (BARTLETT) DOTEN, b. Plymouth 9 March 1748/9; d. there 19 Nov. 1802 in 53rd yr.; dau. of Amaziah and Lois (Doty) Harlow, a descendant of Pilgrim Edward Doty. She m. (1) Plymouth 16 Oct. 1766 Isaac Bartlett by whom she had John. She m. (2) Plymouth 1 June 1779 Thomas Doten.

He m. (3) Plymouth 31 March 1803 PATIENCE (HOLMES) DIMON, b. ca. 1751; d. Plymouth 15 April 1819 in 69th yr. She m. (1) Daniel Dimon.

He m. (4) Plymouth 27 May 1821 PHEBE (PEARSON) DOTEN b. Plymouth 1755; d. there 1855 ae 99y 4m 15d; dau. of William Bendick and Phebe (Holmes) Pearson. She m. (1) Plymouth 22 Dec. 1778 Lemuel Doty by whom she had 5 children.

On 20 June 1825 Ezra Finney was appointed administrator of the estate of Benjamin Warren of Plymouth, gentleman. The inventory was dated 20 June 1825.

The will of Phebe Warren dated 5 Sept. 1837, proved May 1855, names dau. Thirza Sampson; grandson William Peirce, son of her son-in-law John Peirce; and "all her heirs at law."

Children (WARREN) by 1st wife b. Plymouth:

i BENJAMIN[6] b. 12 May 1766
ii REBECCA b. 28 Feb. 1768
iii SALLEY (or SARAH) b. 30 Aug. 1769
iv DAVID (according to WARREN GEN)

References: MD 21:162(b. 1st 3 ch.). WARREN GEN p. 29. PLYMOUTH CH RECS 2:509(2nd m.). (PLYMOUTH) BURIAL HILL pp. 77(d. Jane), 96(d. Lois), 133(d. Patience). Plymouth Co. PR 59:269; 60:117(Benj. Warren); 77:192 (Phebe Warren). PLYMOUTH VR pp. 25(b. Lois), 210(b. 1st 3 ch.), 252(int. 1st m.), 322(4th m.), 356(Lois' 1st m.), 363 (Lois' 2nd m.), 368 (Patience 1st m.), 372(2nd m.), 379(3rd m.), 384(Phebe's 1st m.), 476(d. Benjamin). MF 11:1:198. DOTY GEN p. 171(d. Phebe). VR KINGSTON p. 140(b. Jane). HARLOW GEN pp. 272-3.

1039 BENJAMIN BRAMHALL[5] (Mercy[4] Warren, Benjamin[3], Joseph[2], Richard[1]) b. Plymouth 6 Aug. 1765; d. Quincey 6 June 1848.

He m. Plymouth 22 Oct. 1786 PRISCILLA BURBANK, b. Plymouth 3 Aug. 1766; living 2 Aug. 1848; dau. of Ezra and Priscilla (Savery) Burbank.

The will of Benjamin Bramhall of Quincy dated 2 Aug. 1848, proved 19 Aug. 1848, names wife Priscilla; daus. Mercy Warren Bramhall, Mary Bramhall, Priscilla Sampson, widow of John Sampson, Sarah Kingman, wife of William Kingman; sons William, Silvanus, Joshua and Cornelius Bramhall; Benjamin Bramhall, son of dec. son Benjamin Bramhall of Virginia; Ellis Brewster Bramhall, son of dec. son Charles.

Children (BRAMHALL) all b. prob. Quincy:

i BENJAMIN[6] b. 19 April 1787
ii PRISCILLA (twin) b. 4 April 1789
iii MERCY WARREN (twin) b. 4 April 1789; d. 26 Nov. 1790 ae 1y 7m 7d
iv MERCY WARREN b. 23 Feb. 1793
v CHARLES b. 23 Oct. 1795
vi WILLIAM b. 27 June 1797

vii SYLVANUS b. 29 March 1799
viii JOSHUA b. 12 Jan. 1802
ix MARY b. 7 July 1804
x SARAH b. 5 April 1807
xi THOMAS MURDOCK b. 3 June 1809 (not in will)
xii CORNELIUS b. 9 Sept. 1811

References: PLYMOUTH VR pp. 387(m.), 391(b. Priscilla),450(b. ch.; d. Mercy). Norfolk Co. PR #2447; 81:215-6 (Benjamin Bramhall). (PLYMOUTH) BURIAL HILL p. 65(d. Mercy).

ABBREVIATIONS

ae	aged	n.d.	no date
b.	born	n.f.r.	no further record found
bef.	before	n.p.	no place
bet.	between	N./No.	north
bp.	baptized	NS	Nova Scotia
bur.	buried	N.S.	new style date
ca.	about	O.S.	old style date
Cem./cem.	cemetery	p./pp.	page(s)
ch.	children	pos./poss.	possibly
Ch.	church	PR	probate record
Co.	county	prob.	probably
Col.	colony	pub.	published
Comm.	committee	rec.	record(s)
d.	died	rem.	removed
dau(s).	daughter(s)	repr.	reprinted
dec.	deceased	res.	resided
Dist	district	S./So.	south
d.s.p.	died without issue	sic	copy correct
d.y.	died young	Soc.	Society
E.	east	TR	town record(s)
ed.	edition	unm.	unmarried
G.S.	gravestone	unpub.	unpublished
gdn.	guardian	vol(s).	volume(s)
granddau.	granddaughter	VR	vital records
LE	land evidence	W.	west
LR	land records	wid.	widow
m.	married	-y -m -d	years, months, days
m. int.	marriage intentions		
MS(S).	manuscript(s)		

When no state is indicated after a city or town, the reader should assume Massachusetts. The following two-letter abbreviations are used for states:

CT	Connecticut	NH	New Hampshire
MA	Massachusetts	NJ	New Jersey
ME	Maine	NY	New York
NC	North Carolina	RI	Rhode Island
VT	Vermont		

WARREN KEY TO ABBREVIATED TITLES

ALDRICH GEN
Aldrich, Alvin J. "The George Aldridge Genealogy 1605-1971; vol. 1, Iowa 1971.

BACKUS DIARY
McLoughlin, William G., ed. "The Diary of Isaac Backus." 3 vols. Providence RI, 1979.

BANKS PLANTERS
Banks, Charles E. "The Planters of the Commonwealth." 1930; reprint Baltimore 1961, 1972, 1979

BARKER GEN
Barker, Elizabeth Frye. "Barker Genealogy." New York, 1927.

BARNSTABLE FAMS
Swift, C. F. "Genealogical Notes of Barnstable Families, Being a Reprint of the Amos Otis Papers." Barnstable MA, 1888-90; reprint Baltimore 1979.

BLACKMAN AND ALLIED FAMILIES
Holman, Alfred L. "Blackman and Allied Families." Chicago, 1928.

BOSTON DEATHS 1700-1799
Dunkle, Robert J. and Lainhart, Ann S., "Deaths in Boston, 1700 to 1799." 2 vols. Boston, 1999.

BOSTON NEWS OBITS
"Index of Obituaries in Boston Newspapers 1704-1800." 3 Vols.; Boston, 1968.

BOSTON VR
"Reports of the Record Commissioners." Vol. 9: births, marriages and deaths, 1630-1699; Vol. 24: births 1700-1800; Vol. 28: marriages 1700-1751; Vol. 30: marriages 1751-1809; Boston, 1883, 1894, 1898, 1902.

BOSWORTH GEN
Clarke, Mary B. "A History of the Descendants of Edward Bosworth who Arrived in America in 1634." 6 vols. San Francisco 1926-40.

BRADFORD DESC
Hall, Ruth G. "Descendants of Governor William Bradford." n.p., 1951.

BRAINTREE RECS
Bates, Samuel A. "Records of the Town of Braintree 1640-1793." Randolph MA, 1886.

BURGESS GEN
Burgess, F. "Memorial of Family of Thomas and Dorothy Burgess." 1865.

CAMBRIDGE HIST
Paige, Lucius R. "History of Cambridge 1630-1877." With a genealogical register; Boston and New York, 1877.

CAPE COD HIST
Freeman, Frederick. "History of Cape Cod." 2 vols. Boston, 1858-62; reprint Yarmouth Port MA, 1965.

CAPE COD LIBRARY
Smith, Leonard H. "Cape Cod Library." Baltimore MD 1992.

CHARLESTOWN BY WYMAN
Wyman, Thomas B. "The Genealogies and Estate of Charlestown." 2 vols; Boston 1879; reprint Somersworth NH, 1982.

CHIPMAN GEN
Chipman, A. L. "Chipmans of America." Poland ME 1904.

CHIPMAN GEN (1970)
Chipman, John Hale III. "A Chipman Genealogy." Norwell MA, 1970.

CHURCH DESC
Church, John A. "Descendants of Richard Church of Plymouth, Mass." Rutland VT, 1913.

CLARK FAM
Radasch, Arthur H. & Katherine. "The Thomas Clark Family." n.p., 1962.

COGGESHALL FAM
Coggeshall, Charles & Thelwell R. "The Coggeshalls in America." Boston 1930.

COOKE (THOMAS) GEN
Fiske, Jane Fletcher. "Thomas Cooke of Rhode Island." Boxford MA, 1987.

CT MARR
Bailey, Frederick W. "Early Connecticut Marriages as Found on Ancient Church Records Prior to 1800." 7 vols.; New Haven CT 1896-1906; reprint 1 vol. Baltimore MD 1968, 1982.

CT MEN IN THE REV
"Connecticut Men in the War of the Revolution; War of 1812; Mexican War." West Hartford CT 1889.

CUSHMAN GEN
Cushman, Henry W. "Genealogy of the Cushmans. The Descendants of Robert Cushman, The Puritan, 1617 to 1855." Boston 1855.

DAR PATRIOT INDEX
Published by the National Society of the Daughters of the American Revolution; Washington DC 1966.

DELANO GEN
Delano, Joel A. "The Genealogy, History and Alliances of the American House of Delano." New York 1899.

DELANO GEN (1999)
Cushing, Muriel Curtis. "Philip Delano of the 'Fortune' 1621." Plymouth 1999.

DOGGETT FAM
Doggett, Samuel B. "A History of the Doggett Family." Boston, 1894.

DOTY GEN
Doty, Ethan Allen. "The Doty-Doten Family in America." 2 vols, Brooklyn NY 1897.

DURFEE GEN
Reed, William F. "The Descendants of Thomas Durfee of Portsmouth RI." Vol. 1, 1902; vol. 2, 1905, Washington DC.

DUXBURY BY WINSOR
Winsor, Justin. "History of the Town of Duxbury, Mass. with Genealogical Registers." Boston, 1849; reprint Boston, 1970.

DUXBURY RECS
Etheridge, George. "Copy of the Old Records of the Town of Duxbury, Mass. from 1642 to 1770." Plymouth, 1893.

EARLY REHOBOTH
Bowen, Richard L. "Early Rehoboth." 4 vols.; Rehoboth, 1945-50.

ESTES GEN
C. Estes. "Desc. of Matthew & Richard Estes of Lynn MA, 1894."

FALMOUTH NOVA SCOTIA HISTORY
Duncanson, J.V. "Falmouth, a New England Township in Nova Scotia." Windsor, Ontario 1965.

FAUNCE DESC
Faunce, James F. "The Faunce Family History and Genealogy." Ancestry and Descendants of John Faunce of Purleigh, Essex, England and Plymouth, Mass.; 1967.

FINNEY-PHINNEY
Finney, Howard. "Finney-Phinney Families in America: Descendants of John Finney of Plymouth and Barnstable, Mass. and Bristol, R.I.; of Samuel Finney of Philadelphia, Penn.; and of Robert Finney of New London, Penn." Richmond VR, 1957.

FREEMAN GEN
Freeman, Frederick. "Freeman Genealogy in Three Parts: Edmund Freeman of Sandwich; Samuel Freeman of Watertown; Families of the name Freeman." Boston, 1875.

GEN ADVERTISER
Greenlaw, Lucy H. "The Genealogical Advertiser" a Quarterly Magazine of Family History; vols. 1-4, 1898-1901; reprint Baltimore MD, 1974.

GREAT MIGRATION BEGINS
Anderson, Robert C. "The Great Migration Begins." 3 vols., Boston 1995-6.

HANOVER BY BARRY
Barry, John S. "A Historical Sketch of the Town of Hanover MA with Family Genealogies." 1853.

HANOVER BY DWELLY
Dwelley, Jedediah & Simmons, John F. "History of the Town of Hanover, MA with Family Genealogies." Hanover MA, 1910.

HANOVER FIRST CH
Briggs, L. Vernon. "History and Records of the First Congregational Church, Hanover, Mass. 1727-1865." Vol. 1, Boston, 1895.

HARLOW GEN
Williams, Alicia C. ed. "Harlow Family, Descendants of Sgt. William Harlow of Plymouth MA." Baltimore MD 1997.

HARVARD GRADS
Sibley, John L. "Biographical sketches of graduates of Harvard University in Cambridge, Mass."; vol. 1, Cambridge, 1873.

HATCH GEN
Pack, Charles L. "Thomas Hatch of Barnstable and some of his Descendants." 1930

HATHAWAY GEN
Versailles, Elizabeth S. "Hathaways of America." Northhampton MA, 1970.

HINGHAM HIST
"History of the Town of Hingham, Mass." 3 vols.; Hingham MA, 1893; reprint Somersworth NH, 1982.

IGI
International Genealogical Index, LDS, Salt Lake City, Utah 1984

JENKS GEN
Browne, William B. "Genealogy of the Jenks Family of America." Concord NH 1952.

LITTLE COMPTON FAMS
Wilbour, Benjamin F. "Little Compton Families" published by the Little Compton Historical Society from records compiled by Benjamin F. Wilbour; Providence RI, 1967.

LO-LATHROP FAM
Huntington, E. B. "A Genealogical Memoir of the Lo-Lathrop Family." Ridgefield CT, 1884; reprint 1971.

LORING GEN
Pope, Charles H. "Loring Genealogy" compiled from the chronicles or ancestral records of James Spears Loring from the manuscripts of John Arthur Loring and from many other sources. Cambridge 1917.

MANWARING
Manwaring, Charles W. "A Digest of the Early Connecticut Probate Records." 3 vols; Hartford CT 1902-6.

MARSHFIELD BY RICHARDS
Richards, Lysander S. "History of Marshfield, Mass., with Genealogy." 2 vols.; Plymouth, 1901-5.

MARTHA'S VINEYARD BY BANKS
Banks, Charles E. "History of Martha's Vineyard, with Genealogy." 3 vols.; Boston, 1911-25; reprint Edgartown MA, 1966.

MA MARR
Bailey, Frederick W. "Early Massachusetts Marriages Prior to 1800." 3 vols in 1, 1897-1900 reprint Baltimore MD 1968, 1979.

MAYFLOWER SOURCE RECORDS
"Mayflower Source Records." (from the NEHGR) Baltimore MD, 1986.

MD
Williams, Alicia C., editor. "The Mayflower Descendant: a quarterly magazine of Pilgrim History and Genealogy." Vol. 1, 1899.

ME NH GEN DICT
Noyes, Sybil; Libby, C.T.; and Davis, Walter G. "Genealogical Dictionary of Maine and New Hampshire." Portland ME 1928-1939; reprint Baltimore MD, 5 parts in 1, 1972.

MF
"Mayflower Families Through Five Generations." Published by the General Society of Mayflower Descendants; 20 vols.

MIDDLEFIELD HIST
Church, Edward & Smith, Philip M. "A History of the town of Middlefield, Massachusetts." Menasha WI 1924.

MSSR
"Massachusetts Soldiers and Sailors of the Revolutionary War." 17 vols. Boston 1896-1908.

MQ
"The Mayflower Quarterly." Vol. 1, 1935; a publication of the General Society of Mayflower Descendants.

MIDDLEBORO DEATHS
Wood, Alfred. "Record of Deaths, Middleboro, Massachusetts." Boston, 1947.

MIDDLEBORO FIRST CH
"Book of the First Church of Christ in Middleborough." Boston 1852.

MORTON DESC
Allen, John K. "George Morton of Plymouth Colony and Some of His Descendants." Chicago IL, 1908.

NEHGR
"New England Historical and Genealogical Register." Vol. 1, 1847; published at Boston by the New England Historic Genealogical Society.

NEW HAVEN FAMS
Jacobus, Donald L. "Families of Ancient New Haven." 3 vols., Rome NY 1923, 1927, New Haven CT 1931; reprint Baltimore 1974.

NGSQ
"National Genealogical Society Quarterly." Vol. 1, 1912; published at Washington DC by the Society.

NEW ENGLAND'S MEMORIAL
Morton, Nathaniel. "New England's Memorial." Cambridge 1669; reprinted Boston, 1826.

OLD TIMES
Old Times; a magazine devoted to the early history of North Yarmouth, Maine; 8 vols.; Yarmouth ME 1877-1884.

(PLYMOUTH) ANC LANDMARKS
Davis, William T. "Ancient Lnadmarks of Plymouth." 2nd edition 1899; reprint of Part Two under the title "Genealogical Register of Plymouth Families." Baltimore, 1975.

(PLYMOUTH) BURIAL HILL
Kingman, Bradford. "Epitaphs from Burial Hill, Plymouth, Massachusetts, from 1657 to 1892. With biographical and historical notes." Brookline MA, 1892; reprint Baltimore MD, 1977.

PLYMOUTH CH RECS
"Plymouth Church Records, 1620-1859." 2 vols.; New York, 1920-23; reprint Baltimore MD, 1975.

PLYMOUTH COLONY RECS
Shurtleff, Nathaniel B. & Pulsifer, David. "Records of the Colony of New Plymouth in New England." 12 vols.; Boston, 1855-61; reprint 12 vols. in 6; New York, 1968.

PLYMOUTH CO CT RECS
Konig, David T., ed. "Plymouth County Court Records 1686-1859." 16 vols.; Wilmington DE, 1978.

PLYMOUTH SCRAPBOOK
Pope, Charles H. "The Plymouth Scrapbook." Boston, 1918.

PN&Q
Bowman, George E. "Pilgrim Notes and Queries." 5 vols.; Boston, 1913-17.

RHODE ISLAND 1777 MILITARY CENSUS
Chamberlain, Mildred M. "The Rhode Island 1777 Military Census." Baltimore, 1985.

RI CENSUS 1774
Bartlett, John R. "Census of the Inhabitants of the Colony of Rhode Island and Providence Plantations 1774." Reprint Baltimore MD 1969.

RI GEN DICT
Austin, John O. "The Genealogical Dictionary of Rhode Island, comprising three generations of settlers who came before 1690." Albany NY, 1887; reprint Cleveland OH, 1967 and Baltimore MD, 1969; reprint 1982.

RIGR
Beaman, Alden G., ed. "Rhode Island Genealogical Register." Vol. 1, 1978.

RI VR
Arnold, James N. "Vital Records of Rhode Island, 1636-1850." 21 vols.; Providence RI, 1891-1912.

SAVAGE
Savage, James. "A Genealogical Dictionary of the first settlers of New England, showing three generations of those who came before May 1692 ..." 4 vols.; Boston, 1860-62; reprint Baltimore MD, 1965; reprint 1981.

SCITUATE BY DEANE
Deane, Samuel. "History of Scituate, Mass., from its Settlement to 1831." Boston, 1831; reprint No. Scituate, 1899; reprint Scituate, 1975.

SHARON CT CEMS
Van Alstyne, Lawrence. "Burying Grounds of Sharon CT, Amenia and North East NY." Amenia NY 1903.

SHERMAN DESC
Sherman, Roy V. "Some Descendants of Philip Sherman, the First Secretary of Rhode Island." 1968.

SMALL DESC
Underhill, Lora A. W. "Descendants of Edward Small of New England and the allied families, with tracings of English Ancestry." 3 vols.; Cambridge MA, 1910.

SPOONER DESC
Spooner, Thomas. "Records of William Spooner of Plymouth, Mass., and his Descendants." Vol. 1; Cincinnati OH, 1883.

SPRAGUE GEN
Sprague, Warren V. "Sprague Families in America." Rutland VT 1913.

STETSON DESC
Stetson, Oscar F. "Descendants of Cornet Robert Stetson of Scituate, Mass." Vol. 1; Providence RI, 1933.

STONINGTON CT HIST
Wheeler, R.A. "History of Stonington, Conn. with a genealogical register." London CT 1900; reprint Baltimore MD 1977.

STOUGHTON VR
Endicott, Frederic, ed. "The Record of Births, Marriages and Deaths and Intentions of Marriage in the Town of Stoughton from 1727 to 1800 and in the Town of Canton from 1797 to 1845, Preceded by the Records of the South Precinct of Dorchester from 1715 to 1727." Canton MA, 1896.

SUFFOLK DEEDS
"Suffolk (MA) Deeds." 14 vols.; Boston, 1850-1906.

TABER DESC
Randall, George L. "Taber Genealogy." Descendants of Thomas, son of Philip Taber; New Bedford MA 1924.

TAG
"The American Genealogist." Vol. 1, 1922. Published at Demorest GA.

THOMAS GEN
Raymond, John M. "Thomas Families of Plymouth County, Massachusetts, Genealogies of the Families of David Thomas of Middleboro (1620-1689), John Thomas of Marshfield (1621-1691), and William Thomas of Marshfield (1573-1651)." Menlo Park CA, 1980.

TORREY'S MARRIAGES
Torrey, Clarence Almon. "New England Marriages Prior to 1700." Baltimore MD, 1985.

TRACY GEN
Tracy, Sherman Weld. "The Tracy Genealogy of Plymouth 1623." Rutland VT 1936.

WALPOLE NH HIST
Frizzell, Martha M. "History of Walpole NH." Walpole NH 1963.

WAREHAM FIRST CH
Smith, Leonard H. Jr. "Records of The First Church of Wareham, Mass. 1739-1891." Clearwater FL, 1974.

WARREN GEN
Roebling, Mrs. Washington A. "Richard Warren of the Mayflower and Some of His Descendants." Boston, 1901.

WATERMAN GEN
Jacobus, Donald L. "Descendants of Robert Waterman of Marshfield, Mass." Vols. 1 & 2; New Haven CT, 1939-42. "Descendants of Richard Waterman of Providence, R.I." Vol. 3; New Haven CT, 1954.

WATERTOWN BY BOND
Bond, Henry. "Genealogies of the families and descendants of the early settlers of Watertown (Mass.) including Waltham and Weston." 2 vols.; Boston, 1860.

WATERTOWN RECS
"Watertown Records comprising the third book of town proceedings and the second book of births, marriages and deaths to end of 1737 also burials in Arlington Street Burying Ground." Watertown, 1900.

WEYMOUTH BY CHAMBERLAIN
Chamberlain, G. W. "History of Weymouth with genealogies." 4 vols.; Boston, 1923.

WINDSOR CT BY STILES
Stiles, Henry R. "The History of Ancient Windsor." 2 vols., 1892; reprint Somersworth NH 1976.

WINSLOW MEMORIAL
Holton, David P. and Mrs. Francis K. "Winslow Memorial." 2 vols.; New York, 1877-88.

YORK DEEDS
"York (County) Deeds, 1642-1737." 18 vols in 19; Portland ME, 1878-1910.

INDEX OF NAMES

With a few exceptions, each name in the text is indexed. The names of authors and titles of reference works are not indexed.

Each married woman is indexed under her maiden name and also under her married name(s), showing her maiden name and any previous married name(s) in parentheses. A married woman of unknown maiden name is shown as SMITH Mary (-----).

When variant spellings of a surname occur, they are alphabetized under the more popular spelling, followed by one or more of the alternate spellings.